Lays And Leaves Of The Forest: A Collection Of Poems, And Historical, Genealogical, & Biographical Essays And Sketches, Relating Chiefly To Men And Things Connected With The Royal Forest Of Knaresborough...

Thomas Parkinson (rev.)

6 Albert St. Harrogate
1 June 1882

The Revd J Ackley
The Vicar of Fewston

Revd Sir

I beg to offer for your acceptance a copy of the "Lays & Leaves of the Forest" of which the Church forms the only illustration, of which you are the Vicar. I do not know whether you are acquainted with "~~Mr~~ Parkinson" the author who professes to be a "Forester" but if you are the Descendant of one, you will naturally feel an interest in the Book which I have not yet read, and cannot but feel a warm interest in it, but hope I have some day the pleasure before I go hence, having reached my 82nd year —

I am Dear Sir
Yours truly
Saml Powell

Death of Mrs. S. Powell. — We regret to announce the death of Mrs. Powell, wife of our old and respected townsman, Mr. Samuel Powell, which took place at Craven Lodge, on Sunday. The lamented lady was the only daughter of Arthur Ingleby, Esq., of Crow Nest, and latterly of Autswich, near Settle in Craven. She was married to Mr. Powell on the 27th of May, 1829, and enjoyed a happy married life extending over 54 years. For some time of late, however, Mrs. Powell had been in a delicate state of health, which culminated in her lamented death on Sunday morning. We feel sure our readers will unite with us in the deep sympathy we feel for Mr. Powell in his sore bereavement. + June 24/1883.

The Revd J M [illegible]
Fewston Vicarage
Otley

The Revd J Ashley

The Vicarage

Fewston –

AN

EPITHALAMIUM

OR

BRIDAL HYMN.

MARRIAGE HYMN.

✝✝✝✝✝✝✝✝

NORTH OTTERINGTON

Parish Church, Thornton-le-Moor,

SEPTEMBER 27TH, 1883.

✝✝✝✝✝✝✝✝

ALMIGHTY Father, Who, at first
In Eden's bowers fair,
To man his bride and help-meet gav'st,
And bless'd the primal pair;
Be present at this bridal rite,
O'er every act preside,
And in the mystic union join
The bridegroom and the bride.

O sweet and holy Saviour, once,
In Thy great love benign,
At Cana's marriage feast Thou turn'd
The water into wine;
We call Thee to this marriage now,
O come,—with us abide,—
With all Thy mercies deign to bless
The bridegroom and the bride.

O Holy Spirit, Fount Divine,
  Of all things pure and bright,
The Bride,—the Church,—Thou free'st from stain,
  And grant'st her garments white;
Come shed Thine unction down to-day,
  To comfort and to guide,
And clothe, with Thy pure marriage robe,
  The bridegroom and the bride.

O Heav'nly Giver of ev'ry good,
  At Thy great throne above,
We plead for blessings on this pair,
  And claim a Father's love.
In heat of day, in dark of night,
  O be Thou at their side;
Thy shelt'ring arm through life extend
  O'er bridegroom and the bride.

If long ere death their union break,
  Long may they live to Thee;
If short, O mind Thy promise dear,
  The mourner's God to be.
And grant that when the feast is spread,—
  That of the Lamb who died,—
Among Thy chosen guests may sit,
  The bridegroom and the bride.

O God, mysterious Three in One,
  For hope and mercy given,
Thy name we praise, and hearts upraise,
  To thank Thee, Lord of Heav'n.
Eternal Father, Spirit, Son,
  Our God, Redeemer, Guide,
Thy will be done, Thy glory sung,
  Far as the world is wide.

AMEN.

FEWSTON CHURCH.

LAYS AND LEAVES

OF THE

FOREST:

A COLLECTION OF POEMS, AND
HISTORICAL, GENEALOGICAL, & BIOGRAPHICAL
ESSAYS AND SKETCHES,

RELATING CHIEFLY TO MEN AND THINGS CONNECTED WITH THE ROYAL FOREST OF KNARESBOROUGH,

BY

THOMAS PARKINSON, F.R.HIST.S.

(A FORESTER).

"IN ÆSTU TEMPERIES."

A.D. 1882.

LONDON: KENT & CO., PATERNOSTER ROW.
HARROGATE: R. ACKRILL.

North Otterington Vicarage
Northallerton
June 22nd 1882

My Dear Sir

I have pleasure in again sending you a list of your articles on Dante. It does not take two minutes to make out when the books are at hand. Why have you sent a stamped envelope for so small a matter? —

I ought to have written to you long ago & thank you for your letter on 'Lays & Leaves'. I fear I have been very negligent. I wish the book had not been so marred by 'clerical' and typographical errors. An amateur, like myself, in the correction of 'proofs' ought always to be followed by a skilled "Printer's reader" such as all the large London printing Houses have attached to their establishments but which Ackrill does not possess. I have noted a large number of errata - a list of a few of the more important ones I enclose that you may correct them in your copy if you think fit & have not done so already.

I do not think the book is "selling" very briskly, but I have advertised little & sent few copies for review. My naturalist friends approve of the notices of the Naturalist & of Natural History, - my "historian" friends say some of the Historical papers contain some fresh and interesting matter, - Stubbs approves strongly of the extracts from "a Forester's diary &c" perhaps on the principle that there is least of my own in that Article; while my "Poetic" friends say that some of the poetry is not altogether despicable. — One prefers "The Forester's Return" to any of the others. You, I think, do not dislike "The Dream" & "The Dirge" though you think "The Tryst" the best. I also think it contains a few passages in which the thoughts & expressions approach nearest to poetic ones of any in the book (of my own). — My favourite however is "Sarah" – which no one has taken a fancy to but myself. Three or four of the stanzas [illegible] are somewhat robbed of their smoothness by hasty alterations I made at the last moment in the proofs, & which I now see to be anything but emendations. —

Of course you will publish your "aphorisms". I cannot understand the width & depth of your reading! You seem to go into every mine in the ancient & modern world and there pick up the gems.—

I hope the health of your eldest boy is improved & that he has been able to return to Oxford? My third son got his B.A. at Cambridge on Saturday last. He has been working hard & wants now a little change. Should the weather be fine he & I may be at Hopperdam for two or three days next week. Thank you for your endeavour to obtain for my other son a day's fishing in the Wharf.— Are you intending to run away from Fewston at all this summer?

With kind regards to Mrs Ashley
I am dear Sir
Yours truly
Thos Parkinson

The Revd
J. M. Ashley

Dedication.

TO THEE; around whom all affections entwine,
Whose grace, form, and truth in our spring days of old,
First taught me the love that never grows cold,
And, since thou allowed me to claim thee as mine,
Hast gladden'd the heart which from youth had been thine;
Whose devotion and care, which *that day* will unfold,
Have shed peace on my path more precious than gold,
And ever thy love my breast shall enshrine;
Though cares have oppress'd thee, and suff'ring distress'd;
Thy children arise,—each calleth thee bless'd;
While twenty-five years of our summer have run,
To me thou hast been "Paradisus-in-sun;"*
These Leaves of the Forest, and Lays of our life,
I dedicate to thee,—TO THEE, MY DEAR WIFE.

January 2nd, 1882 A.D.
(Our silver wedding day.)

---

* An old and fanciful play upon the surname: "Paradisus-in-sole," *i. e.* Park-in-sun.

"In labore requies In æstu temperies In fletu solatium."	"Thou in labour our repose Cooling shade when noontide glows, Solace sweet in all our woes."

Missale ad Usum insignis Ecclesiæ Eboracensis
(Sabbatio post Penticostem—Sequentia.)

"Man loves the forest. To the general flame
My breast is not a stranger. I could rove
At morn, at noon, at eve, by lunar ray,
In each returning season, through your shades,
Ye revered woods! Could visit every dell,
Each hill, each breezy lawn, each wandering brook,
And bid the world admire; and when at last
The song was closed, each magic spot again
Could seek, and tell again of all its charms."

—*Gisborne's Walks in a Forest.*

INTRODUCTION.

SOME of the following "Lays and Leaves" have already been published in the Churchman's Shilling Magazine, and local publications. Hitherto fugitive, such are now collected in this volume, and others, not before printed, are added. They represent the literary recreations of the author, in the midst of more important work, and do not profess to be any more than the title given to the book indicates; viz., a few *Lays* sung, by the writer, or by others, to the music of forest rustlings, or to the refrain of forest memories; with *Leaves*—some small and some larger,—some green and some withered,—gathered from its historical and genealogical trees.

The General History of the forest is scarcely touched; many places of interest are not even mentioned; but few of the persons, and families, of influence therein have come within the *purvieu*; and many spots, well worthy of a visit on account of their pastoral scenery, or their rugged wildness, are left unnamed:—though, in passing, let the vale from Bluberhouses Bridge, by West House, toward Thruscross, be named for beauty, and Washburn Head above Hoodstorth for rugged wildness. All these matters and features are found set forth in the admirable, and exhaustive, History of the Forest published, but a few years ago, by Mr. Wm. Grainge, and to it the reader, who would know more of the district, is confidently referred.

There is yet, however, a wide and interesting field open for research in forest lore, to any person with the leisure, the opportunities, and the means, to explore it, especially in the direction of genealogy and family history. There are, the *Beckwith* family of Beckwith and Clint, numerous, and, perhaps, the first in antiquity and forest history; the *Pulleine* family,—prolific branches of which were seated at Fewston, Killinghall, and Scotton, and had among its members two vicars of Fewston at the time of, and immediately after, the Reformation, an archdeacon of Colchester in Queen Elizabeth's time, and an archbishop of Tuam toward the close of the 17th century; the *Day* family of Menwith, one of whom was rector of Topliffe in the last century, and, with others of his name, among the best benefactors to the schools and charities of the district; the *Wood* family, of Swinsty, descendants of the "de la Sales," and the "del Woods" of the 13th and 14th centuries, and who in the 16th and 17th centuries intermarried with the best families of the neighbourhood; and the *Gravers* of Fewston, now forgotten in the forest, but once leading forest men, and numbering among them a Derbyshire vicar, and an archdeacon of Durham; the *Simpsons* and *Smiths* of Felliscliffe and Clint ; the *Biltons* of Bilton and Hampsthwaite; and many other; all,—except a few leading members of each who have found their way into the Heralds' visitations and other records,—awaiting the researches of local genealogists. The antiquarian also, has yet a field open for his investigations, in the Druidical rocks at Almas Cliff and elsewhere;

in the extensive earthworks, probably British, near Norwood; in the barrows, or burial mounds, known as "Pippin. Castle," and in the identification—an able contribution towards which has lately been made by Mr. William Grainge,—of the site of the Royal residence of the Saxon *Ella*, and of the place thence named *Elsworth*. And to the topographer, and more general historian, there are yet, comparatively unexplored, the rolls, and other records of the Forest Court at Knaresborough, and the Forest and Liberty wills, and other testamentary documents, lately removed to Somerset House, London.

The Lays, and scattered Leaves, which have been gleaned from this field by the writer, are here offered to the public, in hope that other workers may yet follow in the same track; that to many Foresters, and others connected with the Forest, the perusal of these gleanings may yield some instruction and pleasure; and that to strangers, into whose hands they may fall, they may be a means of exciting an interest in a district—on many accounts—well worthy of interest. And here, for the benefit of any who may visit those western parts of the forest, chiefly spoken of, let Hopper Lane Hotel be mentioned. Standing in the midst of the scenes described, it is truly an "Hostel" in the old and best sense of the word, on whose window might be written, as Shenstone wrote,

"Whoe'er has travell'd life's dull round,
Where'er his stages may have been,
May sigh to think he still has found
The warmest welcome at an inn."

It is not in itself without interest. Dating back for more than a century, as a large posting house on a chief road from Lancashire to York, it has received at one time or other, most of the noted men of the north and west,—

many of whom seem to have taken a delight in inscribing their names on the glass of its windows, where they may yet be read.* Mr. Ward himself,—the owner and host,—belongs to an old and respected forest family, whose friendship the family of the writer has enjoyed, and valued, for over a century.

For a considerable portion of the information in these "Leaves," the writer is deeply indebted to the Rev. J. W. Darnborough, M.A., rector of South Otterington; for permission, most readily and courteously given, to search the Forest records at Knaresborough to the Messrs. Powell; and to the Rev. Robert Collyer, D.D., of New York, for the plate of Fewston church, which, as the only published view of that House of God, will be doubly valuable if, as seems too probable, the church be doomed to the destruction which has already overtaken the village. To these the writer here begs to make due acknowledgment, and to express his thanks.

A few of the "Lays," it will be noticed, *e.g.*, "The Forest Church," were written before the transformation of the Washburn valley by the construction of the reservoirs. The writer has thought it best to give them unaltered, though they occasionally picture scenes, which now are greatly changed, or no longer exist.

North Otterington Vicarage,
22nd March, 1882.

---

* The following inscriptions may be noted as typical of their class.

"Good fare in this House, 1807."

"James Black, Sept. 1848."

The next is a very enigmatical one :—

"Cuthbert the Great bought 30,000 horns, 15th July, 1814. Witness, J. Parkinson."

CONTENTS.

ERRATUM.

Page 193, line 11 from the bottom (Note), for 1867 A.D., read 1876 A.D.

THE FOREST.

"From Wharnside Hill not far, outflows the nymble Nydd
Through Nythersdale, along as sweetly she doth glide
Tow'rds Knaresburg on the way . . . . . .
Where that *brave forest stands.*
Entitled by the town.

—DRAYTON'S POLYOLBION.

THE Royal Forest of Knaresborough, of which these lays are sung, and whence these leaves are gathered, is a range of country about twenty miles in length and eight in width, diversified with mountain and moor, rocky eminences and fertile valleys, and extending from Knaresborough, westward and south-westward, to the heather-clad hills overlooking Bolton Abbey.

In the earliest times it was a rugged and wild district, rich and luxuriant wood-land in its valleys and dells; but its upland and exposed parts, covered with fern and heather and gorse and rushes, as now.

A place, verily suitable, and sought as a refuge, for the superstitions of the Old British and Saxon creeds! Within its bounds there remain the druidical rocks, and rock altars of Great Almas Cliff, Little Almas Cliff, Brandrith and Roggan. While, but just beyond its margins, are those of Brimham on the north, Chevin and Rumbold's Moor on the south, and Simon's Seat on the west.

In mediæval days, though embracing, within its precincts, but one or two modest castlets or Forest Lodges, and three parish churches (Pannal, Hampsthwaite, and Fewston), it was surrounded by feudal strongholds, and ecclesiastical establishments, of the first magnitude. The Castle of Knaresborough of the Lords of the Forest, Spofforth of the Percies, Harewood of the Gascoigns, Ripley of the Ingilbys, Barden and Skipton of the Cliffords, Dog Park of the Vavasours, stood but just beyond its bounds. And so stood, also, the great abbey of Fountains, the priories of Bolton and Knaresborough, the nunnery of Arthington, the Archiepiscopal palace of Otley,—and, at no great distance, the abbey of Kirkstall on the one side, and the great foundation of St. Wilfrid (Ripon) on the other.

Even at, or very soon after, its palmiest days, as a Royal Forest, the lowlands and valleys seem to have been enclosed and cultivated; but wide, wild, uncultivated tracts of great extent, remained open and unreclaimed, until near the end of the last century.

In 1770 A.D., an Act of Parliament was obtained for enclosing the open parts of the Forest. The usual disputes, and the strife of competing interests of such occasions, took place, and gave rise to the following *jeu d'esprit* by an anonymous author, yet worth preservation.

" *Verses on the intended enclosure of the Forest.*"

"The question heretofore proposed,
Was, that the Forest be enclosed.
It is a calculated thing,
To serve the public and the king.
No longer would the dismal cries,
Be heard, for want of due supplies :
Instead of dangerous bogs and rushes,
Of fens and briars, whins and bushes,
Plenty of grass and corn would spring !
The very fields would laugh and sing !
Say then, and freely speak your mind,
And tell me how you are inclined :
But let me whisper in your ear,
Be sure as we're collected here,
Whether the "Ayes" prevail or "Noes,"

The Act is pass'd—we must enclose.
Some doubts indeed, and seeming flaws,
A tedious delay may cause,
In settling bound'ries, right and wrong,
Betwixt the multifarious throng:
But sages, learned in the laws,
To clear up doubts, and heal the flaws,
Are in the self-same Act appointed,
By Commons, Peers, and King anointed.

Another Meeting now they call,
Claimants appearing, one and all;
Counsel attend the time and place,
To justify each client's case;
And others too, call'd arbitrators,
To settle all disputed matters.
They eat and drink from day to day,
And joyous pass the time away.
The latter sort consult, explain,
and then adjourn,—to meet again.
At last, they leave all matters so,
The Agents know not what to do.
They seem indeed resolved to sell,
But right, or wrong, they cannot tell.

Another Meeting now they call,
And offer terms to please 'em all.
But lo! How diff'rent the event!
Rejected all, with one consent.
The Law,—the glorious law's the thing,—
Must judge 'twixt subject and the king.
And when for hearing, all is riper,
Alas! poor Forest pays the piper."

After this enclosure, nothing remained of the Forest, as a forest, except the name.

Modern times have brought other innovations. Early in the century,—utilizing the water power of its rivers and streams,—manufactories of flax, and other materials, were erected near Bluberhouses, at Thurscross, and other places, only, however, to languish and pass away on the advent of steam power. Within the past few years the Washburn valley has been invaded, and taken possession of, by the Corporation of the town of Leeds, who have swept away many old land marks, and transformed the principal portion of the valley into a chain of reservoirs, which, for picturesqueness and extent, are not unworthy the name of mountain lakes.

The greatest change, however, has been in the rise of one of its obscure hamlets into the fashionable, world-famed, town of Harrogate, where the healing waters of a forest *dene*, and the bracing breezes of the forest air, are sought by every class from almost every clime. The logical connection, between this town's attractions, and its patrons, was aptly expressed by the humorous writer of an epistolary poem in the last generation, thus—

"It is proper, I vow,
And, dear Simon, you know
They would not hither repair,
Did the people not find
That both body and mind
Are improv'd, by those waters and air."

Of local "characters" and "celebrities," the Forest and its capital, Knaresborough—from which it cannot well be dissevered,—have had a full share: Eugene Aram, Blind Jack of Knaresbrough, Peter Barker the blind joiner of Hampsthwaite, and one whose fame is even wider, Mother Shipton, may be named. Innumerable chap books, and Baring Gould in his "Yorkshire Oddities," have duly chronicled their lives and doings. With regard to Mother Shipton; those persons who may be at all disturbed by her supposed prophecies, are advised to consult the original edition of them, (and that not written until more than 100 years after her death), preserved in the British Museum, and lately printed, in a handy form, by Mr. W. H. Harrison, of London. They will there see how few and insignificant the so called prophecies were until augmented by popular fancies and exaggerations.

The feelings, with which the present writer regards "the Forest" and its associations, are aptly expressed, *mutatis mutandis*, by a poet and topographer of no mean power a century ago, Thomas Maude, Esq., born at Harewood on its borders, when writing of his native vale of Wharfedale.

**" Forgive me, *Reader,* if in mood serene,
I deck my native banks with cheering green;
Bestow a smile upon the finny stream,—
My vernal pastimes, and autumnal theme,
Point to the glades, where erst my wand'ring sight,
First roused the waking gleams of soft delight,—
Dreams though of fairy hue, I trace the time,
And strongly recognize the feast sublime;
Fling to the howling winds the murky lore,
That aims to rob me of the precious store.**

**What if, I, toyful, with ethereal ray,
Life's passage strew to cheat the dreary way,
Or, if in mirth's sweet bounds, I breath the gale,
Drink at her fount, nor step the moral pale;
By all the order of the spheres I ween,
On that fair ground no peccant spot is seen."**

***Verbeia, or Wharfdale.*—A poem published in 1782 A.D.**

THE FOREST CHURCH.

"How beautiful they stand,
Those ancient churches of our native land!
Amid the pasture fields, and dark green woods,
Amid the mountain clouds and solitudes;
By rivers broad that rush unto the sea:
By little brooks, that with lisping sound,
Like playful children, run by copse and lea!
Each in its little plot of holy ground.
How beautiful they stand,
Those old grey churches of our native land!"

AWAY in the forest, and far from the throng,
Of the world's surging crowd, and hurry around,
Where Washburn, in peace, rolls its waters along,
And the brooklets, at play re-echo the sound,
O'erlooking dark alder and silvery birch,
On forest hill-side stands the forester's church.

In thrice hallow'd ground, in beauty it stands,
Around it most sacred memories cling;
From the exile, away, in his far distant land,
It draws the heart's yearnings on light'ning's wing.
And precious the seed laid beneath the green sod,—
'Tis reverenced by man, as hallowed to God.

'Tis the house of our Father,—our forefathers' church!
O could we recall, through the long roll of years,
Which hide from the ear and the eye's deepest search,
The bride's happy smile, and the widow's hot tears,
With joy's gladsome praise, and affliction's deep calls,
Beheld, in the past, by its time-beaten walls!

At its sacred font, upon infant and sire
Alike, in succession, were solemnly poured
The baptismal water, the Divine Spirit's fire,
With grace from on high in covenant showered,
When to children of earth, in mercy, was given
The birthright of sons and daughters of heaven.

At its altar their bridal pledges were bound,
Their vows and their loves with blessing were sealed;
And there, too, in the Holy Supper, they found
To their souls their dear Saviour revealed.
Through weal and through woe, by His hand they were led,
With the heaven-sent bread sustained and fed.

There, in prayer devout, oft meekly they knelt,
And bowed, their Redeemer's name to adore;
With heart, as with voice, sang the praises they felt,
Or, seated, they thought the Divine lessons o'er.
Their faith and their prayer thus hallowed the spot,
Shall it be by their child profaned or forgot?

Where the evening shadows of its chancel fall,
They, father and son, in dust, are at rest;
To their ear temptation's soft voice brings no call,
Nor are they by care, or earth's trials, oppress'd.
Gone for aye are their sorrows, and dried their tears,
Their murmurs are stilled, and forgotten their fears.

O grant to me, Father, such grace in my way,
  That where'er I wander, where'er I may dwell,
I may live, work, and die, a victor as they,
  Then "happy the journey, for I shall be well." *
Though my dust may be laid afar from their side,
From its Guardian's eye no distance can hide.

With theirs it will rest till God's sons are revealed,
  His kingdom of glory fulfilled in love,
Then, however far scattered, wherever concealed,
  He'll rebuild it—a temple—meet for above;
In beauty and life, ne'er to die, 'twill arise
From its cell upon earth, to His home in the skies.

Till then, let the pile in piety reared,
  Where, a child, I learned in worship to bow,
By children's children through centuries revered,
  By their sons e'er be loved and guarded as now!
Oh! see that it stand, by profane foot ne'er trod,
The church of our fathers—the house of our God!

* A collateral ancestor of the writer, who died in 1670, A.D. directed the words "Felix iter a seculo ad cœlum, illic sanus ero," to be cut on his tomb, still existing, though covered by the tiles, in the chancel of the church of Carleton in Craven.

MEN OF THE FOREST 500 YEARS AGO.

"Time rolls his ceaseless course. The race of yore,
Who danced our infancy upon their knee,
And told our marvelling boyhood legend's store,
Of their strange ventures happ'd by land or sea,
How are they blotted from the things that be?"
—Sir Walter Scott.

THE following list of men, inhabiting the parts of the Forest to which the "leaves" chiefly relate in the 2nd year (June 1378, to June 1379) of King Richard II, is, on many accounts, of very great interest. It is a portion of the collector's roll or list, for a subsidy, or voluntary poll-tax, granted to the king from the laity, in the wapentake of Claro, in the West Riding of the County of York. The roll for the whole county, taken from the records of the King's Exchequer, has lately been printed by the Yorkshire Archæological Society.

The amount collected from each person is some indication of his means and position. It will be noticed that four pence (iiij.d), equivalent to about 3s. 4d. of our money, is the sum paid by the large majority; though several rise to (vj.d) six pence, and only four to above that sum, viz., John Gyott and his wife, of Beckwith, 12d.; Thomas Turpin and his wife, of Killinghall, 12d.; Adam Beckwith and his wife, of Clint, 2s.; and *Percyuallus Pensax*, of Beckwith, 40d.

The great interest of the roll, however, consists, in its giving the names of the inhabitants of the Forest, in the days of its forest glory, 500 years ago, and enabling those, who are acquainted with the names of the present families, to see how many descendants of the old inhabitants yet linger within its precincts, after all the changes and chances of five centuries.

A second source of interest is found in the many valuable illustrations, which the roll affords, of the origin, and the manner of formation, of surnames, at a time when such names were coming, or had very lately come, into general use.

In the foot notes to the following pages, many instances of these points of interest are indicated, and many others will be easily detected by the reader.

The original list is in Latin, and although here translated (except the word "de" meaning "of") the original etymology of the surnames and names of places is retained.

TOWN OR CONSTABULARY OF CLINT, INCLUDING THE PRESENT TOWNSHIPS OF CLINT, HAMPSTHWAITE, FELLISCLIFFE, AND POSSIBLY NORWOOD AND HAVERAH PARK.

(1) Richard Wilson de Clint and his wife 4d.
William, his son ... ... 4d.
John de Derby and his wife ... 4d.
Thomas Atkynson and his wife ... 4d.
John Wilson and his wife ... ... 4d.

---

(1) The origin of those surnames which arose from designating a person, over and above (sur) his own Christian name, by that of his father, and sometimes of his mother, with the addition of "son," is aptly shown in many of the names in this list. Richard Wil-son, Thomas Atkyns-son, Adam Alice-son, &c., that is, Richard, the son of Will; Thomas, the son of Atkins; Adam, the son of Alice.

The origin of another class of names—that of persons receiving their surname from the name of the place at which they resided,—is illustrated by such as John de Beckwith, William de Rouden, Thomas de Farnhill, that is John of Beckwith, &c., &c. The "de" was almost invariably soon dropped out, and the names became John Beckwith, William Rowdon, Thomas Farnhill, &c.

William del Hall and his wife	...	4d.
Adam Aliceson and his wife	...	4d.
William Bayok and his wife	...	4d.
John de Bekwith and his wife	...	4d.
Richard, his servant	...	4d.
William Plenteth and his wife	...	4d.
Adam de Beckwith and his wife	...	ij.s.
Thomas, his servant	...	4d.
John, his servant	...	4d.
John Tredegate and his wife	...	4d.
Henry Tailliour and his wife	...	4d.
Isolda de Riddyng	...	4d.
Julia, her daughter	...	4d.
Johanna, daughter of Thomas Nelson		4d.
Simon Agasson and his wife	...	4d.
Richard Nelleson and his wife	...	4d.
(2) William del West and his wife	...	4d.
William Rede and his wife ...	...	4d.
John Harebroune and his wife	...	4d.
William Webster and his wife	...	4d.
John Blome and his wife ...	...	4d.
Robert Tilleson and his wife	...	4d.
John Py and his wife ...	..	4d.
Robert de Whelehous and his wife		4d.
John de Swanlay and his wife	...	4d.
John Hobson and his wife ...	...	4d.
William Godythson and his wife	...	4d.
John Somyer and his wife ...	...	4d.
Henry Lawe and his wife ...	...	4d.
William Lawson and his wife	...	4d.
John Lawe and his wife ...	...	4d.
Robert Lawe and his wife ...	...	4d.
(3) Thomas de Trees	...	4d.

(2) "Del" a contraction of "de la." William de la (or del.) West is William of the West, soon shortened to William West.

(3) "Trees" is now an interesting Elizabethan house in the township of Norwood, and near to the western boundary of Haverah Park. It was for many generations the home of the substantial yeoman family of Jeffray.

	Roger Ffleccher and his wife	...	4d.
	Thomas, his son	...	4d.
	Robert Woderoue and his wife	...	4d.
	William Basseham and his wife	...	4d.
	John, the son of Roger and his wife		4d.
(4)	John Cowhird and his wife ...	...	xij.d.
	Richard Carter and his wife..	...	4d.
	William Brennand and his wife	...	6d.
	William de Gateshened and his wife		vj.d.
(5)	Johanna Lytster	...	vj.d.
	Alicia Schutt	...	4d.
	Julia of Couton	...	4d.
	Robert Lillyng and his wife...	...	4d.
	John atte Gate	...	vj.d.
	William Sergeaunt and his wife	...	4d.
	John Gryme and his wife ...	...	4d.
	Matilda de Hirst	...	vj.d.
	Alicia Rote	...	4d.
	William de Wattes and his wife	...	4d.
	John Webster and his wife ...	..	vj.d.
	Thomas Dawe and his wife ...	...	vj.d.
	Henry Hikson and his wife	...	4d.
	John Rote and his wife ...	...	4d.
	Matthew Brabaner and his wife	...	vj.d.
	Richard del Hall and his wife	...	4d.
	Adam Laycan and his wife ...	...	4d.
(6)	John Thekester and his wife	...	4d.
	Agnes de Goukthorp ...	...	4d.
	Benedict Sporrett and his wife	...	4d.
(7)	Agnes Parcour	...	4d.
	William Smert and his wife...	...	4d.
	Thomas de Ffarnhill and his wife	...	4d.
	Thomas Lax and his wife ...	...	4d.

(4) Cowhird, from the occupation of a cow-herd; now contracted to Coward.

(5) "Lytster," a dyer; now Lister.

(6) Thekester, probably "thek" or "thack" *i.e.*, thatch, and "ster" meaning "the thatcher."

(7) Parcour.—The park keeper; now Parker.

	Thomas Scargill and his wife	...	4d.
	Thomas del Hall and his wife	...	4d.
	Thomas Been and his wife ...	..	4d.
	William de Roudon and his wife	...	4d.
(8)	Richard Polayn and his wife	...	4d.
	Robert Sporrett and his wife	...	4d.
	Thomas Batlyng and his wife	...	4d.
	Thomas Parcour and his wife	...	4d.
	William Nanson and his wife	...	4d.
	John Robynson and his wife	...	4d.
	John de Kirkeby and his wife	...	4d.
(9)	Agnes Nelledoghter	...	4d.
	John Loucok and his wife ...	...	4d.
	John de Wattes and his wife	...	4d.
	William Waller and his wife	...	4d.
	William de Ffarnhill and his wife	...	4d.
	Thomas de Mallum and his wife	...	4d.
	Thomas Wright and his wife	...	vj.d.
	John Caluehird and his wife	...	4d.
	Alexander del Cote and his wife	...	4d.
	William Gryme and his wife	...	4d.
	John Hanson and his wife . .	...	4d.
	Richard Maundby and his wife	...	4d.
	Thomas Nelleson and his wife	...	4d.
(10)	William Stubbe and his wife...	...	4d.

---

(8) "Richard Polayn," the same as Pullein, Pulleyne, &c. This very old, numerous, and influential, forest family is said to have received the name from "Pullus," a colt, or young horse, the early ancestors having had charge of the Royal Stud kept in the Forest. The crest given in Glover's visitation, as that of the Scotton branch of the family, is. "A colt's head erased sable, bridled or." The name has also been said to be of Welsh origin, viz., Ap Ullin,—*i.e.*, the son of Ullin.

(9) "Nelle-doughter," curious as showing the use of the word "daughter" in a similar manner to that of "son," the daughter of Nelle, as Nelleson was the son of Nelle.

(10) William Stubbe, that is, "Stob" or "Stub," the root end or stump of a bush or tree. This is an ancestor, at this early date, in the forest, of its most illustrious son in the present century, the Rev. William Stubbs, D.D., Regius Professor of Modern History in Oxford, and Canon of St. Paul's,

(11) William Lely and his wife ... ... 4d.
Robert Batelying (?) and his wife ... 4d.
Henry of Wyndill and his wife ... 4d.
Richard de Ffarnhill and his wife ... 4d.
John Alaynson and his wife... ... 4d.
John Scayff ... ... 4d.
Robert Nanson and his wife ... 4d.
Robert Horner and his wife ... 4d.
William Schutt and his wife ... 4d.
William Ingelsant and his wife ... 4d.
(12) John de Fellesclyff and his wife ... 4d.
John Ingelsant ... ... 4d.
Thomas Ingelsant and his wife ... 4d.
Robert Brennand and his wife ... 4d.
Henry del More and his wife ... 4d.
Richard Yong and his wife ... ... 4d.
William Yong and his wife ... ... 4d.
Agnes de Derlay ... ... 4d.
Thomas de Raghton and his wife (Cissor) vj.d.
Thomas de Salmon and his wife ... 4d.
William, son of Richard Nelleson (Smyth) vj.d.

THE TOWN OR CONSTABULARY OF THUSCROSS, INCLUDING THURSCROSS, THORNTHWAITE, MENWITH, PADSIDE AND DARLEY.

John de Burley and his wife ... 4d.
William Inglesant and his wife ... 4d.
Richard de Dowes and his wife ... 4d.
Geoffrey, the son of John Menwith... 4d.
Robert Blaunche and his wife ... 4d.
William Syre and his wife ... ... 4d.
William Turnour and his wife ... vj.d.
Benedict Dikson and his wife ... 4d.
William, son of Robert Menwith ... 4d.
Thomas Carter ... ... 4d.

(11) "Lely," probably from the village of "Leathley" locally pronounced, still "Lely."

(12) Felliscliffe, a hamlet in Hampsthwaite.

(1)	Alicia Arkill	4d.
	John de Heghlay and his wife ...	4d.
	Thomas de Heghlay and his wife ..	4d.
	Richard Souter and his wife ...	4d.
	Richard Ffleccher and his wife ...	4d.
	Alicia de Wyndeslay	4d.
	Robert, her son	4d.
	John de Lethom and his wife ...	4d.
(2)	William de Thakwra and his wife ...	4d.
	John de Thakwra	4d.
	John Luff	4d.
	Thomas de Menwith...	4d.
	Thomas Dikson	4d.
	John de Skreuyngham	4d.
(3)	Richard Smythson	4d.
	Henry de Slyngesby and his wife ...	4d.
	Thomas de Crauen	4d.
	John Lemyng and his wife	4d.
	Adam de Thornthwayt	4d.
	Henry Watteson	4d.
	John de Tesedale	4d.
	John Pullayn and his wife	4d.
(4)	Elias de Morehous and his wife ...	4d.
	Thomas Dalay and his wife	4d.
(5)	Richard Schiphird and his wife ...	4d.
	John de Thurescroft...	4d.

---

(1) The eminent Saxon thane who owned Clint and part of Bilton in the time of the Confessor was named Archil; Alice Arkill was probably a descendent.

(2) "De Thackwra," Thackura, or Thackeray, was a homestead and rivulet, on the south bank of the Washburn, between Fewston and Bluberhouse. It probably means the "thatch mere." Dropping the "de" we get the name, made so world-wide by one of its illustrious bearers, William Makepeace Thackeray.

(3) Smythson—afterwards spelt "Smithson," a well-known, and at one time wealthy family.

(4) Elias of the "More," or "Moor-house." A respected name still left; Moorhouse.

(5) "Schiphird" *i.e.* sheep herd. The "ship" or "skip" form of the word is yet found in the name of Skipton.

(6)	Thomas del Holme and his wife ...	4d.
	John Bates and his wife	4d.
	John Adamson	4d.
	Richard del Marche	4d.
(7)	John Tymble and his wife	4d.
	John de Kirkeby and his wife ...	4d.
	John de Marche and his wife ...	4d.
	Adam Willeson	4d.
	John Ffleccher and his wife ...	4d.
	Richard de Slyngesby and his wife...	4d.
	John de Ingeland and his wife	4d.

THE TOWN OR CONSTABULARY OF TIMBLE, INCLUDING TIMBLE, FEWSTON, AND BLUBERHOUSES.

(1)	Richard atte Garthend	4d.
(2)	John de Studfold	4d.
	Richard Gyll	4d.
	John Vescy	4d.
(3)	John Spynk	4d.
	John Couper	4d.
	John de Poterton	4d.
	Alicia Cragwyf	4d.
	Alicia Brathwayt	4d.
	John de Iles, junior	4d.
(4)	John de Hardolfsty	4d.
	Adam Schephird	4d.
(4)	Stephen de Hardolfsty	4d.

(6) "Del Holme," *i.e.* of the holm or flat land by the water. The name Holmes is yet common.

(7) "John Tymble," a place-name with the "de" already dropped. Robertus Timbril did homage to the Archbishop of York at Otley for land in Timbild, in 1298 A.D. John de Tymble did the same in 1315 A.D. Surtees Society's, Vol. 49.

(1) Richard at the garth end. The name possibly lingers in that of the family of "Garth."

(2) John of the stud-fold.

(3) There is still the name of Spinks-burn: a brook and also hamlet, near Fewston.

(4) Hardofsty, now Hardisty, and Hardisty Hill. The family named from this place is still numerous.

	John de Suthill	... ...		4d.
(5)	Isabella Polayn	... ...		4d.
	John, her servant	... ...		4d.
	Agnes, her servant	... ...		4d.
(7)	Thomas de Bestan	... ...		4d.
	John Tailiour	... ...		4d.
(8)	Thomas de Wyndoghs	... ...		4d.
	Henry, his son	... ...		4d.
	Thomas Gybson	... ...		4d.
	Thomas de Plumland	... ...		4d.
	John, the son of Roger	... ...		4d.
	Richard Tailiour	... ...		4d.
(9)	Emma Prestwoman	... ...		4d.
	Agnes Webster	... ...		4d.
	John Webster, (Textor)	... ...		vj.d.
	Roger de Rypon	... ...		4d.
(10)	Robert Grauer	... ...		4d.
	Johanna Vickerwoman	... ...		4d.
(11)	William Vickerman	... ...		4d.
	Robert atte Brigg	... ...		4d.
	William Yong	... ...		4d.
	John Wright	... ...		4d.

(5) Polayn, the same as Pulleine; shewing this wide-spread family at Fewston at this early date, and in the position of employing two house-servants.

(7) "de Bestan." "Bestham" or "Beestan," the home of the wild beasts, is a name given in Doomsday Book to a place of some importance at that time. It is frequently mentioned afterwards up to one hundred and fifty years ago, when it appears as "Beeston Leighs," and "Beeston Leas" in old documents in the possession of the writer. The identification of the place is now difficult. It was certainly in that part of the valley of the Washburn, which lies between Cragg Hall and the village of Fewston.

(8) "de Wyndough," now Wydrah probably.

(9) Probably servant in the house of "the priest;" compare "Priestman."

(10) "Robert Graur or Graver." The family of Graver was, up to the middle of the 17th century, one of the principal families in Fewston. The name has now altogether disappeared.

(11) "Vickerman" and "Vickerwoman," probably the man servant and woman servant of the Vicar.

(12)	William Ketilsyng	...	...	...	4d.
(13)	Roger Wright	...	...	...	4d.
(13)	John Wrightson	...	...	...	4d.
(13)	Elena Wrightwyf	...	...	...	4d.
(14)	William de Megill	...	...	...	4d.
	Robert Whyteside		...	...	4d.
(15)	Thomas de Bland	..	...	...	4d.
	Adam, son of Hugo	...	...	...	4d.
	Roger Hobson	...	...	...	4d.
	William Brouneherd		...	...	4d.
	Henry Grauer	...	...	...	4d.
	Alicia Hobeler	...	...	...	4d.
	Wymerk de Bland	...	...	...	4d.
	John de Goukthorp		...	...	4d.
	Robert Milner	...	...	...	4d.
	John Tayte	...	...	...	4d.
(16)	Robert de Brame	...	...	...	4d.
	Alicia de Bekwyth	...	...	...	4d.
	Robert Goukeman	...	...	..	4d.
	William de Rypon	...	...	...	4d.
	John de Batheby	...	...	...	4d.
	Thomas de Trees	...	...	...	4d.
	John Isakson...	...	...	...	4d.
	John Rede ...	...	...	...	4d.
(17)	Robert Ayredy	...	...	...	4d.
(18)	John Schorthose	...	...	...	4d.
	John de Iles, senior	...	...	...	4d.

(12) "Ketilsyng," that is Ketel's (a Saxon Thane) "ing" or meadow Now Kettlesing.

(13) "Wright." John, Wright's son; Ellen, Wright's wife.

(14) Megill: A hamlet in Fewston township.

(15) "Bland Hill" is yet a hamlet in Norwood township.

(16) "de Brame." Brame, Braham, Brane, is an ancient place mentioned in Domesday Book) in the township of Plumpton. There is also "Brame Lane" in Norwood township.

(17) "Ayredy," probably a "bye" or "nickname,"—Ay'-ready—always on the alert or ready.

(18) "Schorthose," i.e, "short stocking" or hose; another nickname.

(19)	Robert de Gyll	4d.
	John Wayneman	4d.
	John Ryder	4d.
(20)	Margaret Webster (Textrix) ...	vj.d.
	John Patefyn	4d.
	John de March	4d.
(21)	Thomas de Holyns	4d.
(22)	William de Thakwra	4d.
	Robert de Herefeld	4d.
(23)	William de Bramley	4d.

THE TOWN OR CONSTABULARY OF KILLINGHALL, INCLUDING KILLINGHALL, PANNAL, BECKWITH, BECKWITHSHAW, HARROGATE, AND BILTON.

	John Rudd	4d.
(1)	John Schutt and his wife	4d.
	John Boller and his wife	4d.
	William Rutt...	4d.
	John Prudd and his wife	4d.
	Robert, son of Thomas, and his wife	4d.
	Thomas de Stockeld...	4d.
	Thomas Turpyn and his wife ...	xij.d.
	William Turpyn and his wife ...	4d.
	Robert, son of Thomas Turpyn ...	4d.
	Richard de Bekwith and his wife ...	4d.
	John, son of Ade Taillour and his wife	4d.
	John Milner and his wife	vj.d.
	John de Stockeld and his wife ...	4d.
	John Wright	vj.d.

---

(19) "de Gyll," "The Gill" emphatic, Gill Bottom, is, or was, a hamlet in Norwood.

(20) "Webster,"—a plain instance of a trade-name :—A weaver.

(21) "Holyns," i.e., "Hollins,"—a place in the parish of Hampsthwaite.

(22) See Ante.

(23) "de Bramley," *i.e.*, of the "Bram" or "Brame" field. The de being dropped, it is now the well-known forest name of Bramley.

(1) A curious name still common about Harrogate.

(2)	Robert Fflesshewer and his wife ...	4d.
	Robert Edeson	4d.
	Robert de Clifton and his wife ...	4d.
	William Ffuke and his wife... ...	4d.
	William Malson and his wife ...	4d.
	Johanna de Drewesogh	4d.
	Alicia Turpyn	4d.
	William, son of William	4d.
	Robert, his son	4d.
	John Cortman and his wife	4d.
	Thomas Lambe and his wife ...	4d.
	John Lambe and his wife	4d.
	Robert Grayne	4d.
	Robert de Lonesdall...	4d.
	Margaret West	4d.
	Adam del Hill and his wife	4d.
	William Yong and his wife	4d.
	Beatrice de Hill	4d.
	Walter, her servant	4d.
	William de Corby	4d.
	John de Corby, senior	4d.
	John de Corby, junior	4d.
	John Baychour (carpenter)... ...	vj.d.
	Beatrice Turpyn	4d.
	Julia Tailliour	4d.

BEKWYTH—HAMLET DE KYLYNGALL.

(1)	Benedict de Skelwra	4d.
	John, his servant	4d.
	Richard de Skelwra and his wife ...	4d.
	Emma, his daughter	4d.
	Robert de Skelwra and his wife ...	4d.

(2) "Ffleshewer," probably "Flesh cutter" or "butcher;" but more probably "fleche" (French) an arrow, and "Flech-hewer," an arrow cutter; now Fletcher and Flesher.

(1) "de Skelwra," *i.e.*, of the "mere," or perhaps, "island," on the Skell.

(2)	William Ffoloufast and his wife	...	4d.
	Guditha Ffoloufast ...	... ...	4d.
	Matilda de Whetelay	... ...	4d.
	Enota Lambe...	... ...	4d
	Benedict, her son	... ...	4d.
(3)	John de Vsburn and his wife	...	4d.
	John de Hathrusty and his wife	...	4d.
	Robert Douff and his wife ...	...	4d.
	Benedict Wilson and his wife	...	4d.
	Agnes, his daughter...	... ...	4d.
	Richard de Clapham and his wife	...	4d.
	John de Beckwith and his wife	...	4d.
	William de Scalwra and his wife	...	4d.
	William Anny . . . (?) and his wife		4d.
	Robert Atte (?) . . . and his wife		4d.
	John del Gyll	... ...	4d.
	Robert Alayn and his wife ...	...	4d.
	John de Neusom and his wife	...	4d.
	John Nelson ...	... ...	4d.
	William Scayff and his wife	...	4d.
	William de Mosse and his wife	...	4d.
	Alicia, his daughter ...	... ...	4d.
	Walter Hathrusty	... ...	4d.
	John del Hill and his wife ...	...	4d.
	Galfrid Mosse and his wife ...	...	4d.
	Adam Rute and his wife	... ...	4d.
	Geoffrey, his son	... ...	4d.
	John de Lethelay and his wife	...	4d.
	Matilda Mareschall ...	... ...	4d.
	Agnes Vnderbank	... ...	4d.
	Adam Chilray and his wife ...	...	4d.
	Richard de Chilray and his wife	...	4d.
	Benedict Scott and his wife...	...	4d.
	Geoffrey, his son	... ...	4d.
	Richard del Brote and his wife	...	4d.

(2) "Followfast," possibly a nickname: or it may be "de Follifoot," the village of that name.

(3) "de Vsburn," i.e., of Ouseburn.

	William de Merston and his wife ...	4d.
	John de Brocton and his wife ...	4d.
	John de Hoton and his wife ...	4d.
	John Robynson	4d.
	Richard Johnman and his wife ...	4d.
	Geoffrey Johnson and his wife ...	4d.
	Elena, who had been wife of John de Mos	4d.
	Robert de Mos, junior	4d.
	Adam Ffox and his wife	4d.
	John Ffox and his wife	4d.
	John Colyer and his wife	4d.
	Robert Breuster and his wife ...	4d.
	Alicia de Staueley	4d.
	Robert de Mos and his wife ...	4d.
	Thomas Hudson and his wife ...	4d.
	John Benbarn and his wife	4d.
	John Hudson and his wife	4d.
	Alicia de Deen	4d.
	William de Bek and his wife ...	4d.
	Richard de Swynton	4d.
	Roger de Depedale and his wife ...	4d.
	William del Wode and his wife ...	4d.
	Robert Jeppeson	4d.
	Johanna, servant	4d.
	Robert Thompson (Webster) and his wife	vj.d.
	John Webster	vj.d.
	William Pensax and his wife ...	4d.
	John of Pensax	4d.
(4)	Richard de Ffolyfayt	4d.
	Adam Symson	4d.
	Agnes Dynnyng	4d.
	Richard Milneson and his wife ...	4d.
(5)	Percyuallus Pensax	xl.d.
	William, his son	4d.

(4) "de Folyfayt," of Follifoot, near Spofforth.

(5) Percyuallus Pensax. This contribution to the tax, 40d., is equivalent to 33s. 4d. our money and represents the rank of esquire or franklin.

William Doegeson and his wife	...	4d.
John de Ergham	...	4d.
Robert Gybson and his wife	...	4d.
William, son of William and his wife		4d.
John Gyot (Faber) and his wife	...	xij.d.
Matilda de Bekwith	...	4d.
William del Bank	...	4d.
Thomas Hudson and his wife	...	4d.
Richard de Merston and his wife	...	4d.
Richard Wilkes	...	4d.
Richard del Bek and his wife	...	4d.
Benedict Gilleroth and his wife	...	4d.
John Derlof and his wife ..	...	4d.
William Legett and his wife	...	4d.

SOME FOREST MEN IN 1504 A.D.

In a law suit in 1504 A.D., by which it was sought to eject Sir Robert Plumpton, the Master Forester, from his estates in the neighbourhood, the following men bore witness in his behalf. They may be taken as the leading men, in the forest and neighbourhood, at that time. With the exception of about the first twelve names, which are those of knights and gentlemen in the vicinity, nearly all are easily recognised as those of forest families—some of whom had their representatives in the foregoing list of 1378 A.D., and many have still their representatives at the present day.

William Gascoigne,	Knight.
Christopher Ward	,,
Henry Vavasor	Esquire.
Thomas Pigot	,,
Henry Ughtred	,,
Thomas Fairfax	,,
Richard Maulevery	,,
Richard Kyghley	,,

Nicholas Gasgoigne	Esquire.
Robert Chylton	,,
Thomas Ratcliffe	,,
Walter Baylton	,,
Thomas Nawdon	,,
Walter Woode	,,
William Lindley	Gentleman.
Richard Wode	,,
Launcelot Wode	,,
Percival Lindley	,,
George Oglesthorpe	,,
Edmund Richworth	,,
Robert Oglesthorpe	,,
Thomas Knaresborough	,,
William Aldborough	,,
Robert Knaresborough	,,
William Scargill	,,
Raufe Moure	,,
John Douning	,,
William Scargill, yonger	,,
William Dickenson	Yeoman.
Thomas Saxton	,,
Thomas Wood	,,
John Graver	,,
Thomas Dickinson	,,
John Hardistie	,,
William Payer (?) Paver	,,
William Beshe	,,
Robert Dickinson	,,
Nicholas Atherton	,,
Thos. Dickinson	,,
Roger Dickinson	,,
John Beckwith	,,
Robert Gelsthorpe	,,
William Beaston	,,
John Graver, yonger	,,
Stephen Hardistie	,,
Raufe Stanfield	,,

Stephen Gyll	Gentleman.
Robt. Richardson	„
Myles Gyll	„
Myles Wood	„
Robt. Dickinson	„
John Gefray	„
John Pullaine	„
Thomas Kendell	„
Stephen Beaston	„
John Fairborne	„
James Wod	„
Percival Whitehead	„
Thomas Bradebent	„
William Robinson	„
John Exelby	„
Robt. Wayde	„
James Holynaghe	„
James Helme	„
John Scaife	„
Thos. Bayldon	„
Edmund Mydlebroke	„
Richard Barker	„
Henry Readshaw	„
Will: Shutley	„
John Swale	„
Robt. Folyfote	„
Thomas Kyghly	„
Richard Coundall	„

and others.

One hundred and fifty years later, viz., in 1651, A.D., a project was started by the principal inhabitants of the Forest to purchase the manor, and lordship, thereof, from the Duchy of Lancaster. The particulars are given by Grainge. Although the project came to nothing, the following list, of the twenty-five forest men elected by the others to represent them in the transaction, enables us to see who were some of the leading men at that period, and to compare their names with those on earlier lists. They were

Thomas Stockdale, Esquire	Proposed for Trustee.
Robert Atkinson	,,
John Burton	,,
William Hardistie	,,
Richard Roundell	To be Feofees.
Thomas Wescoe	,,
Henry Clint	,,
Arthur Burton	,,
William Burton	,,
Robert Atkinson	,,
William Mann	,,
Francis Day	,,
Leonard Atkinson	,,
Henry Robinson	,,
Thomas Skayfe	,,
Marmaduke Bramley	,,
Stephen Gill	,,
Samuel Midgley	,,
George Ward	,,
John Matthews	,,
George Spence	,,
Anthony Pulleine	,,
Thomas Simpson	,,
John Raynowdes	,,
Arthur Hardistie	,,

These lists of their forefathers, 500, 380, and 230 years ago, will be scanned with interest by foresters to-day; and they will recognise many a name still honoured among them, and many of which it is true "the place that once knew them, knows them no more."

THE WILD ANIMALS OF THE FOREST.

"But see ye not yon fallow deer,
From their ferny covert peer,
Roused with the blush of dawn?
The meek does mincing as they tread,
The stags, with gallant antlers spread,
Stalking a-field, with lordly head;
They cross the dewy upland near,
With watchful eye, and wakeful ear,
Snuffng the breath of morn!"
—W. H. LEATHAM.

N the days of our Saxon and Danish forefathers, the wide tract of country extending from below Knaresborough, on the east, to

"Roggan's heath-clad brow"

on the wild moors, above Bolton Abbey, on the west, and from the Wharf, and the Washburn, on the south, to the Nidd on the north, was owned by two Saxon noblemen, Gamelbar and Gospatric.

At the time when Doomsday survey was completed, about 1086 A.D., these lords of the soil had been dispossessed by the Norman William; and he, and two of his foreign followers, Gilbert Tyson, and William de Perci, (founder, at Spofforth, of that noble family in England), were the new lords of the district. On the forfeiture, in the following reign, of Tyson's fee to the Crown, nearly the whole of what is now the forest, came again into the royal hands. In all probability it was in this (Rufus's) reign, or in that of his successor, Henry I., that the lands were "afforested," and became, henceforth, the Royal Forest of Knaresborough.

The wild animals then existing, and numerous, in the district were, the wolf, wild boar, wild cattle, (which Whitaker says were then called *Oryx*, and identical with the Aurochs or wild bulls of Lithuania), deer or stag, roebuck, hare, fox, badger, beaver, polecat or foumart, (foul marten), and the smaller animals still existing.

For the better protection of the animals, and especially of the deer, and for the convenience of chase, it was not unusual to form within the extensive forests of Norman and Plantagenet times, enclosures or parks. The fences or hedges for these were formed of cleft pales of oak.

This appears to have been done, at a most suitable spot, in the Forest of Knaresborough, soon after its formation. The enclosure, or hedged portion, of the forest was called "Heywra," from *haie* or "*hey*," a hedge (Norman French) and "*wra*" or "*roe*." *Heywra* would thus mean the enclosure, or park, of the deer or roe. Now it is *Haverah*.

This park, situated some six miles to the west of Knaresborough, was reached from thence by a road, or "*gait*," or "*gate*," across the unenclosed forest. From this circumstance we receive the name "Heywra-gate," *i.e.*, the pathway to "Heywra." The word has been so transformed that it is scarcely recognizable, and certainly has lost some traces of its significant origin, in the world-wide name of Harrogate.

The mention, found in books and documents, of the wild animals of this forest, is not frequent, but sufficient to indicate their presence through several centuries.

In the beginning of the 13th century, St. Robert of Knaresborough (b. 1160 A.D., d. 1218 A.D.), was inhabiting his hermit's cell near that town, and several of his miracles, or reputed miracles, were wrought in connection with the wild animals of the forest.

Wolves are alluded to in two passages, in an old metrical life (written about 1400 A.D.) of the Saint.

William de Stuteville, to whom the king had granted the lordship of Knaresborough and its forest, on one occasion, discovering the hut of the Saint erected in his domains without his permission, swore

"Dicens domum ut deleret
In spelunca ut speret,
Feras ferre ac hac feret
Latet in latibulo.

Tunc Robertus hic auditis,
Ait autem satis scitis
Non movebit me invitis
Lupus de hoc lapide."

Translated thus:—

"Saying he would his house destroy,
Wait in a cave and him annoy;
Wolves he'd bring and them employ
Out from his hiding place.

Then our Robert, on this hearing,
Well you know, says he, nought fearing,
Hence no *wolf*, God-right revering,
Shall ever me displace."

The other passage, alluding to the presence of these animals in the neighbourhood, is describing the lamentation which took place on the death of St. Robert :—

"When the news was further spread,
Stayed the sad crowd with their dead;
Weeping sore, in forest dread,
Was made by thousands many.

* * * * * * *

Crowds are round with cowl and hood,
Poor, and powerful, and good,
Him to mourn in sorrowing mood,
Maids, husbands, widows seek.

'Who from *Wolves* our lov'd homes freed?
Who for his own did intercede?
Who with words our souls did feed?'
Thus grieved they ever speak."

Rewards were paid by the monks of Bolton Priory, as appears by their books—and whose territory adjoined the forest on the west—for the destruction of wolves. One was paid for, as slain, in the year 1306 A.D.

Among the shields of arms, at one time, existing in Plumpton Hall, was one bearing, "a fess between three wolves' heads, erased, gules." The Plumptons were Chief Foresters for several generations, and these were, most probably, the suggestive arms of that officer. Further northwards—in the county of Durham—in the time of Bishop Geoffrey Flambard, who died in 1128 A.D.,—wolves must have been exceeding numerous, for Laurence of Durham, who wrote about 1150 A.D., mentions that in a single winter 500 foals, out of 1600 belonging to the Bishop, in that county, were slain by them.—*(Surtees' Society, vol. 70, p. 62).*

In the "Life of St. Robert" there is a very early mention of the *Wild Cattle* of the Forest.

On one occasion the hermit was in want of a cow "for the needs of his poore." He hied him to "the Earl"—the lord of the forest at that period—and asked the bestowal of one. A wild one of the forest was granted, so wild, and untameable, that no one durst approach her. Robert, however, put "a band" round her neck, and led her home like a lamb.

"Gave the Earl thereon to Robert,
One fierce wild one in the desert,
Her he brought and nought was hurt,
She gentle as she could be.
Home he led her, the said peers
Were astonished, eyes and ears,
Minds were moved with sudden fears
As awed as they should be."

In an old English metrical life of the Saint the event is thus described:—

"Quomodo vaccam domavit."

"Off a myracle wylle I melle,
That I trow be trew and lele,
Of Sayntt Robertt; anes, as I rede,
Off a cow he had nede,
For hys pormen in his place;
Tharefor to the Erll Roberd gayes,
And for a cow he com and craved.
He graunte hym ane that wytles raued;
He bad hym to hys forest fare,
'And syke a cowe tak the thare,
I halde hyr wylde, maik thou hyr tame.'
Robert rayked and thider yode,
And faud this cowe wyttles and wode;
Styll she stode, naythinge stirrand;
Roberd arest hyr in a band,
And hame wyth hyr full fast he hyed;
Marvayle them thoght that stood besyde.
Byrde and best all bowed hym tyll,
Ever to wyrke after hys wyll."

The late Rev. John Storer, in his "History of the Wild Cattle of Great Britain, remarks on this narrative:—"I have given this account in full because I think it affords the strongest proof of the existence of wild cattle in the forest of Knaresborough at a very early period . . . . This writer (of the life of St. Robert) about the year 1400 A.D., relating events which took place about the year 1200 A.D., makes 'the fierce wild cow,' supposed to be utterly irreclaimable, ranging through 'the desert,' according to one version of the story, and in 'the forest' according to another, a principal actor in the narrative. I feel sure that the narrator was quite aware that such cattle existed in the times of which he wrote, and in all probability, in the age in which he himself lived, and that those for whose benefit he wrote knew this full well. If this had not been the case, his narrative would have been destitute of the first elements of credibility; and knowing as we do, what the forest breed was on all sides, we may safely assume that this wild cow was of the same description and colour also; for as the wild cattle were always alike in that respect, ancient writers seldom thought it necessary to mention that particular."

The colour alluded to was white, with black or red noses, red inside the ears, and either hornless, or horns tipped with black. The story of Robert and the wild cow was once so popular that a picture of the scene, in stained glass, was set up in Knaresborough Church so late as the year 1473 A.D.

The wild bulls were, as is well known, the most formidable among wild animals, and the most dangerous in the chase. Scott describes them

> "Through the huge oaks of Evandale,
> Whose limbs a thousand years have worn,
> What sullen roar comes down the gale,
> And drowns the hunter's pealing horn?
>
> Mightiest of all the beasts of chase,
> That roam in woody Caledon,
> Crashing the forest in his race,
> The mountain bull comes thundering on.
>
> Fierce on the hunter's quivered band,
> He rolls his eyes of swarthy glow,
> Spurns, with black hoof and horn, the sand,
> And tosses high his mane of snow.
>
> Aimed well, the chieftain's lance has flown;
> Struggling in blood the savage lies;
> His roar is sunk in hollow groan—
> Sound, merry huntsman! sound the *pryse!**

But to proceed. The *Stags* of the forest were a source of great annoyance at one time to St. Robert. They broke through his hedges, intruded among his corn, and ate or trod down much of it. The saint informed the earl of this. His reply was, "I give thee full permission, Robert, to shut them up in thy barn until thou hast received full restitution for thy losses." Robert took a switch, and drove the intruders, like lambs, into his barn, and then went and told the owner what he had done. This being more than the earl had bargained for, he with-

* A note blown at the death.

drew his gift, but bestowed three of them on Saint Robert if he would use them instead of oxen to plough his land. Robert took them, yoked them, and their docility in the work was the admiration of all.

At a much later date than that of St. Robert, viz., in 1428 A.D., an enquiry was held at Ripley, to obtain proof that William, son of Thomas Ingleby, of that place, was of the age of 21 years, on the 8th day of June in that year. William Beckwith deposed that he remembered the date enquired into "because the day before the birth of the said William Ingleby, he, the said William Beckwith, was sauntering alone in the Forest of Knaresborough, when he slew there a *certain great stag*, and afterwards conveyed it to Thomas and Alianore Ingleby, the parents of the said William."

And again in a similar proof of the age of John Ingleby, in 1455 A.D., born on the festival of the Translation of St. Thomas, 1433 A.D., son of William Ingleby, deceased; Robert Apilton, aged 60 years, stated that he recollected the day of the birth of the said John, "because he was walking from the village of Ripley to the village of Hampsthwaite on that festival, and by the way, in the wood called Harlow Wood, he *killed a fallow deer*, and carried the same to the house of John Pullaine."

About the same time, in 1439 A.D., when Sir William Plumpton was master forester, there were one hundred and sixty head of wild deer in the park at Heywra.

Some forty years later, viz., in 1484 A.D., the following letter was written, by the Earl of Northumberland, to Sir Robert Plumpton, then master forester:—

"Right hartely beloved cousin, I commend me unto you, and desire and pray you to caus a bucke of season to be taken, within the forest of Knaresborough under your rule, and to be delivered unto this bearer, to the behaulfe of the mawer (Mayor) of the Cyte of Yorke and his bredren, and this my writting shal be your warrant. * * * * Written in my manor at Lekinfield, the xxviii. day of Juyn.

Yor Cousin,

HEN. NORTHUMBERLAND."

D

We hope the "Mawer of the Cyte of Yorke and his bredren" enjoyed their venison from Knaresborough Forest.

It is to be feared that not seldom in those lawless days, in spite of chief forester, and warden, and verderer, and bedell, "a bucke of season," or out of season, was taken without lordly warrant.

Deer-stealers, and outlaws, found a refuge in the fastnesses and woods of this forest as they did in those of others.

In 1302 A.D., a precept was issued by Edward I., commanding an enquiry to be made concerning malefactors and disturbers of the peace within the chase of Knaresborough; and also of those who fly there, and those who without license sport in the same, and all transgressors; and if convicted, commanding the same to be committed to prison within the Castle of Knaresborough.

Even the notorious Robin Hood and his merry men all, are believed by Mr. Hunter, the historian of Hallamshire, to have occasionally resorted to this forest, finding

> "When shaws beene sheene, and shradds full fayre,
> And leaves both large and long,
> It is merrye walking in the fayre forrest,
> To heare the small birdes songe;"

And more than "to heare the small birdes songe," to exercise their bow-skill upon the Royal deer.

As a protection against such, and possibly, also to serve as a hunting lodge to the Royal and other sportsmen, duly warranted to take "a bucke of season," there was erected in the upper part of Heywra Park, toward the end of the second Edward's reign, or early in that of his successor, a tower or fortified castlet, known afterwards as John of Gaunt's Castle. The ruins of it are still to be seen. It is first mentioned in 1334 A.D., (9th of Edward III.) when it is designated "fortallicii Regis Heyra." About forty years after this date, viz., in 1371 A.D., the Forest and Honour were granted by Edward III. to his son John of Gaunt, Duke of Lancaster, and they have formed, ever since, a portion of that Duchy. This accounts for the Castlet bearing the name of this renowned son of Edward.

The ruins of another similar forest fortress are to be seen at the north-western extremity of the district. Padside Hall, an erection of the time of Elizabeth, occupies the greater part of the area which this castlet formerly occupied, and is built from the old materials. Some portions of the older building yet remain, but now and for long

> "The tim'rous deer have left the lawn,
> The oak a victim falls;
> The gentle traveller sighs when shown
> Those desolated walls."

On at least two occasions the Royal denizens of the forest enjoyed the honour of a Royal huntsman.

About 1209 A.D., King John* was on a hunting expedition in the neighbourhood, and took the opportunity, as we learn from the life of St. Robert, of paying a visit to that hermit in his cell, near Knaresborough; and Edward II., in 1323 A.D., from an itinerary of his of that date, was at *Heywra* for three days. What for, if not for the purposes of the chase?

It is impossible to fix any date at which the various wild animals ceased to inhabit the forest. The wild cattle are not mentioned after the 13th century. Wolves were probably not extinct in the 14th, indeed there are traditions of their existence three centuries later. Deer there were in 1654 A.D., for William Fleetwood, serjeant of the Duchy of Lancaster, was plaintiff in a suit against Ellis Markham for destruction of some deer, game, and trees in Haverah or Heywra, Park, at that date. The last wild boar is said to have been slain in the Boar Hole, in Haverah Park, in the reign of Charles II. By the middle of the reign of Elizabeth, however, say 1580 A.D., probably all (except very rare specimens indeed) the larger wild animals were gone.

---

* King John was at Knaresborough, on Thursday, May 30, 1209 A.D., on Wednesday and Thursday, June 13th and 14th, in the same year; again on Friday and Saturday, September 7th and 8th, 1212, A.D., and again Friday and Saturday, September 12th and 18th, 1213 A.D.

At the Sheriff's Torne of the forest, held in 1576 A.D., there were several "paines set," bearing on the subject, *e.g.*, no person "having with him dogg or bytche, and carrying any bowe, bolte, or arrow, or any other engine or devise," should, without license, go about to kill any "woodcock, hare, coney, pheasant, partridge, or other beast or foule" in the said forest.

No mention, it will be noticed, is made of any animal larger than hare, coney, &c.; and henceforth alike are

"The hunter and the deer, a shade."

They have not, however, passed into "the shadow land" without leaving abiding evidence, of their former presence in the forest, stamped upon the names of the places in which they abounded.

One name, pointing to the district as a wild beasts' home, even before the forest, as such, was formed, has a special significance; viz., that of "Bestham" or "Beast-haim." It occurs as the name of a manor, or place of importance, in Doomsday Book, and several times afterwards, and may possibly be identified with Beeston, or Beaston, or Beaston Leas, of comparatively modern times. And if so, this once well known refuge for the wild beasts was a portion of the Washburn valley, between Fewston and Cragg Hall. Many old documents mention Beaston Leas or Leighs as being there.

There can be no doubt about the significance of the still well known names of "Swinden," the "dene" or valley of the swine; or the kindred ones of "Swinsty," and "Swin-cliffe;" or of Barden, *i.e.* "Boar-dene," just beyond the forest boundary on the west; or "Boar Hole" in Haverah Park. Darley, *i.e.* Deer-ley, the field of the deer; Ray-Bank, or Roe-Bank, near Thruscross; Beaver-dike, near the ruins of John of Gaunt's Castle; "Padside," or Pate-side, (*Pate*, a badger), and "Badger Gate" on Timble Ings, all in like manner tell their own story. And, as we have already seen, "Hey-wra" was the park of the wra, or roe, though now disguised as Haverah and Harro.

Nominally the district remained a Royal Forest up to the time of its enclosure, under Act of Parliament, in 1771 A.D.; but long before this date it had practically ceased to be a refuge for the wild beasts, or to be used for the chase. As we have seen, its larger animals were extinct; and besides losing its chief fauna, it had been denuded, in a great measure, of its green woods and forest monarchs. This is said to have been brought about chiefly by the existence of smelting furnaces, for lead, and iron, in the neighbourhood. Thoresby, writing in 1703 A.D., makes this entry in his diary:—

"The Forest of Knaresborough did abound with '*minera ferri*.' It was once so woody, that I have heard of an old writing, said to be reserved in the parish chest at Knaresborough, which obliged them to cut down so many yearly as to make a convenient passage for the wool-carriers from Newcastle to Leeds. Now it is so naked, that there is not so much as one left for a way-mark."

To this cause, rather than to any other, is to be attributed the denudation which laid Harrogate open to the sarcasm of Sydney Smith, "Harrogate is the most heaven-forsaken country under the sun. When I saw it there were only nine mangy fir-trees there, and even they all leaned away from it."

This certainly has no application to the place now. Harrogate has become again, under the fostering care of the art of landscape gardening, more than of forestry, a place of luxuriant groves and avenues.

And in spite of destruction's unsparing hand, in many of the remoter parts of the district, there are still wild recesses and dells, and places where "the forest primeval" yet waves; and oaks, which may have sheltered the Royal deer, yet flourish, and sycamore groves spread their grateful shades, all worthy of ancient forest fame.

And some among the arboreal patriarchs, could they but tell us what they had seen, might say, as Mrs. Hemans has made such a one to say—

"I have seen the forest shadows lie
 Where men now reap the corn;
I have seen the kingly chase rush by,
 Through the deep glades at morn.

With the glance of many a gallant spear,
 And the wave of many a plume,
And the bounding of a hundred deer,
 It hath lit the woodland's gloom.

I have seen the knight and his train ride past,
 With his banner borne on high;
O'er all my leaves there was brightness cast
 From his gleaming panoply.

The pilgrim, at my feet hath laid
 His palm branch 'midst the flowers,
And told his beads, and meekly prayed,
 Kneeling, at vesper hours.

And the merry men, of wild and glen,
 In the green array they wore,
Have feasted here, with the red wine cheer,
 And the hunter's song of yore.

And the minstrel resting in my shade,
 Hath made the forest ring,
With lordly tales of the high crusade,
 Once loved by chief and king.

But now their noble forms are gone,
 That walked the earth of old;
The soft wind hath a mournful tone,
 The sunny light looks cold.

There is no glory left us now,
 Like the glory with the dead:—
I would that where they slumber now,
 My latest leaves were shed!"

Yes! the days of the "merry green-wood" are gone. The foresters pursue the even tenour of their lives in the peaceful cultivation of the fields, where their forefathers guarded, or hunted, or perhaps stole the king's deer.

Yet there are few foresters whose eye will not kindle, and the old forest spirit leap within them, at the trolling of the Wensleydale forester's (Mr. G. M. J. Barker) song:

Hurrah for the Forest! Hurrah for the free!
Our home is the wood-land, our shelter the tree,
Our couch is the fair mossy lawn;
No clock to us telleth the coming of day,
But when larks are singing "we up and away!"
Through the soft rosy splendour of dawn.

The rich dwell in splendour, —the poor till the soil—
We heed not their pleasures,—we brook not their toil,
Nor envy their elegant cheer;
Beneath some old oak tree our banquet we spread,
With the green turf beneath us, and green boughs o'erhead,
And our feast is the flesh of the deer.

Then fill we full goblets, our comforts to crown,
With France's choice vintage, or ale berry-brown,
While nothing embitters the bowl;
But heart with heart joining, we clasp hand in hand,
And joyfully quaffing, "to Friendship's true band,"
The blithe songs of our Forestry troll.

* * * * * * * *

Deep, deep in the forest, beneath the dear shade,
Where love rock'd our cradles, our last homes are made,
When we sink into death's heavy sleep.
And should no proud tomb mark the Forester's grave,
Above his green hillock thick oak branches wave,
And true friends at his burial weep.

Deceit lurks in cities, in pomp there is pain,
Amid honours, the honour'd oft sigheth in vain,
For a peace that he never must see:
But free from ambition—disclaiming all strife.—
Undisturbed are our minds as untroubled our life,
Then—"Hurrah for the Forest and Free."

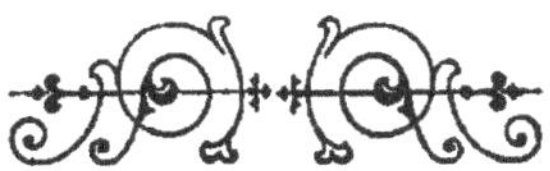

THE HUNT.

"'Waken lords and ladies gay,
The mist has left the mountains grey,
Springlets in the dawn are streaming,
Diamonds on the brake are gleaming;
And foresters have busy been,
To track the buck in thicket green;
Now we come to chant our lay,
'Waken lords and ladies gay.

'Waken lords and ladies gay,
To the greenwood haste away;
We can show you where he lies,
Fleet of foot and tall of size;
We can show the marks he made,
When 'gainst the oak his antlers frayed;
You shall see him brought to bay,
'Waken lords and ladies gay."

—*Scott.*

THE rising sun sends forth its lights,
In many a golden ray,
To crown the cliffs on Almas' heights
With blush of waking day.

Now gleam, now shade, plays o'er Bland Hill,
As morn pursues the night;
And autumn mists by Fewstone mill
Give place to silvern light.

The goss'mer's webs, on whin and hedge,
Are spread—a beauteous sight;
And dewdrops gleam, on tree and hedge,
As clear as diamonds bright.

The deer—buck, hind, and fawn—at ease,
  By Bestham's wood are laid;
No sound, as yet, disturbs the peace
  Of forest's tangled glade.

Another hour! how changed the scene!
  On morning's breeze is borne
O'er hill, and dale, and village green,
  The blast of hunter's horn.

As music loved in forest home,
  Is heard the hounds' deep bay;
Plompton—chief forester—is come
  To hunt the stag this day.

The forest, waking with a bound,
  Sends up a ringing cheer;
And quick, from house and hamlet round,
  The foresters appear.

From Norwood, Elsworthe, Padside Green,
  In haste they hurry forth;
From Timble, and its Ings, they're seen,
  From Thurscross and Hoodstorth.

The shepherd stalks* from Bluber moor,
  The warden from the Gill;
And miners quickly hasten o'er
  The heath from Greenhow Hill.

In troops, o'er Ketel's Head and Ing,
  The men of Hampsthwaite swarm;
And, toiling through the gorse and ling,
  They run by Long Stoop farm.

From Greyston plain, and Oak Beck side,
  The swineherds are not late;
By Strayling *ville*, o'er moorlands wild,
  They come from Heywra-gate.

---

* Persons, whose employment leads them to have to walk much among the tall, trackless, heather acquire a gait, or mode of walking, which may aptly be described by this word.

From Swincliffe Top, and Swarcliffe height,
  The Smith's and Bilton's haste;
With hunting spear and quiver dight,
  O'er Cold Cotes moorland waste.

They're there from all the forest through,
  No man behind doth lag;
Fairfaxes of Newhall and Scough,
  And Franklands of the Cragg.

Beckwith and Pulleine hear the call,
  And stand with hounds in leash;
There's Robinson, of Swinsty Hall,
  And Day, of old Day Ash.

John Jeffrey, of "The Trees," is there,
  And Stubbs of Whitewall Nook,
Guy Palmes, of Lindley, th'sport to share,
  Hath come o'er moor and brook.

Will Wood, of Timble, too is out,
  John Breary of Bland Hill;
E'en Parson Smithson joins the rout,
  And Graver from the *ville*.

Soon men and hounds, a merry throng,
  Are on the move; and, hark!
With lusty shout and hunters' song,
  They make for Heyra Park.

The woods are drawn by John O'Gaunt's,
  The Beaver dell is past;
The herds are startled in their haunts
  As a buck breaks ground at last.

At clarion blown on huntsman's horn,
  The shout rings loud and far;
They rush through tangled brake and thorn,
  By field and echoing scar.

The wild boar dashes from his lair,
  'Mong leaves and rotting logs;
The grey fox scuds, with timid hare,
  From crash of men and dogs.

The graceful stag, without a check,
  Now bounds o'er Old Camp ridge,
Down Worstall Crags, o'er Wydrah Beck,
  And 'cross by Bedlam Bridge.

Then on, and on, as arrow sent,
  He flies by Coppice Sike,
Thence skirts the side of Fewston Bent,
  And 'long the Busky Dike.

By Upper Cragg, o'er Watling Street,
  He speeds by Lane Ends wood;
And, pressed by the hunters fleet,
  There crosses Washburn flood.

Before him fly the startled flocks,
  As o'er the heath he takes,
Along the hill by Brandreth rocks,
  And 'mong the golden brakes.

The sun has reached to half its height,
  As down 'neath Hangon Hill,
The hunted beast, in hunters' sight,
  Seeks rest in Redshaw Gill.

But there no shelt'ring spot he finds,
  But breaks toward Brown Bank,
As hunters' shouts come on the wind,
  And foam drops from his flank.

With panting tongue, by Bramley Head,
  He drags a weary way;
By moor, and moss, and brooklets' bed,
  He treads the mountains grey.

In Cappishaw's bright amber stream,
  He cools his heated limbs,
As 'cross its pool in sunlit gleam,
  He quickly—madly—swims.

Still on he toils by Whit-Moor ends,
  And Thurstan's holy cross,
By where the waning Washbrook wends,
  At Hoodstorth's sparkling foss.

Past Harden Beck, away, away,
He gains the deep Ray Bank,
And there, at length, he turns to bay,
'Neath rocks 'mid brackens dank.

The deep-mouthed hounds rush on in cry,
But fear to close around,
As right and left his antlers fly,
Till gore bestrews the ground.

But soon they end the mortal fray,
His frantic strength is fled;
They seize,—they tear,—and win the day,—
The noble beast is dead!

Then quick, with shouts both loud and shrill,
The hunters gather round;
From crag to crag, and hill to hill,
Echoing horns resound.

Many a chase that day they run,
And many a one before;
But ne'er a chase like this they won,
On forest, hill, or moor.

The sun goes down o'er Roggan's height
Before their sport they end;
The day is passing into night,
As homeward, slow, they wend.

The hunters' moon is mounted high,
Few signs of day remain,
A thousand stars bedeck the sky,
Ere all their homes attain.

* * * * * * *

Long years of change have come and gone
Since there such day was seen;
Where thick woods waved the sun hath shone,
And now are pastures green.

Where then the red buck bounded free,
Till roused by hunters' horn;
There now but spreads the hedgerow tree,
Or waves the rip'ning corn.

Where royal lodge, in haughty power,
Arose with battled wall,
There now but stands the ivyed tower,
Or yeoman's crumbling hall.

The names well known and famed of yore,
Have fled, or waned, or died;
Day, Beckwith, Frankland, are no more,
And many a one beside.

But oft a root, though hid away,
By *shoot* is not unknown:
And Fairfax, Stubbs, and Thackeray,
Are names the world doth own.

E'en yet, in hall, by lane, or gill,
Of sires whose course is run,
The grand old forest blossoms still,
With many a worthy son.

Long may its sons, as men of God,
For Church and Country stand,
As England's yeomen ever stood,
The bulwarks of the land.

[This ballad contains grave anachronisms, excusable only under poetic license. It is not probable that many, if any, wild beasts, even of chase, survived in the Forest later than the 16th century. The personal names introduced into the ballad belong to the former half of the 17th century.]

The hunt even yet penetrates occasionally into the forest glens, if we may judge from the following account, taken from the *Yorkshire Post* of January 12th, 1881:—

"YORK AND AINSTY HOUNDS. — A correspondent writes: — Unlike most other packs of hounds, to which, judging from the oft-occurring accounts of their performances—bad, good, and indifferent—a 'remembrancer' is evidently attached to the staff of officials, the York and Ainsty very rarely go over their ground again on paper. However, the sport on Thursday last, January 6th, was so exceptionally remarkable, that I must send you an account of it, having had the good fortune to be out on that day. The hounds met at Bishop Monkton, drew Bishop Monkton Whin blank. We then drew the low coverts at Copgrove, and found immediately; a real good fox went away by the low grounds straight for Copgrove, turned to the right up the hill, left Burton Leonard village on the left, and the coverts to the right, ran to South Stainley, crossed the Ripon road, on through Cayton Gill to Shaw Mill, and went to ground close to Winsley; time, 1 hour and 20 minutes; distance as the crow flies, seven miles. We then drew Clint Wood. Here a gallant fox was found, and was off without an instant's delay. He went over the river immediately, close to Hampsthwaite Bridge, where we crossed. He then went by Birstwith to Kettlesing, towards Blubberhouse Moor and Hardisty Hill; the hounds ran into a deep gill, near West End, where it was impossible for horses to get down. It was thought that the fox might have got to ground in the gill. The huntsman therefore dismounted, and went down the gill on foot, to try and mark him, but he here found that some of the hounds were missing, and afterwards ascertained that five couple had slipped out at the end of the gill, and it was supposed had killed their fox alone on the moor, two miles further on, between Bramley Head and Simon's Seat. It was now quite dark, and time had not been taken, but the distance as the crow flies is close upon ten miles, leaving off at least 40 miles from the kennels. Both master and huntsman had reason to be proud of the bitch pack on that day, for they worked magnificently. Altogether the York and Ainsty have had very good sport this season, accounting for plenty of foxes, and having had some rattling good gallops—in fact quite above the average. I am told that the master is greatly pleased with his new huntsman, and from what I have seen myself and heard from others, he has every reason to be so."

The Master of the York and Ainsty Hounds bears the honoured forest name of Fairfax—Col. Fairfax.

SAINT ROBERT,
THE HERMIT OF KNARESBOROUGH.

"Our Lord that likened is to a lamb,
I beseech Thee where I sit,
Visit that Thou would my wit,
With wisdom of Thy worthy Sell,
Through living truly for to tell
Of Saint Robert that heremit,
Was approved here perfitt;
Beside Knaresburgh in a skene,
In a renes closed himsene;
And full devoutly he lay
In contemplation night and day."
—*Metrical Life of St. Robert, 14th cent.*

IN the ballads, romances, and even the history of most nations, men of ascetic lives, nazarites, hermits, and such like, hold a place in ecclesiastical chivalry analagous to that held by crusaders, knights, Knights Templars, &c., in social and national chivalry. The lives of many such have been written, and form no unimportant part of mediæval and modern literature.

The life, however, of *St. Robert, the hermit of Knarcsborough*, seems, as to modern days at least, to be an exception. The influence he exercised in his time, and the veneration in which his name was long held in Yorkshire, were very considerable. Yet the short sketches, which have been given of his history, have been confined to books which only come into the hands of few. And this, since the revival of a taste for archæological and mediæval subjects, is the more to be wondered at, because there exists, buried in monastic legends and writings, a considerable amount of material ready for use.

There is a MS. life of him in Latin triplets, probably the work of one of the monks of Fountains Abbey, another metrical one, in old English, most likely by a brother of the Priory of Holy Trinity at Knaresborough, and also one in Latin prose, all dating about the beginning of the fifteenth century. These are now in the library of the Duke of Newcastle. They were placed at the disposal of the late J. R. Walbran, Esq., when compiling his "Memorials of Fountains," and in a note to this able work is found the most reliable sketch of the hermit's life which has been given. The old English version has been printed for the Roxburgh Club. The whole of these sources of information are freely put under contribution for this paper; the spelling of the old English being more or less modernized, and a free rendering of the Latin triplets substituted, except in one or two instances, for the original. There is also "Vita Roberti de Knaresburg, per Richard Stodeley scripta," among the Harleian MSS. in the British Museum, but whether this be a copy of any of the above, or an independent record, the writer has not had the opportunity to ascertain.

St. Robert's parents resided, during the latter half of the twelfth century, at York. His father was Sir Toke Flouris, who was at least twice mayor of that city. According to the Latin history, the name of his wife, Robert's mother, was Siminima, but the early English MS. gives it as Onnuryte :—

> "Some time in York his life to lead,
> Of a righteous man, I reade,
> Docens Flos, I understand
> Men called him when he was livand,
> And his wife, dame Onnuryte."

It has, however, been thought by some that "Toke," or "Coke," was really the paternal name, and that the family was originally "De Tokeliffe," or "De Cokeliffe."

That there should be some uncertainty, on such a point, will surprise no one, who knows how unfixed were surnames at that time.

Robert was the eldest son, and was born about 1160 A.D.

Little of his early life is recorded beyond that he was an exemplary child, and a studious youth. The Latin biographer says,—

> "Hic adultus mansuetus,
> Fuit factus qui facetus,
> Pulchris puris ac repletus,
> Ornamentis morum.
> Pius, prudens, ac perfectus,
> Et a plebe predelectus,
> Factis sedis nec infectus
> Fuit viciorum."

On attaining the requisite age he was admitted to holy orders, but never advanced beyond the sub-diaconate.

> "But why nay mey orders he toke,
> Find I noght brefed in my boke."

After some time, during which a brother of his appears to have become an inmate of the Cistercian Abbey of Newminster,* in Northumberland, Robert joined the same brotherhood, and was there invested with the habit of the Cistercian novitiate. Here, however, he remained only eighteen weeks.

> "Four monthes and two weke mare,
> Robert reved with monkes there;
> And then like maid mildest of mode,
> To York again full mildly rode,
> To his friendship and his friends."

A monk's life thus not suiting him, he, after a time, determined to try that of a hermit. He selected for this purpose a romantic spot near Knaresborough, about

* The abbey of Newminster was founded by Ralph de Merley, in 1138 A.D., with a colony of twelve monks from Fountains, one of whom, St. Robert of Newminster (often confounded with the subject of this sketch), was the first abbot.

eighteen miles westward of his native city. Hither, leaving the "landes and goodes of his father, to whome he was heire, as eldest sonne" (Leland), he withdrew himself secretly from his parents' home. Providence appears to have smiled on the step, for when—

"He came to Knaresborough,
There an hermit, Robert fand,
Devout in a rock dwelland,
That a knight had been before,
That kin, and towne, and his store,
All had forsaken, child and wife,
And there as hermit led his life."

This man, who had thus forestalled Robert in the place, was known as St. Giles. He already had provided himself a cell — a cave in the rock on the northern side of the river Nidd, — about a mile below the town. To this kindred spirit Robert gladly joined himself.

The place, which these men had thus selected for their abode, was one which, in almost every detail, meets Spenser's description of a hermitage :—

"A little lowly hermitage it was,
Downe in a dale, hard by a forest's side;
Far from resort of people that did pass
In traveill to and fro; a little wyde
There was an holy chapelle edifyde,
Wherein the holy hermite dewly wont to say
His holy things, each morn and eventyde:
Thereby a christall streame did gently play,
Which from a sacred fountain welled forth alway."

The river Nidd, after pursuing its "unquiet" course from its source at the foot of Whernside in the western moorlands, through Nidderdale, breaks out, at Knaresborough between high and rugged limestone cliffs, into the open vale of York. On the top of one of these cliffs stood, and still stand the ruins of, the strong castle built by Serlo de Burg soon after the Conquest, and in which for a time the murderers of Archbishop a'Becket found a refuge.

A considerable portion of the town of Knaresborough stands on rocky terraces, sloping down to the water. To the south, and away for many miles to the west, stretched, in the days of St. Robert, the almost impenetrable *forest.*

> "The nimble Nyde,
> Through Nythersdale, along as sweetly she doth glide
> Tow'rds Knaresburg on her way,—
> Where that brave forest stands
> Entitled by the town."—*Drayton.*

On the opposite side of the river, and facing the cliffs in which the hermits had fixed their residence, rises, like an enormous sphinx out of the opening plain, a precipitous rock — its sides now clothed with underwood — called Grimbald's Crag.

A more suitable spot, therefore, for a hermit's cell, could not have been found. The cave, which formed part (probably at first the whole) of the hermitage, is now known as *St. Robert's Cave.** It is completely shut in by trees and underwood. A rudely formed stair, partly hewn in the natural rock, leads down through the dense foliage to the mouth. The cave itself is of an irregular circular shape, sufficiently large, as to area, to form a comfortable room. The roof is solid rock, and so is the floor. At one end of the apartment there is a recess, which may have served for a pantry, the places for the shelves being yet visible. Outside, to the right-hand of the doorway, a long seat is cut, also in the solid stone, while above it the face of the rock contains some indications of another, and larger room, having been partly hewn out, and partly formed by masonry built against it. A little to the left of the entrance, but only separated from the rock by about two feet, are the foundations of a small chapel, of hewn stone. Of this chapel, more hereafter. The whole in-

---

* This cave has been given notoriety in modern times by being the scene of the murder, for which Eugene Aram, the hero of Bulwer Lytton's novel, and of Hood's poem, "The dream of Eugene Aram," was executed.

voluntarily recalls Dr. Percy's description of the hermitage at Warkworth:—

"And now, attended by their host,
The hermitage they viewed,
Deep-hewn within a craggy cliff,
And overhung with wood.

"And near, a flight of shapely steps,
All cut with nicest skill,
And piercing through a stony arch,
Ran winding up the hill.

* * * * *

"Then, scooped within the solid rock,
Three sacred vaults he shows:
The chief a chapel, neatly arched,
On branching columns rose."

But to return now to St. Robert. The compact between him and St. Giles did not long bear the strain of close fellowship. St. Giles very soon withdrew himself and returned to the world.

" Langer liked him not that life,
But as a wretch, went to his wife,
As hound that casts off his kit,
And, aye, turns and takest his vomit."

Thus was Robert left in sole possession. How long he lived alone in the cave there is no record; probably not long, but soon betook himself to a wealthy lady in the neighbourhood (probably a Percy of Spofforth Castle) for assistance.

" Ad matronam tunc migravit,
A qua quidem impetravit
Vite victim nec negavit,
Dare necessaria."

This lady bestowed upon him a small chapel, dedicated to St. Hilda, and as much land as he should be able to dig. It would appear, however, that he had now associated others with himself, as companions or helpers; for the lady's grant is made—

"To thee and thy poor men alway,
Against my gift shall no man say."

The place of this chapel and hermitage, is about two miles from his cave-dwelling in the rock. It is still known as St. Hile's Nook, and, so late as 1843 A.D., the foundations of the chapel were removed, and used in the erection of the Roman Catholic church at Knaresborough. Here again Robert remained only about a year. The reason for his desertion is thus related:—

> "It befell upon a night
> Fell thieves came with main and might;
> His bower they brak, and bare away
> His bread, his cheese, his sustenance,
> And his poore men's purveyance.
> Havand in his mind always
> How God his gospel says,
> 'If fools pursue you, false and fell,
> In a city where you dwell,
> Flee unto another than;'
> Therefore Robert raise and ran,
> And sped him unto Spofford town
> To sue God with devocione."

Spofforth, the place to which "he ran," is a village near, and the castle there was a residence of the Percy family, one of whom his patroness probably was. His sojourn at the place was a temporary one. The importunity of large numbers of people annoyed him, and his popularity led him to fear lest he should fall into temptation to vain-glory. He therefore accepted an opportune invitation from a cell of Cluniac monks at Hedley, in the adjoining parish of Bramham, to join their brotherhood.

Neither, however, did their mode of life suit him. His austerity rebuked their laxity. Though—

> "His life to leil men gave great light
> As does a stere upon a night,"

they gave him no agreeable time of it at Hedley; but—

> "On him they raise all in a route,
> And bade this blessed man go out;
> At him they were baithe wrath and ork,
> Baithe in cloister and in kyrk."

He therefore left them, and returned to the ruined chapel and cell of St. Hilda, thinking it—

"Better to beld with beastes wyld
Than with merred men unmylde."

The lady who had before befriended him did so again. She gladly welcomed him back to the spot she had before given him, and at once she set "men of crafte" to work to build (or rebuild) for him "a honesthalle," and "mansiones for his men gert mák," and—

"A laithe for Robert's sake,
His swine, his cattel into bringe."

The number of men now forming his brotherhood was four. Two were employed to till and cultivate the land around their dwelling; one accompanied Robert about the country begging alms for the community and for the poor; and the fourth was a kind of general help.

He is said at this time to have spent whole nights in prayer, aud that the little sleep he permitted himself to take was taken upon the bare ground. His clothing consisted of one long garment, white in colour, probably that of the Cistercian novitiate, made of undyed wool, but so thin as "to serve him rather as a cover for his nakedness than a protection from the cold." His food was bread made of barley meal, with broth of herbs, varied by a few beans seasoned with salt once a week. His daily employment was—

"To begge and brynge pore men of baile,
This was his purpose principale."

One day about this period, while he was sleeping upon the flowery grass, his mother, who had lately died, appeared to him,

"Pale and wan of hide and hue."

She told him that for usury and other sins she was suffering great torment, and must continue to do so until set free through his prayers. This greatly troubled him, and for a whole year he ceased not to make intercession on her behalf. At the end of that time she again appeared to him, with a happy and shining face, to thank him and announce her deliverance. She then proceeded to—

> "Wend to wealth that never shall wane,
> Farewell! I bless thee, blood and bain."

A very similar circumstance, the reader may remember, is related of St. Perpetua, who suffered martyrdom as early as the year 205 A.D.

Robert was not allowed to remain undisturbed at St. Hilda's. The words of his patroness in her grant—

> "Against my gifte shall no man say,"

proved untrue.

The times were those in which often—

> "Might was right,"

and men were content with—

> "The simple plan,
> That they should take who have the power.
> And they should keep who can."

In 1177 A.D., the king (Henry II.) granted the wardship of the castle and manor of Knaresborough to William de Stuteville. This baron,—

> "Lord of that land, both east and west,
> Of frith, and field, and of forest,"

probably soon after his grant, was riding through the forest, and came upon Robert's "honest halle." He asked of his attendants, "Whose was that building?" They replied, "that it belonged to—

> "Ane hermite, that is perfite,
> Robert, that is no rebellour,
> A servante of oure Savioure."

"No," replied the baron, "not so, but an abettor and harbourer of thieves." Then he ordered the place to be demolished, and the hermit banished from the forest. The attendants were most unwilling to molest "the holy hermite," and delayed to execute the order. But Stuteville passed the same way a few days afterwards, and, seeing the buildings yet standing, was mad with fury, and ordered their instant destruction.

> "Then they durst no langer byde,
> But unto Robert's housying hyed,
> And dang them downe, baith less and maire,
> Nothing left they standing there."

Again, by violence, deprived of his dwelling, Robert for some time wandered from place to place in the forest, but at length returned to the shelter of the cliffs near Knaresborough. Probably not, however, to his original cave, but to an excavation in the rock which is now known as St. Robert's Chapel, and also as the Chapel of St. Giles. Whether this chapel was the work of St. Giles, or of St. Robert during his former residence near, may be doubtful. Much, if not all, that is now to be seen in it, is of more modern date than either of them. The cavern is cut entirely out of the limestone rock; on the face of the rock at the right hand, as the door is approached, is sculptured the figure of a Knight Templar, armed, and in the act of drawing his sword to defend the entrance.

> "Carved in the rock, and near the door,
> An armed warrior stands,
> Who seems to guard the sacred place
> From rude and hostile hands."

The doorway is a somewhat rudely constructed pointed arch; the window to the left of it (entering) is an insertion in the Perpendicular style, and therefore later, than the other parts of the chapel. It was probably brought from the ruins of the neighbouring priory of the Holy Trinity after the suppression of that house in A.D. 1539. The interior measurement of the chapel is given as 10 ft. by 9 ft., and the height 7 ft. 6 in. The roof is groined; the altar—opposite the door—remains complete; over it is a recess cut in a rock, probably for the crucifix. In the altar slab, near the front edge, there are two holes for the sacred relics. In the centre of the floor, and immediately in front of the altar, there is a large hole, probably also for relics. On the walls there are three or four rudely sketched faces, and apparently the work of a much more recent hand than any of the other decorations. In many respects this singular, almost, I believe, unique chapel, is intensely interesting to the ecclesiologist and archæologist.

To this place St. Robert came, or returned, after the destruction of his hermitage at St. Hilda's. He formed himself a dwelling, at the front of the cave, by means of stakes and the boughs of trees. And hither—

> "Highe and lowe unto him hyed,
> In soth for to be edifyed."

But again his enemy, the lord of the adjoining castle, passed that way—

> "Withe hound, and hawke upon his hond,"

and seeing the smoke curling up from Robert's hut, he again asked, "Who dwelt there?" The reply was, "Robert the hermit." "What, that same Robert whom I not long ago since expelled from my forest?" Again he was answered, "It is the same." Then he sware a mad oath that he should at once be driven away again.

But in the middle of the following night there appeared to the baron a fearful vision. Three men, "blacker than Ynd," stood by him in his chamber. Two of them carried a fearful instrument of torture, and the third, a tall powerful man, had in his hand two iron clubs. This man bid the baron rise and take one of the clubs and defend himself, "for the wrongs with which thou spites the man of God, because I am sent here to fight thee on his part."

> "Fears the lord—his whole frame shakes,
> Horror deep his mind o'ertakes,
> Vanished they as he awakes,
> Who rushed in wrath to rend him."

The hermit's dwelling was saved; as soon as the morning dawned, Stuteville hastened to the cell, and,

> "In the cavern he low bow'd,
> His transgression disallowed,
> Gave the land, an owner proud,
> To Robert and guest-friends."

The land thus given him was all that which lay between his cell and Grimbald's Crag. This would be a considerable quantity, including what is now the site of the ruined priory; and, to enable him the better to cultivate it, there was added to the grant the gift of two oxen and two horses, with as many cows And also, from Christmas to the morrow of the Epiphany, in every year, Robert was to have food from the castle for thirteen poor men; and, at all times, all necessary alms for the needy.

Now the hermit dwelt undisturbed. His enemy's ire had been turned to his advantage, and even he "had been made to dwell at peace with him."

Large numbers of people—the feeble, lame, maimed, deaf, and blind—flocked to his cell to seek his intervention and blessing. And about this time his brother Walter, who had risen to be mayor of York, came to visit him. But being ashamed, and grieved, to find him in so miserable a dwelling, he endeavoured to induce him to change his solitary life, and again join some religious house. But Robert would not hear of it. His brother, upon this, sent masons and other workmen of divers kinds, "who built for him a *little chapel* in honour of the *Holy Cross*, of hewn stone, and prepared a house where he might receive pilgrims and the poor."

There can be little doubt that this *house* was the apartment of which traces remain, in front of the cave which had been the original habitation of St. Giles and himself. The record runs thus:—

"Walter built for him a cell,
And St. Crux's fair chapelle;
Newly anew endowed it well
With gifts that shew'd kind will."

This Chapel of the Holy Cross was the one, the foundations of which were uncovered about forty years ago, and to which allusion has before been made, close to the entrance of the cave. Being thus more fitly provided with chapel and cell by Walter, hither Robert once more removed from his hut by the Chapel of St. Giles, and here he spent the remainder of his life.

The foundations of the Chapel of the Holy Cross are still tolerably perfect. The length of it has been about 16 ft. 6 in., the width 9 ft. 3 in. The floor at the east end is raised for the altar, the steps to which, with the bottom of the walls, buttresses, and stairs down to the river, are all to be seen In front of the altar steps, in the midst of what may be designated the nave, is a stone coffin or grave, hewn in the floor of solid rock. This no doubt was prepared for the hermit's last resting-place, and here probably his body did for long generations rest, but when the rubbish was cleared away at the time the foundations were laid bare, the grave was found uncovered and empty.

"The green tree o'er the altar bends
  Mid grass and nettles tall;
Deeply her sigh the midnight sends
  Along the ruined wall.
Of sainted memories calm and bright,
  No legend needs to tell,
For story's pen must fail to write
  What ruin paints so well.

But once more to return to the life of the hermit. On taking up his abode, in this more commodious hermitage, he took also to himself a companion, in the person of Ivo, who is said to have been a Jew. The call of Ivo by St. Robert is thus described:—

"Whilst one day he walked about,
Ivo joined him relieved from doubt;
By his voice he called him out,
  With me and mine take part.

But before long, yielding to the temptation of Satan,—

"Ivo with Robert soon has strife,
So withdrew from desert life."

But as he was making haste in his escape, in passing through a wood, he stepped on a rotten bough, which caused him to fall into a ditch and break his leg. Robert, being made aware of the accident, hastened to the spot, and smiling at Ivo's plight, rebuked him for his fault, and reminded him that, "no one putting his hand to the plough, and looking back, is fit for the kingdom of God." Ivo humbly confessed his error in deserting his friend, and begged his pardon. Robert bid him—

> "Wretched, seek my habitation,
> Blessed and free for contemplation,
> Long and long God's domination,
> Thou by thy prayer hast won."

He then touched the backslider's leg, and it was restored safe and sound. They never parted more until Robert died, and were worthy brothers in self-mortification. Ivo often went to York to gather alms for the poor, and even in the severe weather of winter he walked barefoot, and his footsteps could be traced along the frozen road by the blood which flowed from his feet.

> "York by road, snow o'er the top,
> Barefoot he walked to, without stop,
> Blood distilling, drop by drop,
> Full deeply stained the ground."

About this period five robbers attempted to break into the hermit's sacred premises, and were suddenly struck dead for their temerity.

Even the animal creation felt St. Robert's power and obeyed his behests. The same thing has been related of others; *e.g.*, stags came out of the forest to draw the ploughs of St. Leonor, and stags drew the Irish hermit Kellac to his grave; they came of their own will out of the forest to supply the place of cattle that St. Colodoc had lost; and the most ferocious wild beasts are said to have crouched at the feet of Macarius, Hilarion, and others. So was it with Robert.

Once, when collecting alms, he asked the lord of the forest for a cow. One, so wild and ferocious that no one dare approach her, was given him. At once he went after her into the forest, and, going up to her, put a band round her neck, and led her home gentle as a lamb. One of the attendants, seeing the animal so easily tamed, proposed to get her back from the hermit by subtilty. The master did not approve of the attempt; nevertheless the man determined to make it. He went to Robert as a beggar with distorted face, and counterfeited lameness in both hands and feet, and, telling a piteous tale of wife and children dying for want, implored him to give him the cow. "God gave and God shall have," was his reply, "but it shall be with thee as thou hast feigned." So when the counterfeit cripple would have driven off his prize, he found himself so lame both in hands and feet that he was unable to move. Seeing this judgment upon him, the man cried out, "O Robert, thou servant of God, forgive my trespass and the injury I have done." He was instantly forgiven, and the use of his limbs restored to him.

This story and the following one formed the subjects of coloured windows set up in Knaresborough Church in 1473 A.D. — 250 years after the hermit's death.

Robert suffered great damage by the stags from Knaresborough Forest breaking down and trampling his corn and other crops.

"Often stags made fierce attacks,
Cut up corn fields in their tracks,
All the earth their wildness racks
Except where each one rests.

Again Robert went to the lord of the forest, and desired that they might be restrained. "I give thee full permission," replied De Estuteville, "to shut them up in thy barn."

"Answers he with ill design,
Christian, shut up the stags as thine,
That with chaunts thou mayest refine
Them yet untam'd by pains."

Robert, taking a small stick in his hand, proceeded into the fields and drove the wild deer into his barn like so many lambs, and shut them up.

"Seeks he the plain, his barn is filled,
Stags being brought from fields well tilled,
Joining in, as beasts well skilled,
They snort with hallowed chime."

He then went to inform the baron what he had accomplished, and desired to know what next should be done with them. Finding that more had been done than was intended, permission was only given him to retain three of them, for use instead of oxen to draw his plough. Robert thanked the donor, and went home and yoked them to his plough. Their submission and docility at this work were daily seen and admired by all who passed by.

More than once he had to contend with Satanic visitants in his cell. One—

> "Aboute his house this harlotte hyed,
> His devocions he defyed;
> All the vessels that he fand
> He tyfled and touched them with his hand,
> His pott, his panne, his sause, his foule,
> With his fingers, fat and foule."

The details of these visitations are perhaps better untold; suffice it to say, that the visitant was once driven away by being sprinkled with holy water, once by the sign of the cross, and finally by the hermit's staff.

In 1203 A.D., De Stuteville, lord of the castle and forest of Knaresborough, died, and for his good deeds was buried at Fountains Abbey. The charge of these royal possessions was, soon after, handed over by King John, to Sir Brian de Lisle, who, proving a great friend to Robert, induced the king (John) and his court, when he came to hunt in the royal forest, to visit him in his cell.* The king came with a great concourse of nobles. When they entered, the hermit was at prayer, prostrate before the altar of his chapel. He did not rise, though aware of the presence and dignity of his visitors, until De Lisle went to him and whispered, "Brother Robert, arise quickly; our lord King John is here, desirous to see thee." Then he arose, and said, "Show me which of these is my

* King John was at Knaresborough, Thursday, May 30th, 1209 A.D., again on Wednesday and Thursday, June 13th and 14th, 1209 A.D., on September 7th and 8th, 1212 A.D.; and on September 17th and 18th, 1213 A.D.

king." One of his peers, "a knight, outpoured much talk, and this beside,"—

> "Ask the king out of his store
> Thee to bless this day with more,
> That by his grant here as before
> You may with yours abide."

He declined to do so; but taking up an ear of corn from the floor, he addressed the king, "Art thou able, O my king, by thy power, to create such an ear as this out of nothing?" The king replied he was unable to do so. "Then there is no king," answered Robert, "but the Lord only." Some of the attendants said, "This man is mad;" others, "Nay, he is wiser than we, since he is the servant of God, in whom is all wisdom." John was not offended, but rather pleased at the blunt address of St. Robert, and said to him, "Ask of me whatever is necessary for thee, and it shall be given."

> "Answered Robert thus the speaker,
> 'Silver and gold to me Christ's seeker,
> Earthly gifts none can be weaker
> To meet our transient need.'"

But Ivo, when the king had departed finding that no alms had been taken, and mindful also of their successors, ran or sent after him, and the king conferred upon them as much land, of the waste in the adjacent wood, as they could cultivate with one plough, by way of alms to the poor; and also, free liberty to cut and take fire wood and bedding.

No sooner was this grant brought under cultivation, than the rector of the parish demanded his tithe therefrom, and said,—

> "Tythe exemption don't assert,
> Straight bring thy corn and hay."

But Robert,—

> "This expressly he denied,
> And to the rector quick replied,
> 'None I'll pay, and so decide;
> Don't ask for them, I pray;'"

And because the rector, who was also at that time the

head of Nostel Priory, insisted upon its rights, Robert foretold for him no good,—

> "Prophesied he,—thou book wearer,
> Thy own tongue, tho' now a tearer,
> Shall be torn from this, thou swearer,
> And so he made his misery."

Robert's own end at last drew near. When the monks of Fountains Abbey had warning thereof, they hurried to his cell, bringing with them the full habit of their order in which to invest him, hoping thus to secure his body for burial in their monastery.

> "The monks of Fountains came full tyte,
> And with them brought a habit white,
> And said, 'Robert, this sall thou have
> With thee when thou goest to thy grave.'
> Robert said, 'Sirs, *when I deghe*
> *Mine own clothing sall suffice for me.*'"

He was, however, certain, and he warned Ivo and his other friends, that on his death the monks would endeavour to gain possession of his body, and said that his own desire was to be buried where he had lived.

> "Here will I rest my time in dust,
> And to the King and Queen I trust,
> To the Triune God as just,
> To take my case commended."

Having charged his friends with regard to this, and other matters, and told them if necessary to call in the civil power to protect his body, and having given his blessing to Ivo and others standing weeping by, then—

> "Into Thy hands, my Maker, I
> Now yield up my soul and die.
> Crossed himself, no groan, no sigh,
> And so gave up the ghost.
> Present is the angel choir,
> All around seized the Spirit's fire,
> To high heaven praise rises higher,
> They join'd who love the most."

Then—

> "Ivo closed his eghe with makyll care.
> And wept for him baithe less and maire."

And, if the reader will pardon a quotation from the Latin prose life of the saint,—"Yvo cum astantibus lugubres voces cum crebris singultibus emittentes, dixerunt, 'Heu, heu! ad quem in tribulationibus et pressuris constituti ibimus.' Defuncto itaque beatæ et dignæ memoriæ patre nostro, Roberto, advocato, et patrono spirituque suo ad summæ felicitatis eternitatem vocato, sanctuque corpore ipsius exanimi relicto, idem cum omni diligentia properavit ad humandum."

The death took place on the 24th of September, 1218 A.D. As the holy man had foreseen, so soon as his death was known, the monks of Fountains came to get, if possible, possession of the body, in order to enshrine it in their own abbey. Again they brought with them the habit of their order in which to enfold it. When they attempted to carry it off, Ivo and other friends urged the expression of the hermit's own wish, that he should be buried where he had lived. This the monks met by the reply, "that it was more convenient and decent that the body of so great a man should be interred in a more solemn resting-place than in that barren and desolate spot." However, acting on the suggestion of Robert given before his death, Ivo and the brotherhood besought help from the castle, which was granted them, and thus by force of arms they prevented the carrying off of the body. The monks were compelled to retire to their monastery, defeated, and in sorrow at the loss of what would have been to them so great a treasure.

When Ivo and the other brethren committed it to the tomb, multitudes gathered from all the country around to pay the last honours to one who had been to them so great a benefactor.

> "Crowds are round with cowl and hood,
> Poor, and powerful, and good,
> Him to mourn in sorrowing mood,
> Maids, husbands, widows, seek.

"Who from wolves our loved homes freed?
Who for his own did intercede?
Who with words our souls did feed?
Thus grieved, they ever speak.

"Ivo next with greatest care
Did, with much beside prepare
(Himself and many a helper there),
In earth our saint to place."

The saint was thus buried where he had desired, in the Chapel of the Holy Cross, built for him by his brother, "in a tomb before the altar."

It does not appear that St. Robert was ever formally canonized, although from within a short time of his death he has always been designated "Saint." The following lines convey this intimation:—

"Yet his tomb gives attestation,
Where our Saint has veneration,
That it is no fabrication,
Which us our book assures.

"Tho' not canonized a Saint,
God through him regards each plaint;
Prayed to, removes our every taint,
With many wondrous cures.

According to the "Anglican Calendar," published by J. H. Parker, the Festival of St. Robert was May 23rd. His influence long survived in the north. Pictures of the scenes of his life were valued, even set up in churches,* and his tomb was a place of pilgrimage for such as were supposed to have been benefited by his help in life.

Matthew of Paris, under the year 1238 A.D., says:— "Eodem anno claruit fama Sancti Roberti heremita apud Knaresburg, cujus tumba oleum medicinale fertur abundatur emisse." Walbran thinks that the source of this supposed "medicinal oil" may probably be referred "to the solution of the resinous substance with which the cover to the grave may have been fixed."

---

* In Morley Church, near Derby, there is a window of six lights filled with scenes from the Life of St. Robert of Knaresborough.

The list of cures wrought at the tomb is a long one; let it suffice to give the closing lines of one of the lives of the Saint;—

> "And to conclude them all in sere,
> All that had hurt anywhere,
> Or any sickness, all were saved,
> This heal, because they of him craved.
> They may be glad, and blithe that has
> Syke a patron of their place."

How long Ivo, who succeeded St. Robert in the hermitage, lived, there is no record. In 1227 A.D. Henry III. "granted and confirmed to brother Ivo, hermit of the Holy Cross at Cnaresburg, and his successors, forty acres of land in Swinesco, which his father, King John, had given to brother Robert, formerly hermit of the same place."

Ivo appears, however, to have had no regular successor, and the property of the cell fell into the hands of the lord of the forest, or manor, under the king. This, in 1257 A.D. was the Earl of Cornwall, who in that year founded at Knaresborough a society called the Friars of the Order of the Holy Trinity, whose object seems to have been similar to that of St. Robert. Upon this society the earl bestowed "the chapel of St. Robert, and all that land which King John gave the said Robert in his lifetime." And upon a portion of the land,—a fair meadow by the river and under the shelter of the cliffs, about midway between St. Robert's Chapel and St. Robert's Cave,—the society erected their priory. The foundation is also frequently designated "The Minister and Brethren of St. Robert of Knaresborough." Their revenues were divided into three parts, one for their own support, one to relieve the poor, and the third to redeem such Christians as should be captive in the hands of the heathen in foreign lands.

The house does not appear to have increased very much in wealth. At the time of its suppression in 1539 A.D., it consisted of a prior (Thomas Kent) and five brethren, the annual revenue being estimated at but £30 10s. 11d., in addition to which, however, the minister and brethren possessed the right of patronage of the three forest churches, viz., Fewston, Hampsthwaite, and Pannal, and of one other besides, Whixley.

The only remains of this priory now left are a small portion of the foundations, and some carved stones scattered about, or incorporated in, the adjoining farm-house and buildings.

The example here given is a fair picture of hermit life in this country before the Reformation, and of the manner in which such recluses were regarded and dealt with by the people. Much that is incredulous in the records, which have been preserved to us, may be explained and accounted for, without necessarily concluding that the subjects of them were all hypocrites or wilful deceivers. They probably themselves believed the marvels which they are said to have wrought. Their lives at least fulfilled a want, taught a needed lesson, and counteracted a danger to which a lawless age was especially prone, the lesson that there is for man "another life," and the danger that there is to man, left to his own ways, of forgetting that there is another life.

As to the men who recorded the lives and legends of the holy men, they no doubt believed what they wrote; and they wrote in the full conviction that others would believe them also. And so others did believe them, and took them as matters of fact, according to which they practically ruled their lives, and according to which the lives of the nation were more or less ruled.

But these men, having done their work, have with their influence, for a time at least, passed away,—

> "The old order changed giving place to the new;
> And God fulfilled Himself in many ways."

Whether finally changed and passed away or not may be doubtful. "An age," to use the words of the late Canon Kingsley — "an age of luxury and unbelief has been succeeded, more than once in history, by an age of remorse and superstition. Gay gentlemen and ladies may renounce the world as they did in the time of old, when the world is ready to renounce them. We have already our nunneries, our monasteries, of more creeds than one; and the mountains of Kerry, or the pine forests of the Highlands, may some day once more hold hermits, persuading themselves to believe, and at last succeeding in believing, the teaching of St. Anthony, instead of that of our Lord Jesus Christ, and of that Father of the spirits of all flesh, who made love, and marriage, and little children, and sunshine, and flowers, the wings of butterflies and the song of birds; who rejoices in His own works, and bids all who truly reverence Him to rejoice in them with Him. This is not more impossible than many religious phenomena seemed forty years ago, which are now no fancies, but powerful facts."

WAR TIMES IN THE FOREST.

"Bella! horrida bella!"
(Wars! horrid wars!)

VICTORIOUS Roman legions have, in the far off days when Rome was the mistress of the world, tramped through this district, then almost forest primeval. From Olicana, (Ilkley) over the moors by Middleton, and across the Washburn, between Bluberhouses and Cragg Hall, then away by Ketelsing Head, to Isurium, (Aldborough) ran one military road; and again from Cataractonium, (Catterick) by Ripley, and Harlow, and Rigton, and Castley, to Burgadunum, (Adel) are to be traced the remains of another.

At Bank, or Bank Slack, near Norwood, and at other places, there are earthworks of probably British origin. These, if not military camps, must have been works of defence for the native villages or encampments: and thus indicate wars, or states of disturbance and unrest, the memory, or record, of which has passed away.

In more historic times, the forest—as a Royal Forest—had, in all probability, its origin in the devastations of war.

It was in 1069 A.D., that the Norman William, provoked by the rebellion of the men of Yorkshire and Durham, against his newly established rule, swore his favourite oath, "by the splendour of God," he would exterminate the whole inhabitants of the district. In that and the succeeding year he proceeded to do it. From York to Durham he ravaged the country, sparing nothing. Houses and churches and villages were swept away. The women, the aged, and the children who escaped death at the hands of his soldiers or executioners, were left homeless, foodless, and friendless, to die of cold and famine. By one means or another 100,000 persons are said to have perished. "It was a horrible spectacle," says an old chronicler, (Roger Hovedon), "to see on the high roads, and public places, and at the doors of houses, human bodies eaten by worms, for there remained no one to cover them with a little earth."

For nine or ten years, the country remained perfectly desolate. William of Malmsbury—another chronicler—writing of it during those years, says, "Should any stranger now see it, he laments over the once magnificent cities, the towers threatening heaven with their loftiness, the fields abundant in pasturage and watered by rivers,—and if any inhabitant remains, he knows it no longer." Thus during those years, and, in some parts, for many years longer, the ground remained untilled, for there was not a man to till it.

That some of the remote parts of the district, now the forest, escaped the worst sufferings of this devastating war—from their remoteness, and the scantiness of their human inhabitants—is probable; but that other parts suffered severely—perhaps the full force of it—is certain.

Doomsday Book, completed some ten or twelve years afterwards, is evidence indisputable. There, of Bilton, parts of Brame and Rossett, of Beckwith, of Killinghall, of Clint, and of Rigton, the entry is "Wastum est,"—"It is waste." In these places, we may safely conclude, were witnessed all the horrors of which the old chroniclers speak. Other places show a depreciation in value from the times of Edward the Confessor.

The greater part of the forest lands then belonged to the king, or to Giselbert Tyson. Those of Tyson were afterwards forfeited to the king's successor, Rufus. This state of things no doubt prepared the way, for the formation of the district, into a Royal Forest, probably early in Henry I.'s reign.

We pass over the disturbed times of Stephen, of Richard I., and of John. Sir Walter Scott, in *Ivanhoe*, graphically pictures the social state in that period. There is no reason to suppose the forest escaped the lawlessness any more than other parts of the country did. And there, as elsewhere, obtained,

> "The good old rule,
> . . . The simple plan,
> That they should take, who have the power,
> And they should keep who can."

INVASION OF THE SCOTS.

At the time of the Scottish wars of the Edwards, the forest was, as a forest, at its best estate; though more than once it suffered severely at the hands of the northern invaders.

On Midsummer Day, 1314, A.D., was fought the disastrous battle of Bannockburn. Who does not remember Bruce's address to his army, as given by Scotland's immortal bard?

> Scots, wha hae wi' Wallace bled,
> Scots, wham Bruce has aften led,
> Welcome to your gory bed,
> Or to victory!
>
> Now's the day, and now's the hour;
> See the front o' battle lour:
> See approach proud Edward's power—
> Chains and slavery!
>
> Wha will be a traitor knave?
> Wha can fill a coward's grave?
> Wha sae base as be a slave?
> Let him turn and flee!
>
> Wha for Scotland's king and law
> Freedom's sword will strongly draw,
> Freeman stand, or freeman fa',
> Let him follow me!

By oppression's woes and pains!
By your sons in servile chains!
We will drain our dearest veins,
But they shall be free!

Lay the proud usurpers low!
Tyrants fall in every foe!
Liberty's in every blow!—
Let us do or dee.

The Scotch, under Bruce, completely defeated the English under the weak Edward II. The king and his army fled, and the north of England was left for several years undefended to the ravages of the victors.

In the spring of 1318 A.D., they poured into this part of Yorkshire under Sir James Douglas. Northallerton and Boroughbridge were burnt; Ripon was saved by the inhabitants paying a ransom of 1000 marks—an enormous sum in those days,—and Knaresborough was taken and burnt. The tower of the church still bears the marks of the fire kindled against it, in the vain hope of bringing it to the ground, and destroying the fugitives who had taken shelter therein.

The forest suffered terribly as the invaders swept through it, and the neighbouring districts, to Skipton. Holinshead says, "After they had tarried here (at Ripon) three daies they departed thence and went to Knaresbro', which town they burnt, *and beating the woods, into the which the people were withdrawn with their goods and cattell, they got a great bootie*, and returning home by Scipton in Craven, they first spoiled the towne, and after burnt it, and so marching through the countrie came back into Scotland with their spoiles and prisoners without anie resistance."

After this raid, nearly all the townships in the forest petitioned the king, for a remission of taxation, on the plea that, their houses had been burned, and their cattle and goods plundered by the Scots. Knaresbro', Scriven, Boroughbridge, Minskip, Timble, Fewston, Thruscross, Menwith, Clint, Felliscliff, Birstwith, Hampsthwaite, Killinghall, Rosehurst, Bilton and Nidd, all petitioned for remission. And, after inquiry made, the king returned answer to his taxing officers at Knaresbro':—"We therefore, pitying their desolate and depressed condition, forgive them the farms and rents which they are bound to pay to us, at the term of St. Michael last past; which amount to the sum of sixty and twelve pounds three shillings and sevenpence, as by the aforesaid investigation more fully appears. And, therefore, we command you fully to discharge the said tenants from their farms and rents due to us, even so far as the before-mentioned sum."

For the same reason, the Abbot and brethren of Fountains Abbey excused their tenants in Rigton and Stainburn from payment of rents.

The churches and church property suffered equally with the rest.

At Pannal the invaders took up their abode in the church, and burnt it when they departed.

The response to a mandate, by Archbishop Melton, for a re-taxation of the churches destroyed and wasted by the Scots, states, "Eccle de Pannail ad nihil taxatur, quia Scoti ibi hospitabantur, et combusserunt in recessu duo." (Reg. 7 Aug., 1318.)

Hampsthwaite Benefice was valued in 1292 A.D. (Pope Nicholas's taxation) at £5, but in 1318 A.D. at nothing, "owing to the ravages of the Scots."

Fewston, the third Forest Benefice, in 1292 A.D. was worth £20 per annum, but in 1318 A.D. only one-third of that sum, viz., £6 13s. 4d., no doubt for the same reason.

We may be sure it was long before the foresters of those days forgot the terrible devastation wrought by these northern neighbours! No memorial of the scourge, however, now remains, so far as the writer is aware, unless the memory still lingers in the name of a lane at Thurscross, called the Scots lane.

FEUD WITH THE ARCHBISHOP'S MEN.

Passing over more than a century—let us hope, of peace—we come to the year 1439 A.D., when the foresters entered into a small war on their own account.

It would seem that, as free foresters or King's tenants, they claimed exemption from all tolls and charges on their goods at the markets throughout the kingdom. The tolls at Otley and Ripon, the two nearest market towns, belonged to the Archbishop of York, whose officers disputed the foresters' claims, and attempted to collect from them the lawful charges. Then, on July 22nd, the forest men, to the number of 700, with the tacit consent of Sir William Plumpton, chief forester, and under the lead of Thos. Beckwith, John Fauks, William Wakefield, and John Beckwith, of Killinghall, "in manner of war and riotous-wise, entered the town of Otley, during the fair then being held, and put the Archbishop's officers in great fear, and told them that they should not take, ask, nor receive any toll of any men of the said forest." The dispute went on evidently very "riotous-wise" on the foresters' part, until May, 1441 A.D., when the Archbishop determined to assert his authority at the fair then to be held at Ripon. For this purpose he gathered a large number of men from Tynedale, Hexham, Otley, and other places, and "kept the towne of Ripon like a towne of warr," against the foresters; and the Archbishop's men "went roving up the said towne, and downe, and they said openly (it was the most continuall language they had during the said faire), 'Would God these knaves and lads of the forest would come hider, that we might have a faire day upon them!' and other words of great scorne, rebuke and provoking." The forest knaves and lads, however, did not that day give them their chance; but two days afterwards, May the 5th, 1441 A.D., they, under Thos. Beckwith, John Fauks, and Ralph Pulleine, laid wait for them at Boroughbridge, and Thornton Bridge, near there, as they went on their way to York, and gave them such a warm reception, that some "escaped down a long straite lane, and some by breaking of a hedge into a field, upon whom the said misdoers (foresters) followed, and drove them into a mire-more neere hand, the space of half-a-mile fro' Helperby, noising and crying, 'Sley the Archbishop's carles,' and 'Would God we had the Archbishop here.' In the which pursuits, assaulte and shote, there was slain by the said misdoers, one Thomas Hunter, gentleman, and one Thomas Roper, yeoman, servants of the Cardinal Archbishop." The matter would appear to have been, in the end, amicably settled between the contending parties, for nothing further seems to have come of it.

WARS OF THE ROSES.

Next came the disastrous Wars of the Roses. The battle, in which the forest men were most concerned, was that of Towton, or Saxton Field, fought on March 29th, Palm Sunday, 1461 A.D.

"Towton we now approach, of sanguine slain,
A woe-worn village, weeping o'er its plain.
No laurel here shall emblematic grow,
No verdant wreath bedeck the victor's brow.
Erase, ye demons foul, the tragic page;
Hide from the muse's ken your hostile rage;
Where horror vaunts each character of death,
In all the attitudes of parting breath;
And grimly dreadful stalks the mourning ground,
Promiscuous dealing havoc wide around;
Bid Cock's pure stream with civil gore to glide,
And Wharfe, a peeress of the liquid tribe."

—T. Maude.

Henry VI. lay at York. Edward IV., with the king-maker, Warwick, was advancing northwards to meet him. On the 12th of March, Henry issued an order from York to Sir William Plumpton, Sir Richard Tunstall, and Sir Thomas Tresham, "to summon all liege men of *the forest and demesne of Knaresborough*, and to set out with them to meet the enemy." On the following day, March the 13th, a second order followed, and straitly charged "our trusty and well-beloved knight, Sir William Plumpton, to repair to the Royal presence with the array, in all haste possible." We can well imagine how, from village to village, and from hamlet to hamlet, flew the messengers on this occasion, summoning the forest to arms!

"Ah! then and there was hurrying to and fro,
And gathering tears, and tremblings of distress!
* * * * * * *
And there was mounting in hot haste; the steed,
The mustering squadron, and the clattering car,
Went pouring forth with impetuous speed,
And swiftly forming in the ranks of war."

Sir William Plumpton, with his son and heir, and their forest array, joined the army on the Lancastrian side within a few days; and on the 29th the opposing forces met—100,000 Englishmen!—on Towton Field, near Tadcaster—

"Where the red rose and the white rose
In furious battle reel'd;
And yeomen fought like barons,
And barons died ere yield.

Where mingling with the snowstorm,
The storm of arrows flew;
And York against proud Lancaster
His ranks of spearmen threw.

Where thunder like the uproar
Outshook from either side,
As hand to hand they battled
From morn till eventide.

Where the river ran all gory,
And in hillocks lay the dead,
And seven and thirty thousand
Fell from the white and red."

Sixty thousand Red-rose Lancastrians met forty thousand White-rose Yorkists. All the evil passions aroused by ten years of civil war were focussed on this field. It was a stern hand-to-hand fight, begun in a blinding snowstorm, in the narrow valley of the Cock. No quarter was given; the snow became crimson with blood, and the waters of the rivulet were tinged with it when they entered the Wharfe, two miles distant. Thirty-six thousand men were left dead and dying when that Sunday evening closed! Who remembers not Shakespeare's description of the scene!—

King Henry VI. "Now sways it this way like a mighty sea,
Forced by the tide to combat with the wind;
Now sways it that way, like the self-same sea,
Forced to retire by fury of the wind:
Sometime the flood prevails; and then the wind;
Now, one the better; then, another best;
Both tugging to be victors, breast to breast,
Yet neither conqueror, nor conquered;
So is the equal poise of this fell war.
* * * * * * * * *

Enter a son that has killed his father, dragging in the dead body.

Son. Ill blows the wind that profits nobody,—
This man, whom hand to hand I slew in fight,
May be possessed with some store of crowns.
* * * * * * * * *
Who's this? O God! it is my father's face,
Whom in this conflict I un'wares have kill'd;
O heavy times begetting such events!
From London by the King was I pressed forth;
My father, being the Earl of Warwick's man,
Came on the part of York, pressed by his master;
And I, who at his hands received my life,
Have, by my hands, of life bereaved him—
Pardon me, God, I knew not what I did!—
And pardon, father, for I knew not thee!—
* * * * * * * * *

Enter a father who has killed his son, with the body in his arms.

Father. Thou, that so stoutly has resisted me,
Give me thy gold, if thou hast any gold:
For I have bought it with an hundred blows,—
But let me see:—is this our foeman's face?
Ah, no, no, no, it is mine only son!—
* * * * * * * * *
O, pity, God, this miserable age!—
What stratagems, how fell, how butcherly,
Erroneous, mutinous, unnatural,
This deadly quarrel daily doth beget!—
O, boy, thy father gave thee life too soon,
And hath bereft thee of thy life too late!

The white rose prevailed; the Lancastrians were defeated and fled. How many of the forest men fell, we know not, but we are certain it must have been many. Their young leader, the son and heir of Sir William Plumpton, was slain, and Sir William himself taken prisoner. We may be sure many forest homes were desolate; that many husbands, fathers, sons and brothers, friends and lovers, never returned; and that the Easter of that year was one of lamentation and woe. The wail of the forester of the north after Flodden, would well have applied to Knaresborough Forest after Towton—

"I have heard of a lilting, at our ewes milking,
Lasses a lilting, before the break of day;
But now there's a moaning, on ilka green loaning,
That our braw foresters are a' wede away.

At boughts, in the morning, nae blythe lads are scorning;
The lasses are lonely, dowie, and wae;
Nae daffin, nae gabbin, but sighing and sabbing;
Ilka ane lifts her leglen, and hies her away.

At e'en at the gloaming, nae swankies are roaming
'Mong stacks, with the lasses, at bogle to play;
But ilka ane sits dreary, lamenting her deary,
The Flowers of the Forest that are a' wede away.

At harrest, at the shearing, nae youngsters are jeering,
The bansters are rankled, lyart and grey;
At a fair, or a preaching, nae wooing, nae fleeching,
Since our braw foresters are a' wede away.

O dool for the order, sent our lads to the border:
The English, for anes, by guile gat the day.
The Flowers of the Forest, that ay shone the foremost,
The prime of our land, lies cauld in the clay.

We'll hear nae mair lilting, at our ewes milking,
The women and bairns are dowie, and wae,
Sighing and moaning, on ilka green loaning,
Since our braw foresters are a' wede away."

RIOT IN 1489 A.D.

Twenty-nine years afterwards, viz., 1489 A.D., the men of the forest were again summoned to arms, this time by Sir Robert Plumpton, the master forester, and Sir William Gascoigne, to assist the Earl of Northumberland, then threatened by rebels at his seat at Topcliffe.

Henry Percy, the fourth Earl, as Lord-Lieutenant of Yorkshire, was the unwilling agent of Henry VII., or rather of his ministers, Empson and Dudley, in the attempt to enforce an unpopular poll-tax, for raising a subsidy to France. He protested to the King against it. To his protest came the reply, that "not a penny should be abated, and that he must see to its exaction to the uttermost farthing." The men of the neighbourhood of Thirsk were specially active in opposition. The Earl, however, called a meeting there; and it was probably in anticipation of disturbance on this occasion that the forest men were summoned. The Earl rode into the town surrounded by a body of the gentlemen of the county and retainers, and was received with mingled cheers and hisses. The reading of the King's message, however, so incensed the populace, that a riot commenced. Northumberland and his friends retired with all haste to his house at Topcliffe, four miles distant. But the incensed mob followed, and, probably before the great body of his defenders could be gathered, the house was broken into, and the Earl, and many of his household and friends murdered.

"Trustinge in noblemen, that wer with hym there,
Bot all they fled from hym for falsehode or fere.
* * * * * * * * *
All left alone, alas! he fawte in vayne;
For cruelly amonge them ther he was slayne."
—SKELTON.

What part the foresters played on this occasion is uncertain. It is scarcely probable, however, that they turned traitors; for at the final suppression of the insurrection, which began with this riot, at the Battle of Ackworth in 1492 A.D., Sir Robert Plumpton was present, and we may well infer his forest followers also, and took part on the Royal side.

THE CIVIL WARS.

Few incidents connected with the forest in the Civil Wars in the 17th century, appear on record. Possibly it was in the happy position of having no history during that time. Royalist and Republican garrisons were in the neighbourhood—at Knaresborough, and at Skipton—and made occasional raids upon the foresters. In 1644 A.D., such a raid was made upon Swinden Hall, the residence of Walter Bethell, Esq., by a party from the Royalist garrison at Knaresborough, who plundered the place of all available property, and totally destroyed the house.

In the previous year (1643 A.D.), according to an old tract of that date, the same party were guilty of outrages at Otley, and on the open parts of the forest. "The last week, there is a garrison of horse and foot layd at Knaresbro', where they began to fortify the town, and pillage and utterly ruin all the religious people in those parts and round about them. On Friday seven-night last, three troops, and some other forces, of which many were French, came from the garrison and pillaged Otley, and there barbarously used some honest women of that town; and in their retreat to Knaresbro', upon the *open forest* they took a man and a woman,—the man they wounded, and beat cruelly, and before his eyes ravished the woman."

Charles Fairfax, of Menston, in a letter to Lord Ferdinand Fairfax, dated January 6th, 1640 A.D., (Fairfax correspondence) mentions the presence of a body of military in the forest, of whom the foresters had mistrust. "Upon Christmas Eve last, was brought into the parish of Fewston, Captain Langley's Company, heretofore billeted about Harrogate, but now unequally dispersed in that parish. They had no good report before they came, yet I hear not of any great enormity since their coming though they be many weeks behind with their pay, for which they have their Captain (a man of ill government still at Harrogate) in suspicion. The Lieutenant, Captain Rouse, a complete gentleman, who has served as Major at the Isle of Rhè, has a special care and vigilant eye on them. It is much to be feared we shall have ill neighbours in them, and when their landlord's provisions fail them, that they will cater for themselves."

About this time, and probably by these "ill neighbours," an attack was made upon Cragg Hall, near Fewston. It belonged at this time to the Rev. Henry Fairfax, and, in all probability, it was some sturdy puritan tenant of his, who (according to tradition), had declared of the marauders, that, "their hearts were as withered as Jeroboam's hand,"—an indiscreet speech, which, when reported to them drew attention to his dwelling, and led to the plunder of his goods, and probably would also have led to the loss of his life, had not one of the recesses of the old hall afforded him an asylum which eluded all their researches. The ancient oak door, still *in situ*, with its massive bolt, resisted all efforts at ingress that way, and still bears the honourable scars inflicted at the time. Ingress, however, was gained otherwise, and the place pillaged and robbed. A valuable stud of horses, tradition says, alone was saved, by their being hid in a thick grove of alders by the river a short distance away.

In 1644 A.D. took place the fatal battle—fatal to the Royalist cause—of Marston Moor, near York, when—

"On Marston Heath
Met front to front the ranks of death;
Flourished the trumpets fierce, and now
Fixed was each eye, and flushed each brow;
On either side loud clamours ring—
'God save the Cause!' 'God save the King!'
Right English all they rushed to blows,
With all to win, or all to lose."

After the battle, the Royalist garrison at York was permitted to retire to Skipton. Sir Henry Slingsby, of Scriven, relates in his Diary with regard to them, "*Upon Knaresborough Forest* we made a handsome show with those troops of our guard, for we marched with their colours, but not with above six or seven score men, namely: one of Col. Titmas's, one of Sir William Girlington's, and one of mine, with such only of the Prince's (Rupert's) men as were left in York, and Sir Thomas Glenham's nine colours."

Since those unhappy times, now two hundred and forty years ago, the Forest has known, by experience, none of the miseries of war; and long may it continue to know nothing of them; and long may each forester be spared to dwell under his vine and his fig tree, and

> "From toil to win his spirit's light,
> From busy day, the peaceful night;
> Rich, from the very want of wealth,
> In Heaven's best treasure,—peace and health."
>
> —Gray.

SONNET.

THE YORKSHIRE ABBEYS.

IN sheltered vales, or mid green meadows wide,
Ivy-clad, or grey, the mouldering ruins stand,
Rich in historic lore; in death e'en grand!
By crystal Wharf, or rapid Derwent's side,
By Skell's fair stream, or Ure, or Rye's clear tide,
Fair Bolton, Fountains, Jervaulx, Bella-land,*
Rievaulx, and Hilda's House by Whitby strand,
A past re-call our age may not deride.
The pious zeal that gave,—the skilful hand
That reared, — the fertile brain that rev'rent planned
The massive tower, and arch, and long drawn aisle,
Yet live, and speak, in every sacred pile;
Their silent tongues rebuke the mammon greed,
Which chills the zeal of a far purer creed.

* Bella-land—the mediæval name of Byland.

THE FAIRFAXES IN THE FOREST.

"An illustrious house, —a house that for learning and valour has no peer among the families of Yorkshire."—*Canon Raine.*

IN "Walks through the City of York," by the late Robert Davis, F.S.A., lately published by his widow, we are told, that, early in the 13th century, one of the magnates of that city resided in a house in Nether or Lower Ousegate, near the foot of Ouse Bridge. It was a *stone* house, and so a house of importance in those days, when stone houses were rare. The name of this city magnate was William Fairfax. His son, also named William, was more than once bailiff of York—an office next in dignity to the mayoralty. The father was undoubtedly an opulent citizen, though his name does not appear as the holder, at any time, of any municipal office. He was farmer of the Royal Mint, in York, and had considerable property in the city. Before the close of the reign of King John (1216 A.D.) he possessed also estates in the Ainsty.

"Now this gentleman," continues Mr. Davis, "is, I think, memorable for this reason. He was the progenitor —the earliest ancestor of whom we have any account, the stock from which sprang all the branches,—of the great Yorkshire family of Fairfax, a family of whom the county, and indeed the whole kingdom, has reason to be proud. And we, citizens of York, may perhaps be allowed to share that pride, when we reflect that the many illustrious persons who bore the name of Fairfax all trace their origin to one, who was a merchant of York, and dwelt in the street of Nether Ousegate, in the parish of St. Michael at Usebrig end, six centuries and a half ago."

It is by no means the object of the present writer to even sketch the history of this illustrious family. This has already been done by other and abler pens. But, "a forester" may venture to advance, on behalf of his fellow foresters, a claim to a share in that pride which Mr. Davis claims for his fellow citizens of York—seeing how closely several members of the family have been connected with the forest.

At Walton, near Tadcaster, and Steeton in the Ainsty, and the neighbourhood, the family has flourished from the time of this William of York, to this day.

At the beginning of the 16th century there was again a William, *Sir* William Fairfax of Steeton. Then a young man he, under romantic circumstances, succeeded in carrying off, from the care of the Abbess of Nun-Appleton, a youthful heiress—Isabella Thwaites,—to whom he was married at Bolton Percy in 1518 A.D. This lady brought, to her husband, among other possessions, her ancestral domain of Denton in Wharfedale.

The eldest surviving son of this match, Thomas Fairfax, born 1521 A.D. inherited Denton, and resided there. Among his seven sons and five daughters, were Thomas his successor, and Edward the poet and translator of Tasso, of whom more will be found elsewhere. He appears to have been the first of the family to acquire any direct interest in the Forest of Knaresborough. *New Hall*, near Fewston, in a detached part of the parish of Otley, was the first possession. How, or at what date, acquired is not ascertained. It previously belonged to the ancient and influential forest family of *Pulleine*. The first mention found of it belonging to the Fairfaxes, is when Sir Thomas Fairfax, by will dated 1599 A.D., left it, at the request of his eldest son Sir Thomas, to Edward Fairfax, the poet, who soon afterwards took up his abode there.

Sir Thomas Fairfax the elder, died in 1599 A.D. and was succeeded by his son, the second of that name, who had married in 1582 A.D. Ellen, daughter of Robert Aske, of Aughton. In 1627 A.D. he was created Baron (or Lord) Fairfax of Cameron. Of a family of twelve children, of whom three sons were slain in the wars abroad, and a fourth died also abroad, there were *three* who claim our attention on account of their after connection with the forest. These were, *Ferdinando*, who succeeded his father as second Lord Fairfax, *Henry*, the fourth son, and *Charles*, the ninth son.

After the loss of his other, his soldier-sons,—about 1621 A.D.—the bereaved father seems to have thought somewhat lightly of the survivors. Dr. Matthews, Archbishop of York remarked to him, on one occasion, "I have great reason to sorrow with respect to my sons; one having wit and no grace, and another having grace and no wit, and a third neither grace nor wit to guide him aright."—"May it please your grace," replied Fairfax, "Your case is sad but not singular; I am also grievously disappointed in my sons. One (Ferdinando) I sent to the Netherlands to train him for a soldier, and he makes a tolerable country justice, but is a mere coward at fighting; my next (Henry) I sent to Cambridge, and he proves a good lawyer, but a mere dunce at Divinity; and my youngest (Charles) I sent to the Inns of Court, and he is a good divine, but nobody at the law." He had hope, which was somewhat shaken before he died however, of his then young grandson—the future Parliamentary General,—for he was heard about this time to call aloud to him, "Tom, Tom, mind thou the battle; thy father is a good man, but a mere coward at fighting. All the good I expect, is from thee."

FERDINANDO FAIRFAX (THE 2ND. LORD) AND HIS "GREATER SON" AT SCOUGH.

At the close of the 16th Century, and the beginning of the 17th, there was residing at Scough, or Skow, Hall—

one of the several "Halls" which had been erected in the forest towards the end of Elizabeth's reign, a family of good position,—and not unknown in county history—named Brearhaugh or Breary. They were also the owners of Menstone Hall, in Wharfedale.

In 1613 A.D. (or 1608 A.D.), John Breary, the last of his name at Scough, died. A rough grit stone tomb to his memory bearing in rude letters, the inscription "JHON BREARY, DIED 1613," is still to be seen in Fewston churchyard. He left a widow with an only child, Mary, then very young. For some reason, the widow and child would appear to have preferred another residence than Scough Hall. Possibly they retired to Menstone, and hence the ancestral home in the Forest was "to Let."

In 1607 A.D. Sir Ferdinando Fairfax, coward though his father thought him in fighting, had made a grand marriage by his union with Mary, daughter of Lord Sheffield, President of the North. During the first few years after the marriage the young couple appear to have resided at York, where their two elder children (daughters) were born. In 1612 A.D. we find them at their father's house at Denton, where was born in that year their eldest son Thomas, who ultimately succeeded his father as the 3rd Lord Fairfax, but is better known as the great Parliamentary General.

Sir Ferdinando and his wife were evidently, however, looking out for a house of their own, and, in the following year, 1613 A.D. we find them with their young family, including the afterwards renowned "Tom," residing at Scough Hall; in all probability tenants to the widow and child of John Breary. An inducement to take up their abode here, may have been the proximity of Scough to Newhall, already the residence of the learned poet and tutor of the family, Sir Ferdinando's uncle, Edward Fairfax.

At Scough were born three children, a daughter, Elizabeth, in 1613 A.D. who afterwards married Sir William Craven, of Lenchurch in Gloucestershire;—à son,

Charles, in 1614 A.D. and another daughter, Mary, in 1616 A.D. afterwards wife of Henry Arthington, Esq., of Arthington.

The baptism of the son, Charles, at Fewston Church, on March 26th, 1614 A.D. was the occasion of a gathering of notables such as the old Parish Church has rarely, if ever, before or since, seen. There would be old Sir Thomas, the grandfather from Denton, Sir Ferdinando, the father, and his aristocratic wife, Edward the great uncle, of Newhall. Sir Guy Palmes, of Lindley, Walter Hawksworth, Esq. of Hawksworth, were the Godfathers; and the child's aunt—another daughter of the Lord President of the North—was Godmother. And may not the illustrious Tom, "a wee toddling thing" of two and a half or three years old, have been there also, a spectator of his baby brother's baptism? How little could that august gathering foresee the fatal day on Marston Moor, just thirty years afterwards, when the elder brother was chiefly instrumental in annihilating the power of his sovereign, and the younger—this Forest-born son of the family,—was mortally wounded, and, five days afterwards died, on, or near, the battle field!

Five or six years was the extent of Sir Ferdinando's residence at Scough. About 1617 A.D. he purchased Steeton—the old family mansion in the Ainsty,—from another branch of the family, and removed thither with his wife and children.

Did that delicate lad—whom he bore away with him from the scenes of his early years at Scough, one is tempted to ask,—did he remember those scenes in after years, when England's greatest poet sang of him

"Fairfax, whose name in arms through Europe rings,
  Filling each mouth with envy and with praise,
  And all her jealous Monarchs with amaze,
And rumours loud, that daunt remotest Kings.
Thy firm, unshaken virtue ever brings
  Victory home, though now rebellions raise
  Their hydra-heads, and the false North displays,
Her broken league to imp their serpent wings!"

Yes, did he in those times of greatness, ever think of his early boyhood at Scough—of riding his first pony across Rowton Wath and over Swinsty Moor, or along Smithson lane and by the humble thatched vicarage, on his way to receive his first lessons from his learned great-uncle at Newhall? Or did he recall, sometimes, that gathering of kinsfolk and friends around the font in the old Forest Church at his sister's, or his baby brother's, baptism? If not in the days of turmoil and strife, perhaps when quieter times came,—in the retirement and rest of the home of his old age at Nun-Appleton—he did recall, and recount to his unhappy childless only child, the wife of the licentious Villiers Duke of Buckingham, of whom it is written that he

> "Never said a foolish thing
> And never did a wise one,"

the scenes and the memories of his childhood's days in the forest.

From his will made in 1667 A.D. with an addition to it on Nov. 11th, 1671 A.D. the day before his death, we learn that his possessions in the forest consisted of the Manor of Rigton with farms there known as "Sproute farme, now in the tenure and occupacon of Francis Ingle," and also "one called Mawson's farme, now in the tenure and occupacon of Thomas Topham or his assignes," and one "other farme called Hardistyes farme, now in the tenure of Richard Hardistye or his assignes," and also "the other farme at Rigton belonging to William Smith, and also the warrant upon the Common there." He mentions also in the same document, "all his right and interest of two leases of the Royalties of the Forest of Knaresborough in the Countye of Yorke."—These properties probably passed ultimately to his successors in the title; but whether they were parted with by them earlier, or not until the general sale of the Yorkshire estates in 1716 A.D. is not known. In a list of the estates sold in 1716 A.D. these are not mentioned —leading to the inference that this interest in the Forest had ceased before that date. Lord Fairfax died Nov. 12th, 1671 A.D. and was buried at Bolton Percy.

THE REV. HENRY FAIRFAX AND CRAGG HALL.

We may now turn to the second surviving son of Sir Thomas Fairfax of Denton and brother of Sir Ferdinando, viz: *Henry* Fairfax, he "who was a good lawyer but a mere dunce at divinity." He became closely united, by property, and perhaps by occasional residence also, with the Forest; and, in spite of his father's bad opinion of his divinity, was the worthy divine of the family.

Henry was born at Denton in 1588 A.D. and educated at Trinity College, Cambridge, of which he became, in 1608 A.D. a Fellow. He vacated his fellowship some years afterwards and accepted the comparatively poor rectory of Ashton-in-Markenfield, in order, there is little doubt, to enable him to take into closer fellowship, a worthy helpmate, Miss Mary Cholmondeley, daughter of Sir Henry Cholmondeley. This also necessitated, with his small living, an application for some further allowance from his father; and in regard to this business there is a characteristic and interesting letter from the lady herself to her affianced husband, in the Fairfax correspondence. It runs as follows:

"To my assured loving cousin, Mr. Harry Fairfax, give these.

"Blessed God, bless our designs, prosper our intentions, and consummate our desires, to His glory and our comforts, if it be His blessed will. I am glad to hear your father is so well pleased, and wish to see him at York, where I hope by good advice to procure the best means to move him for a jointure, which, God knows, is so needful for me to demand, as I fear, if I be denied, we shall both wish you had not thought me worthy of the titles of (dear love), for so dear you are in my esteem as I assure you, you have no cause to doubt the continuance of my firm affection. * * * * * I would say, 'I wish to see you,' but the weather is so unseasonable and the ways so dangerous, by reason of waters, as I will not desire it. I will wear your ring till you take it from me. Humbly beseeching Almighty God, to be with you, I commit you to His gracious protection, that guides my heart unfeignedly to desire myself entirely yours,

"MARY CHOLMELEY.

"P.S.—My mother remembers her love to you, with many thanks for her Christmas provision. My sister Scott commends her kindly to you."

This letter is without date, but was probably written shortly before the marriage in 1627 A.D.

A spare page in a copy of "The works of William Gouge," which belonged to the Earl of Harborough, contains the following inscription, showing the book to have been a gift about this time from the Rev. Henry, to his betrothed :—

"Yorke, 10th, 18th, Ano. Dmi. 1626.

"For Mrs. Mary Cholmeley,

HENRY FAIRFAX."

Then follow two anagrams on her name. Here is one of them.

" Mary Cholmeley.

Anagram, "Oh, I'm all mercy."

"M. My hand, my heart, myself, and what doth make it ;
"C. Claim to be mine, Oh! I'm all mercy, take it."

"Hey. Fairfax."

There are also three manuscript stanzas in the same book which might possibly be of interest to lovers, but space forbids their insertion here.

The book bears on the title page the family motto "Fare : Fac," and throughout are copious M.S. notes by Henry Fairfax, showing that he had read carefully the copy he presented to Mary Cholmeley.*

The following letter, written to her husband during a visit to London some five years after their marriage, manifests no abatement in their attachment.

"To my ever dear loving Mr. Fairfax, parson of Ashton, give these : London.

"My ever dearest Love.

"I received a letter and horse from Long. on Thursday, (Jan. 31st), and will use means to send Procter's horse to Denton. I did not so much rejoice at the safe passage, as at that blessed, and all-sufficient Guide, whose thou art, and whom I know thou truly servest, that hath for a short time parted us, and I firmly hope will give us a joyful meeting. Dear heart, take easy journeys, and prefer thine own health before all other worldly respects whatsoever. Thy three boys at Ashton, are well : thy little Harry is weaned ; all that love us pray for thy safe return.

* Notes and Queries.—*3rd Ser., Vol. viii., p.* 396.

I pray thou beg a blessing for us all, for I must needs commit you to His gracious protection, that will never fail us nor forsake us.

"Thine ever,

"Ashton, Feb. 2, 1632." "MARY FAIRFAX.

Shortly after this time the Revd. Henry Fairfax was transferred to his father's more lucrative—but not rich—living of Newton Kyme near Tadcaster; and at this place, with his estimable wife, he lived in peace through all the terrible commotions and Civil Wars to 1646 A.D. his humble rectory being "a refuge and a sanctuary to all their friends and relations of both sides." Here too the pious, gentle, Christian poet and parish priest, George Herbert, whose friendship he had formed at Cambridge, often visited him.

It was at this period of his life that Henry Fairfax's direct connection with the Forest commenced. We can well believe he had often been a visitor in earlier years to his brother at Scough; and possibly he also—like his nephew,—had sat, an apt scholar, at the feet of his great uncle at Newhall, but a more direct interest was acquired by him in the year 1638 A.D. by the purchase of considerable property in the Forest. This was situated on the sunny side of the Washburn Valley between Fewston and Bluberhouse, and included the site of the ancient "Besthaim."

From documents now in the writer's possession, we learn that on the 23rd day of January, 1638 A.D. "Richard Bannister de le Cragg, gentleman, and Ellen his wife, John Bannister their son and Jana his wife, Ralph Bannister younger son of aforesaid Richard, with Marmaduke Beckwith of Dacre with Thomas Beckwith his son, and Thomas Beckwith of Aldborough, surrendered, in the Forest court at Knaresborough, certain lands and houses called "Bainbrigg Yeate, Low Cragg," "Beiston," and "the Holme and Eshsteades," "scituat, jacentes et existentes in hamlatâ de Fuiston infra villam de Timble et Foreseste de Knaresburg," to the use and behoof of Henry Fairfax of Newton Kyne, clerk, and his heirs and assignes for ever.

In the following year, viz., June 6th, 1639 A.D. there was conveyed to him in like manner by William Frankland, knight of Thirklebie, Henry Frankland, Esquire his son, and Richard Frankland de Fuiston, gentleman, the adjoining estate of "le Cragg," or Cragg Hall, one of the Elizabethan Halls of the Forest.

Thus during the troublous days of the great Civil War, and the Commonwealth, the revered Rector of Newton-Kyme, uncle of the greatest general in that war, the friend of George Herbert, the man of peace and bond of union between contending families, was a chief land-owner in the Forest; and possibly, with an estimable and pious wife, "Mrs. Mary Chomley," he was an occasional resident at Cragg Hall. From a record in the church registers of the parish, he, as well as his father, the old Lord Fairfax of Denton, still living, was interested in the poor of Fewston, and each gave 20s. to their relief.

He removed in 1646 A.D. from Newton Kyme to the richer benefice of Bolton Percy,—which he held till the restoration (1660 A.D.) and then resigned, and retired to a private residence at Oglethorpe, where he died intestate, in 1665 A.D. His wife had pre-deceased him in 1656 A.D. at Bolton Percy, where she was buried, and where an expressive epitaph which he caused to be inscribed on her tomb to her memory, in the Parish Church of that place, may yet be seen.

CHARLES FAIRFAX, ESQ., AND SCOUGH HALL.

We now come to Charles Fairfax, the third of the surviving sons of the first lord, and his connection with the Forest. He is the one of whom his father said "my youngest I sent to the Inns of Court, and he is a good divine but nobody at the law."

The family of Breary of Scough, and Mary Breary the sole heiress of it, have been already mentioned in connection with Sir Ferdinando Fairfax's residence at that place. The young barrister, Charles Fairfax, fresh from

Lincoln's Inn, came within the attractive influence of Mary Breary: and after several years, he and the Forest heiress were married, and occasionally dwelt at her Forest home. At least one of their numerous family, Charles, who died in childhood, was born at Scough Hall, and baptized in 1628 A.D., at Fewston Church. By this marriage Scough and Menstone Halls passed to the Fairfax family. The former probably continued to be occupied by the mother-in-law, Mrs. Breary, for some years. As late as 1640 A.D., Charles wrote to his brother, Lord Ferdinando Fairfax, "My mother-in-law never before now admitted me to any estate at Scoughe." Menston was adopted as the ordinary residence of Charles and his wife. There he lived respected, the genealogist and the antiquarian of the family. He compiled the "Analecta Fairfaxiana,"—containing a full and complete genealogy and sketch of the family,—a copy of which, if now in existence, is very difficult to obtain a sight of. Nor did he altogether abstain from public life. Before the battle of Marston Moor, Oliver Cromwell spent a day with him at Menstone, gaining information from him as to the neighbourhood, their consultations being held, so it is said, seated round a stone table, since removed to Farnley Hall, and now to be seen there. At the time of the Restoration, Charles was a colonel in General Monk's army, and also about the same time Governor of Hull, from the revenue of the port of which Charles the II. granted him a pension.

Among his numerous family, of fourteen children, were the twin sons, John and Henry, born at Menston, October 20th, 1634 A.D. The two as infants, and men, were so exactly alike as to be undistinguishable by their nearest relations. One was a captain in the army, the other (Henry) a clergyman,—noted for his fearless bearing towards Chief Justice Jeffrey in a question of jurisdiction in the appointment of a master to Magdalen College, Oxford, in the reign of James II,—and afterwards Dean of Norwich. It frequently happened that the officer was addressed as the clergyman; and soldiers affirmed to the divine that they had served under him. The Dean is said to have observed, that even their mother was at a loss to distinguish them, as he himself had often received presents from her that were intended for his brother.

In a postscript to one copy of the Analecta Fairfaxiana, Charles Fairfax has left on record the following pathetic prophetical remarks made to him by his father—the aged first lord—a few months before the death of that nobleman in 1640 A.D., expressing his fears as to his grandson, the hopeful "Tom" of earlier days.

"He walking in his great parlour at Denton, I only then present, did seem much perplexed and troubled in his mind: but after a few turns he broke out into these, or the like expressions,—'Charles, I am thinking what will become of my family when I am gone; I have added a title to the heir-male of my house, and shall leave a competent estate to support it. Ferdinando will keep it, and leave it to his son; but such is Tom's pride, led much by his wife, that he, not contented to live in our rank, will *destroy his house.*'"

The wife of Charles, Mary Breary, died in 1657 A.D. and was buried with her family at Fewston, as the following entry in the register there, testifies:

"Mrs. Maria Fairfax, the religious and virtuous wife of Charles Fairfax, of Menstone, Esquire, was buried the 21st day of October, 1657 A.D."

Her husband followed her—and was interred at the same place—in 1673 A.D. The event is thus recorded: "1673 A.D., December, Noble Charles Fairfax, of Menston, Esquire, was buried, the 22nd day." There is also a mural tablet to their memory in Otley Church.

Grainge gives a surrender of Scough in 1664 A.D. but it was only under a settlement on the marriage of Charles Fairfax's eldest son at that date, and the trust was afterwards discharged. It was after the death of the latter—how soon does not appear—that Scough was sold by his representatives. The hall yet stands, an object of interest to Foresters and antiquarians alike.

New Hall had passed away from Edward's family even earlier: and so had Cragg Hall from Henry's. The sale of Scough Hall, therefore, (unless the Rigton property of the third lord was held until the general breaking up the estate in 1714 A.D.)—closed the connection—with one small exception—of this illustrious and noble family with Knaresborough Forest.

The exception referred to is mentioned in a surrender in the Forest court in 1713 A.D by Thomas Fairfax, Esquire, (eldest son of Charles, of Menstone) and Dorothy his wife, and Thomas their heir, of "Two acres of land in the hamlet of Clifton and vill: of Timble to the use and behoof of John (? Stephen) Parkinson his heirs and assigns for ever."

This last small remnant of large estates and influence the writer has been unable to identify.

SONNET

SPRING.

SPRING, bright Easter morn of the circling year,
With freshness of waking day, dawns to fill
With new-life field and garden, copse and gill.
The very air she breathes, buoyant, fresh, and clear,
Proclaims the time of buds and flowers here;
A welcome crowd,—daisy, primrose, daffodil,—
They come, and clothe hedge, mead, and moorland hill,
With blush of May still wet with April's tear.
The lambkins sport; and from thrice happy throats,
Loud rings the morn with sweetest woodland notes.
To labour man rejoicing goes, and leaves
The seed in certain hope of golden sheaves.
All nature wakes, arises, plumes her wings,
And new-life's carol with new vigour sings.

EDWARD FAIRFAX, THE POET OF THE FOREST.

"Edward Fairfax, of Fuyston, Esq., in the forest of Knaresborough, brother of Sir Thomas Fairfax, of Denton. He translated Godfrey of Boulogne out of Italian into English verse; wrote the History of Edward the Black Prince, and other witty eclogues, not printed. He is accounted a singular scholar in all kind of learning, and yet liveth, 1631."

—*Roger Dodsworth.*

EDWARD FAIRFAX, the poet of "that illustrious house,"—and a member of it who shed a lustre upon it, and upon the forest in which he dwelt, second only, if even second, to that shed by his grand-nephew, the great general in the civil wars,—was the son of Sir Thomas Fairfax, the first of that name, at Denton. Sir Thomas Fairfax's wife, and presumably the mother of Edward, was Dorothy, daughter of George Gale, Esq., a goldsmith of York, and also of Askham Grange, near York. It is said *presumably* the mother of Edward, because a doubt hangs over the legitimacy of his birth, and of that of Charles his brother, which, it is feared, may never be cleared up.

The question is an interesting one, and the evidence on both sides may be briefly stated thus:—

1. Dodsworth, the antiquarian, who was most intimate with the family, especially with the third lord, and died in 1654 A.D. styles Edward "the *natural* brother of Sir Thomas Fairfax."

2. In Dugdale's Heraldic Visitation of 1665 A.D. where the family pedigree is signed by Charles Fairfax, of Menston, his uncles Edward and Charles are given with "wavy" lines, intimating, at least, doubtful legitimacy.

3. In the Analecta Fairfaxiana, drawn up also by Charles Fairfax, and in which the relationship is professed to be stated of every member of the family, the issue of the first Sir Thomas are given as—Thomas, Henry, and Ferdinand, two daughters, and then, in a parenthesis, Sir Charles, and Edward.

4. Lord Houghton, in his introduction to a print of the Dæmonology for the Philobiblion Society, adopts the adverse view, and says, "The author (Edward Fairfax), though *illegitimate*, was fully accepted as a member of the noble and historic family of Fairfax."

On the other side of the question it may be said:

1. That the term "*natural* brother," applied by Dodsworth, frequently, if not invariably, at that period meant "true" or "legitimate," or "by blood" as opposed to "by affinity." And, also, it is deserving of notice, that Bryan Fairfax, a learned and painstaking antiquarian of the family, quoting Dodsworth's account of his great relative in a letter to Bishop Atterbury, dated January 12th, 1704-5, A.D. omits the word "natural" altogether; and also states without qualification that Edward was the son of Sir Thomas of Denton.

2. Douglas, in his peerage of Scotland, also, says distinctly, that Edward "was born to Sir Thomas by Dorothy his wife, daughter of George Gale, of Askham Grange, Esquire.

3. The will of Sir Thomas, the father, made a few days before his death in 1599 A.D. and now in the Will Office, at York, it might have been hoped, would have settled the question. But it is far from doing so.

Its testimony is dubious.

After giving the disposition and ordering of his funeral to his eldest son, Sir Thomas Fairfax, whom he also appoints sole executor, he proceeds: "I do give and bequeath to Edward Ffarefax, at the request of my said son Sr. Thomas Ffarfax, all that capitall messuage called Newhall, and all lands tenements, meadowes and pastures with the appurtynances lying and being within the p'ish of Otley and Ffuiston in the Countie of York to the same Newhall belonging, to have and to hold the said capytall messuage . . . and all other the said premises with the appurtenance to the said Edward Ffarefax and the heires of his bodie lawfully to be begotten, and for default of such issue, then I doe give the said messuage and land to my said sonne Sir Thomas Ffarfax, knight, and his heires for evr.—Item: I do give to the said Edward Ffarfax the some of one hundred and fiftie pounds to be paid to him by my executor forth of my goods. Item, I doe give and bequeth to Charles Ffarfax all those my messuages and lands called Brocket-hall, and all my lands in Bradswoth and Weeton, to have and to hold the said messuages and lands with the said messuages and lands unto the said Charles Ffarfax, his executores and assignes, from the anuntiation of our Ladie next after my death, for and during his naturall life, yelding and paing to my said sonne Sr. Thomas Ffarfax knight, and his heires, the yearly rent reserved as now paid for the p'messes att fests and termes accustomed, and I doe also give unto the said Charles one hundred pounds to be paid by my executor."

The reader must now be left to draw his own conclusions as to the question of legitimacy or illegitimacy.

Edward married, but at what date is not known, Dorothy, daughter of ... Laycock, of Coppenthorpe, and sister of Walter Laycock, chief Aulnager of the northern counties. There is evidence that about the date of his father's death, and also that occasionally afterwards, he resided in Kirkgate Leeds, in a house called "The Stocks," near to the parish church: but there can be no doubt that from shortly after the date of his father's will —that is, from within the first few years of the 17th century,—the house of Newhall, left to him under that will, became his ordinary abode.

This house was situated in the township of Little Timble, a detached portion of the parish of Otley, though seven miles from that town. It stood on the southern bank of the Washburn, almost immediately below the village ot Fewston, and on the northern or lower margin of Swinsty Moor. The church and vicarage of the village looked down, from their situation on the northern declivity, directly upon Newhall. The house, or "hall,"—as it existed, with apparently little alteration, until the formation of the Swinsty reservoir, in 1876, A.D. when it was completely removed,—was a plain stone-built dwelling, of two storeys in height on the south or front part facing Swinsty Moor. There was a room on either hand, to right and left of the door in the centre, each with three or four mullioned windows of late Elizabethan date. The roof— covered with the heavy grey slate common in the vicinity — descended almost to the ground behind, and extended outwards considerably, so as to cover the kitchens and other back rooms in the rear towards the river.

This Hall had previously belonged to, and been inhabited by, the Pulleyne family—one of the most numerous and influential families for several centuries in the forest, and at Scotton on the borders of it.

The entries, regarding the Poet's family in Fewston parish registers, commence in the year 1605 A.D., when "Ellen daughter of Edward Fairfax, Esquire, was baptised 12th day of May." Again, in 1606 A.D., "Elizabeth daughter of Edward Fairfax, Esquire, was baptised the 8th of October." The last entry is that of the burial of the widow, and stands thus, "Mrs. Dorothie Fairfax was buried the 24th of January, 1648."

Edward Fairfax himself was living in 1635 A.D. (*vide* two entries in the Court Rolls at Knaresborough), but is believed to have died in that (1635 A.D.) or the following year. Unfortunately the Fewston registers are defective for two or three years at this period, so that no record of the date of death, or of his burial, is to be found.

Bryan Fairfax, a man of letters two generations later, the second son of the Rev. Henry Fairfax, in an account which he wrote of the Poet to Bishop Atterbury, dated March 12th, 1707-8 A.D., says of him, "While his brothers were honourably employed abroad, he stayed at home at his book, and thereby made himself fit for any employment in Church or State. But an invincible modesty, and love of a retired life, made him prefer the shady groves and natural cascades of Denton, and the forest of Knaresborough, before all the diversions of court or camp."

He did not pass his time *ignobili otio*, as appears by the many valuable manuscripts he left in the library of Lord Fairfax, at Denton, both in verse and prose. His great work, and which Bryan Fairfax tells us was "his first essay in poetry when very young," was his translation of Torquato Tasso's heroic poem of Godfrey of Bologne, "out of Italian into smooth and excellent English,—a book highly commended by the best judges and wits of that age, and allowed by the critics of this. King James valued it above all other English poetry; and King Charles, in the time of his confinement, used to divert himself by reading it."*

This praise by the Poet's kinsman has been borne out by the approval and concurrence of the principal English historians and writers, and especially of brother poets, to the present time.

Dr. Johnson noticed the book with great favour.

Hume says "Fairfax has translated Tasso with an elegance and ease, and at the same time, with an exactness, which, for that age, was surprising."

Hallam would name the work, "Jerusalem delivered, *imitated* from Tasso."

Dryden classes Fairfax "among the sweetest of the poets of his age, placing him on an equality with Spencer."

Waller owned to Dryden that he "derived the harmony of his numbers from 'the Godfrey of Bulloigne' which was turned into English by Mr. Fairfax."

---

* Bryan Fairfax to Bishop Atterbury.

Campbell reckons "the Jerusalem delivered" among the glories of the Elizabethan age.

Robert Gould, in prefaratory verses prefixed to the edition of 1687, says—

"See here, you dull translators, look with shame,
Upon this stately monument of fame,
And, to amaze you more, reflect how long
It is, since first 'twas taught the English tongue;
In what a dark age it was brought to light;
Dark? No, our age is dark, and that was bright,
Of all those versions which now brightest shine,
Most (Fairfax) are but foils to set off thine!
Ev'n Horace can't of too much justice boast,
His unaffected easy style is lost;
And Ogilby's the lumber of the stall;
But thy translation does atone for all."

Collins, in his address to Home, the author of "Douglas," says of Tasso and his translator—

"Proceed! nor quit the tales which, simply told,
Could once so well my answering bosom pierce:
Proceed! in peaceful sounds and colours bold,
The native legends of thy land rehearse;
To such adopt thy lyre, and suit thy powerful verse.
In scenes like these, which, daring to depart
From sober truth, are still to nature true,
And call forth fresh delight to fancy's view
The heroic Muse employed her Tasso's art!

How have I trembled, when, at Tancred's stroke,
Its gushing blood the gaping Cyprus pour'd!
When each live plant with mortal accents spoke,
And the wild blast upheaved the vanished sword!
How have I sat when piped the pensive wind
To hear his harp by British Fairfax strung!
Prevailing Poet! whose undoubting mind
Believed the magic wonders which he sung."

As an evidence that the work maintains its pre-eminence to cultivated minds in modern times—the testimony of the Editress (his daughter) of the "Poetical Remains" of the late *Venerable Archdeacon Churton*, may be quoted. She says—speaking of the Archdeacon—"With him, Tasso was a favourite, and not unworthy to be named with Tasso, *Fairfax*, his *unrivalled translator*."

The first edition of the translation of Tasso was published in 1600 A.D., with a dedication by the translator to Queen Elizabeth, in the laudatory style of the times,—

"Wit's rich triumph, Wisdom's glory,
Art's chronicle, and Learning's story,
Tower of goodness, virtue, beauty:
Forgive me, that presume to lay
My labours in your clear eye's ray;
This boldness springs from faith, zeal, duty."

"Her hand, her lap, her vesture's hem,
Muse touch not for polluting them;
All that is hers is pure, clear, holy:
Before her footstool humble lie,
So may she bless thee with her eye;
The sun shines not on good things solely.
* * * * * *

Another edition in 1624 A.D. contained a dedicatory address, also by Fairfax, to Prince Charles,— soon to become the unfortunate Charles I.,—who, as Bryan Fairfax tells us, "in the time of his confinement used to divert himself by reading this book." One stanza, from the five of which the address consists, must suffice as a specimen of it—

"You shepherds on the downs your flocks that keep,
Happy you were, while your Eliza deigned
To dwell amongst you, who so wisely reigned
That never wolf into your folds durst peep;
But now a better fortune have you gained,
For Pan himself is careful of your sheep,
And Charles amidst your cottages doth sleep,
As Phœbus did when he a shepherd feign'd."

Successive editions of the work have continued to appear up to the present time; and, as it is accessible and tolerably well known, it is not necessary to give more than two short extracts from it.

The first is from Book IV., and describes *Armida* in tears at the rejection of her requests by Godfrey and other chiefs:—

"With that she looked as if a proud disdain
Kindl'd displeasure in her noble mind;
The way she came, she turned her steps again,
With gesture sad, but in disdainful kind;
A tempest railed down her cheeks amain,
With tears of woe and sighs of anger's wind;
The drops her footsteps wash, whereon she treads,
And seems to step on pearls, or crystal beads.

Her cheeks, on which this streaming nectar fell,
Still'd through the limbeck of her diamond eyes,
The roses—white and red—resembled well,
Whereon the rory May-dew sprikled lies,
When the fair morn first blusheth from her cell,
And breatheth balm from open'd Paradise;
Thus sighed, thus mourned, thus wept this lovely queen,
And in each drop bathed a grace unseen."

The second extract is descriptive of Rinaldo on the Mount of Olives—

"It was the time, when 'gainst the breaking day,
Rebellious night yet strove, and still repined,
Far in the East appear'd the morning gray,
And yet some lamps on Jove's high palace shined,
When to Mount Olivet he took his way,
And saw, as round about his eyes he twined,
Night's shadows hence, from thence the morning shine
This bright, that dark; that earthly, this divine.

Thus to himself he thought: how many bright
And 'splendant lamps shine in Heaven's Temple high!
Day hath his golden sun, her moon the night,
Her fix'd and wandering stars the azure sky;
So framed all by their Creator's might,
That still they live, and shine, and ne'er will die,
Till in a moment, with the last day's brand,
They burn, and with them burn sea, air, and land."

Among the valuable manuscripts, already alluded to as left behind him by Fairfax, were, "A History of the Black Prince," now, it is feared, entirely lost; "Dæmonology," a discourse of witchcraft as acted in his family, and of which an account is given elsewhere in these "Leaves;" also several letters which passed between him and one John Dorrell, "a Romish priest of no ordinary fame, then a prisoner in York Castle, on several subjects of controversy, as, *e.g.*, the Pope's supremacy, 'infallibility, &c., which deserve to be published." (B.F.)

He also wrote "Certain witty Eclogues"—twelve in number, and, according to Mrs. Cooper (Muses' Library), "all of them written after the accession of James to the throne of England, on important subjects relating to the manners, characters, and incidents of the times he lived in. They are pointed with many strokes of satire; dignified with wholesome lessons of morality and policy, to those of highest rank, and some modest hints even to Majesty itself. As far as *poetry* is concerned in them, the very name of Fairfax is the highest recommendation, and the learning they contain is so various and extensive, that according to the evidence of his son (who has written large annotations on each) no man's reading, besides his own, was sufficient to explain his references effectually."

The son, here alluded to, was his eldest, William Fairfax. The account given of him by the same writer is, that, "he was a very learned but splenetic man, and a kind of tutor, or rather an intimate friend, to Mr. Stanley, who published the 'Lives of the Philosophers;' the greatest part of which work, as well as the 'Notes on Euripides,' truly belonging to Mr. William Fairfax." It may be added he was B.A. of Corpus Christi College, Oxford.

As to his notes upon the Eclogues of his father, nothing is now known. Bryan Fairfax, however, has preserved to us, in his letter, so often quoted, to Bishop Atterbury, the following account (written in 1636 A.D.) from the notes, of the poems themselves:—"These bucolics were written in the first year of the reign of King James, and from their finishing they lay neglected ten years in my father's study, until Ludowic, the late noble Duke of Richmond and Lennox, desired a sight of them, which made the author to transcribe them for his Grace's use. That copy was seen and approved by many learned men; and that reverend divine, Dr. Field, now Bishop of Hereford (Bishop only from December 14th, 1635 A.D., to June 2nd,

1636 A.D.), wrote verses upon it; and these following were written by Wilson, Scotobritannus:

> 'Et Phœbus, castasque doces, Fairfaxe, sorores
> Salsa verecundo verba lepore loqui,
> Ulla nec in toto paruit lascivia libro,
> Pagina non minus est quani tibi vita proba.'
>
> 'Chaste is thy muse as is a vestal nun,
> And thy Apollo spotless as the sun,
> No wanton thought betray'd by word or look,
> As blameless is thy life, as is thy book.'"

Both the book itself and the Bishop's encomium perished in the fire, when the banquetting house at Whitehall was burnt, and with it part of the Duke's lodgings where the book was; but with *my father's help*, I recovered them out of his loose papers, &c."

The fire alluded to thus by the son, must have occurred before his father's—Edward's—death in 1635 A.D.

What has become of the recovered, or reconstructed copies is, unfortunately, now unknown. Mrs. Cooper, whose compilation, "The Muses' Library," was made in 1737 A.D., states that a copy of the Eclogues was then in existence, from which, "by the indulgence of the family, she was permitted to oblige the world with a specimen of their beauties,—a favour, which, she was proud to say, would, in one sense, make her collection complete, since it would be impossible it should be so without."

After much inquiry no complete copy has been found. The *fourth* Eclogue is fortunately preserved, as stated above, in Mrs. Cooper's compilation, and has been reprinted in Knight's edition of the translation of Tasso, and also in Grainge's "Poets and Poetry of Yorkshire."

Another one has, within the last few years, been discovered at the end of a manuscript volume of poems in the handwriting of the third Lord Fairfax, in the Bodleian Library, Oxford. (MSS. Add: vii., B 25). Beyond this, with the exception of two lines of a third one shortly to be alluded to, it is to be feared that the whole of this literary treasure has perished.

The one first printed in the Muses' Library, is entitled "Eglon and Alexis," and is in the form of a dialogue, extending to thirty-eight stanzas, between Eglon a shepherd and Alexis his friend,—wherein under the parable of a fox and a lamb—the wiles of a seducer are pourtrayed with graphic power and caustic satire, while the fearful curse of licentiousness is set forth in words that burn.

The following is an instance, from this poem, of Fairfax's descriptive power :—

"Close to the bosom of a bended hill,
  Of faire and fruitful trees, a forest stood;
Balm, myrtle, bdellium, from their bark distil,
  Bay, smilax, myrtle (Cupid's arrow wood)
Grew there, and cyprus, with its kiss-sky tops,
And Ferrea's tree whence pure rose water drops.

The golden bee, buzzing with tinsel wings,
  Suckt amber honey from the silken flower;
The dove sad love-groans on her sackbut sings,
  The throssell whistles from the oaken tower;
And sporting, lay the nymphs of woods and hills,
On beds of heart's-ease, rue, and daffodils."

Another passage, taken from the conclusion of the poem, in which Alexis is speaking to his friend, mourning over his deluded, suffering lamb, sets forth spiritual truth and comfort, in words not unworthy of their writer :—

"Great is, I grant, the danger of thy sheep;
  But yet there is a salve for every sore;
That Shepherd, who our flocks and us doth keep,
  To remedy this sickness, long before,
Killed a Holy Lamb, clear, spotless, pure,
Whose blood the salve is, all our hearts to cure.

Call for that Surgeon good to dress her wounds,
  Bathe her in holy water of thy tears!
Let her in bands of faith and love be bound;
  And while on earth she spends her pilgrim years,
Thou, for thy charm, pray with the publicane
And so restore thy lamb to health again."

The other Eclogue extant is entitled, "Hermes and Lycaon." It was printed a few years ago by Lord Houghton, for the Philobiblion Society, and has also appeared with some account of its author, by the present writer, in the Churchman's Shilling Magazine. Below it is given in full. The subject matter of it,—again set forth in the form of a dialogue in parable,—are the relative claims, merits, and doctrines of the Church of England, and the Papal Church. As a controversial, as well as poetical work, it merits the highest praise bestowed upon its author. "The argument" and "prologue" are specially beautiful. It is headed, "An Eclogue made by my uncle, Mr. Ed. Fairfax, in a dialogue betwixt tow sheapards."

HERMES AND LYCAON.

The Argument.

"Lycaon his false church extends
Through all the world with pomp and pride;
Hermes the Church of Christ commends
And to her spouse brings home his bride.

The sweatie scythe-man, with his razor keen,
Shore the perfum'd beard from meadows green;
And on each bush and every mossie stone
Jarred Maie's little daughter, Tettrigone,
When to the shadows of a mountain steep,
Lycaon drove his goats, Hermes his sheep.
The shepherds both were lovers, both were young,
Their skill was like in piping, like in song.
The other grooms that heard, hid in the dales,
Were dumb for shame like conquered nightingales.
Oft came the nymphs, and fairy sisters oft
Forsook their mossie beds, and liards soft,—
And oft the half-gods at their music sound,
Came, and their brows with ivy garlands crown'd,
Ye sedgie lakes, and pebble-paved wells,
And, thou, great Pales, in these fields that dwells,
How oft have you, hid in the shady sprays,
Listen'd Lycaon's songs, his loves, and lays!
And you, high-stretched pines and oaks of Jove,
Thou wanton echo, tell-clock of this grove,
How oft did you fair Psyche's praise resound
When Hermes charmed with songs love's bleeding wound.
They sung by course and praised their loves by turns,—
Each cricket loves the flame wherein she burns,—
And whilst their flocks browse on the shrubs and briars,
They tune their pipes, and thus they sing their fires.

Lycaon:

Flora my queen, my joy, my heaven of bliss,
See what my merit and deserving is;
I build thee temples, and I feed thy sheep,
I bring thee gifts, thy words as laws I keep;
My bed is ashes, sackloth is my weed,
I drink with Rechab's sons, with Job I feed.
For all my service and thus suffering long,
Love me, sweet Flora, or thou dost me wrong.

Hermes:

Psyche, my desire, my undefiled, my dove,
O comfort me, for I am sick of love;
Thy sacred temple is this wounded breast;
Sin, error, folly, my service is at best;
Foul leper-spots on all my body grow.
Wipe out these stains, and wash me white as snow.
Clothe me with linen, crown my head with gold,
First make me worthy love, then love me bold.

Lycaon:

Flora was young, a fair few goats she kept,
Ten kings espied her, loved her, with her slept,
And in her sweet embrace such joy they found,
That with three diadems her head they crowned,
And on seven heaps their wealth and treasure laid,
Set her thereon, fell at her feet and prayed.
She forty months and two their service proves,
And takes them for her slaves, not for her loves.

Hermes:

Psyche, my virgin, bore a blessed son;
The dragon chased her; she to desert run,
The fiend a stream of water at her flings,
Earth drunk the flood, she 'scaped with eagles' wings;
Crowned with twelve stars, clothed with glorious sun,
She doth with roes and hinds in Eden run.
There Psyche lives and reigns, in safety blest,
Till time and times and half a time be past.

Lycaon:

Out of the sea a scarlet beast appeared,
Ten horns he had, and seven heads proudly reared;
His forked tail 'gainst all the world made wars;
And smote the third of trees, of floods, of stars.
Flora, this monster caught and tamed his pride,
And on his back, as on a mule, doth ride.
All nations fear the beast and serve the dame,
And sealed are with 's number, mark and name.

Hermes:

Before the gates of Psyche's sheep cote lies
Four wonderous beasts, all full of wings and eyes,
And round about them four and twenty kings
Offer up gold, and myrrh, and precious things.
All these do Psyche's lambs keep, cure, and feed,
And thousand thousands, clad in milk-white weed,
Sing hymns of love, faith, and never cease,
And on his brow each wears the seal of peace.

Lycaon:

Flora once found me sick and hurt to death,
Thrice did she cross me, thrice upon me breathe,
Three times she dipp't me in a living stream,
And salved my wounds with spittle, salt and cream.
A thousand saints she for my guard appoints,
And all my head with oil of balm anoints,
Then makes me master of her flock and fold,
Her goats to keep, or kill, or sell for gold.

Hermes:

Psyche first took me soiled with mire and clay,
Washed in the well of life my filth away;
Thieves robbed me, slew me; of a lamb new slain,
On me she poured the blood,—I lived again;
Since that with bread of heaven, wine of grace,
She diets me,—her lap my resting place;
Her sheep my play fellows, heaven our fold,
Her spouse the door, her voice the key of gold.

Lycaon:

It was the fiftieth year. Flora a feast
Made for all those that loved and served her best;
Her guests were kings and lords of highest birth,
All that were wise and rich upon the earth;
And all that land, or sea, or air afford,
Her caterers took, and therewith filled her board,
And drunk with wine, sucked from her cup of gold,
Were kings and nations, rich, poor, young, and old.

Hermes:

Psyche to supper called the weak, the poor,
The sick, the lazer, from the rich man's door,
And at her board set them with lords and kings;
Her holy steward wine and wafers brings;
They eat and drink by faith, and thirst no more,
Except some guests, forecharged with Flora's store,
Sit there and, spider-like, from roses new,
Draw poison, where the bee sucks honey-dew.

Lycaon:

Flora an orchard had of fruitful treen;
She pared the moss, and kept the branches clean,
She let the fountains in, she killed the worm,
She scarred the birds, she sav'd the blooms from storm;
Flourished the trees, the boughs with apples bent;
She called; her servants to her orchard went.
Gathered to eat; but when she cut the skin,
The fruit was ashes, embers, dust within.

Hermes:

Last year my Psyche had a field of corn;
She scoured the ditches, stopped the gap with thorn;
She tilled the land enough, she sowed good seed;
She stubbed the briars, plucked up tares and weed;
She frayed the crows, she kept the wild boar out;
And when ths sun turned the year's wheel about
She reaped her crop, and when her gain she told,
Found thirty, sixty, and a hundred fold.

Lycaon:

A flock of goats astray from Flora went;
Doris, her handmaid, after them she sent.
But whilst the lass with Thirsis sporting laid,
Her dogs ran forth alone, and soon they strayed;
And like their kind of wolves, of which they sprang,
They slew, and eat, the goats and sucklings young.
Yet some escaped, saved in the woods and rocks;
Doris went home, but thus she lost her flocks.

Hermes:

What Doris left and lost, fair Daphne sought,
And found, and to her mother's sheep fold brought.
There Psyche bound their wounds, and staunched their blood.
At first she gave them milk, then stronger food,
And soon restored their health. Shepherds beware;
Watch, feed, your sheep, charge asketh care.
All that is stolen or slain you must make good,
And Flora's Hylax yet lurks in the wood.

Lycaon:

King Solomon a cedar palace built,
Thatched with tiles, of Flora's tresses gilt;
Her legs were silver posts the house to bear;
Her glorious thoughts the purple hangings were;
Her breast the presence, and her heart his throne;
Her triple crown, as Lord, there sits alone.
Her holy doors ope to each that knocks;
Her hands pure myrrh drops on the bars and locks.

Hermes:

Psyche's fair locks, wrapped in gold of proof,
Of God's high temple is the gilded roof.
Her eyes the crystal windows, through each light
A smiling saint shoots in day's arrows bright.
Her coral lips, the doors that turn and twine
On ruby hooks; her mouth the choir divine;
Her teeth the ivory seats built even and thin;
Her tongue the silver bell that rings all in.

Lycaon:

That royal town where Flora hath her seat,
Stands on seven hills, well peopled, pleasant, great;
Rich in all blessings, all delights that can
Be given by fortune, or be wished by man,
Quinzy the large, Dorad yet seen *(sic)*
Her handmaid be. She is the world's sole queen.
Joy in her streets, life in her temples wide,
And dead and lost is all the world beside.

Hermes:

Psyche's clear city was not raised from dust,
But came from heaven, pure, immortal, just;
Stands on twelve precious stones. Jasper the wall,
Streets gold, gates pearl be, still ope to all
Who taste the tree of life which there does grow.
About the town two blessed rivers flow
Of grace and mercy; over either flood
Lies the fair bridge of faith, hope, doing good.

Lycaon:

O shrill Heptaphones! thou daughter clear,
Tell not these rocks of Flora's doubt and fear;
Write not, Planetus, in to-morrow's stars,
Her future troubles, dangers, losses, wars,
Lest Psyche's shepherds should fore-know her doom,
And kill her goats before her day be come.
These woods are hers, these fields, and folds about;
Then keep them, Flora, till thy lease wear out.

Hermes:

Sitting on Isis' flowery bank, I spied,
On a white horse a crowned monarch ride.
Upon his thigh was writ his wondrous name;
Out of his mouth a sword, two-edged, came.
Flora, her beast, and all her goats he slew,
And in the lake of fire their bodies threw.
This king is Psyche's spouse; with him she went,
And ruled the world, for Flora's lease was spent.

Thus much did Hermes and Lycaon sing.
The heifer let the herbs untouched spring,
Forgot to feed. The stags amazed stood.
The river stayed her speedy flood.
Charmed was the adder deaf, tamed was the lion,
So trees heard Orpheus, dolphins heard Orion."

Of another of the Eclogues, said to have been the fifth, only a scrap, consisting of the two opening lines, is known to exist. The lines are quoted, and thus preserved, in *Gough's Camden*, vol. iii., page 289, Edition of 1806 A.D. They are,

"Upon Verbeia's willow-wattled brim,
As Maspus dressed the wands and wickers trim."

On these lines the following remarks from the notes of the poet's son, William Fairfax, are also preserved.

" *Verbeia*, I take to be the ancient name of the Wharfe which watereth the native county of our family; and I am in this confirmed by an altar so inscribed, which altar is observed by my father some years before Sir Robert Cotton and Mr. Camden came to this monument where it stood at the town of Ilkley. (Woodford in Ward's M.S.) It seemeth probable to me that Verbeia was the supposed nymph of the river, for the altar was erected to her in the water, and there stood as late as the memory of the parents of such as live yet in the house."

As has been already stated, Edward Fairfax died in 1635 or 6 A.D.

His statement of the faith in which he lived, and, we may believe, died, is given in the beginning of his book on Dæmonology thus,—

"I am in religion neither a fantastic Puritan nor superstitious Papist, but so settled in conscience that I have the sure ground of God's word to warrant all I believe, and the commendable ordinance of our English Church to approve all I practise, in which course I live a faithful Christian and an obedient subject; and so teach my family."

It cannot but be matter of deep regret, not only to every forester, but also to every lover of his country's history and literature, that every memorial,—except the portions of his works herein described,—of this learned man, has perished.

If he left a will, it cannot be found. The portion of the parochial register bearing the record of his burial, has been destroyed, or is lost. A marble slab, said to have marked the place of his interment in Fewston Church,—if ever there,—is not now to be seen, and must have perished in the fire by which that church was, in part, destroyed about 1679 A.D. Even the house, which for probably 30 years was the home of himself and his family, has now—every vestige of it—been swept away. Is this to remain the case with the memory of Edward Fairfax? Is *he* to remain

"Unwept, unhonoured, and unsung?"

What say the rich men and women, or the Corporation, of the great town in which, for a time, he dwelt, and who have now, themselves, swept away the last material memorial of him, viz., his forest home—the town of Leeds? This is the age of centenaries. And even a grateful country has ere now erected national monuments to less worthy—less talented—citizens than Edward Fairfax. But if these fail, will no wealthy forester, or Yorkshireman, or Englishman, no lover of his country's fame and literature, wipe away the reproach of the last resting place of the poet of the forest being left without a memorial to mark the spot, or to record his worth and his works! A window, a marble monument in the church, or, better still, the restoration of the whole or a portion of the sacred building in which he worshipped during life, and in which his remains now rest—awaiting the resurrection morn,—would bring honour to the donor, as honour to the recipient of it. The act would be, like mercy,

"twice blessed.
It blesseth him that gives and him that takes."

A TALE OF WITCHCRAFT IN THE FOREST, A.D. 1621.

"Some call me witch,
And being ignorant of myself, they go
About to teach me how to be one; urging
That my bad tongue (by their bad usage made so)
Forespeaks their cattle, doth bewitch their corn,
Themselves, their servants, and their babes at nurse.
This they enforce upon me, and in part
Make me to credit it."—"*The Witch of Edmonton.*"

IT has been said that "witchcraft and kingcraft in England came in and went out with the Stuarts." This, though not true, contains truth. Both existed before James I. ascended the English throne, and neither of them entirely vanished for long after James II. was driven from it. Yet it is certain that a very dark wave of credulity, as to witchcraft at least, passed over this country in the latter half of the sixteenth century, and extended far into the eighteenth, though blackest, perhaps, during the earlier part of the reign of the house of Stuart, *i. e.*, of the seventeenth century. It was not confined to any particular creed or sect. Members of the Church of England, Roman Catholics, Presbyterians, Independents, and Anabaptists, were alike subject to its delusions. The same was the case with all ages and ranks. In A.D. 1594, James, then King of Scotland, and afterwards of England, published his treatise on Dœmonology, of which a modern writer somewhat tartly says, "It contains statements as to making of witches, and their practice of witchcraft, which if true would only prove their revealer to be deep in the councils of Satan, and a regular member or attendant of the assemblages of witchcraft."

About the time when belief in this dark art was at its height, lived Edward Fairfax, the learned translator of Tasso.

Among the MSS. left by him was one entitled, "A Discourse on Witchcraft as it was acted in the family of Mr. Edward Fairfax, of Fuystone, in the county of York, in the year 1621 A.D."

There are several transcripts of this book now in existence in private libraries, and it was printed some years ago for the Philobiblion Society. It reveals a story of supposed witchcraft, which only lacks the tragic end of the accused, to make the witches of Knaresborough Forest as notorious as are those of the Forest of Pendle, in the adjoining county of Lancaster.

Fairfax, the writer, was no ignorant man or superstitious fool. As a poet he has already been spoken of. Lord Houghton, in an introduction to the Philobiblion print, says of him, "Living in a district of Yorkshire which even now is secluded and remote, he placed himself on the highest level of the accomplishments of his age, and he had the peculiar merit of giving to one of the chief classics of a foreign language almost the rank of a classic of his own. In times of turbulent thought and rash opinion he preserved a rare moderation in matters of religion, and writes with equal distaste of the "superstitions of the Papists and the fanaticism of the Puritans." His wealthier relations entrusted him with the management of their estates and the education of their children, as a *discreet, observant, and learned man*, and it would be difficult to find a better representative of the moral and intellectual worth of his generation."

It is on account of containing the observations and descriptions, from a man of his intelligence and position, of the phenomena which were attributed to the machinations of witchcraft, that the book is chiefly interesting and valuable. Moreover, so far as the present writer is acquainted with the literature of the subject, accounts and records of supposed witches and of their doings are numerous, while minute descriptions of the symptoms and sufferings and acts of the victims (as are given in this case) are rare; hence the possession of them on the witness, and from the pen of such a man as Fairfax, is an acquisition to our knowledge on the subject.

The history is in the form of a *diary*, the entries in which are *almost daily* for the greater portion of the time over which they extend, viz., from October 28th, 1621 A.D. to April 11th, 1623 A.D. It is prefaced by an essay of considerable length, which, however far short of carrying conviction to a modern reader, is still a very learned and able defence of the belief in dœmonology.

The opening sentences are worth quoting:—

> "I present thee, Christian reader, a narrative of witchcraft, of which I am a woful witness, and so can best report it. Read this without vindicating passion, and in reading let thy discretion precede thy judgment. I set down the actions and the accidents truly; observe them seriously,—with learning, if thou be furnished that way, if not, yet with wisdom and religion; the inquiry will afford thee matter enough to assure the wise physician that here is more than natural disease, to answer the superstitious ignorant that the actors of this be no walking ghosts or dancing fairies, and to stop the mouths of the incredulous who deny witches; for in this appeareth the work of Satan, — not merely his own, but assisted by some wicked coadjutors by whose co-operation these innocents be thus cruelly afflicted."

In the introduction, the victims of the evil practices are first described to us, and then the women accused of being their tormentors.

Of the former the writer says, "Two of the patients are my daughters, of whom this was the estate when the witches began with them—the elder, Helen Fairfax, a maid of twenty-one years, of person healthful, of complexion sanguine, free from melancholy, of capacity not apprehensive of much, but rather hard to learn things fit, slow of speech, patient of reproof, of behaviour without offence, educated only in mine own house, and therefore not knowing much.

Elizabeth, my younger daughter, an infant of scarce seven* years, of a pleasant aspect, quick wit, active spirit, able to receive any instruction, and willing to undergo pains.

Besides these of mine, one Maud Jeffray, daughter of John Jeffray, yeoman, aged 12 years, hath suffered much from the same hands.

The unfortunate women charged with witchcraft were seven in number. Six are described by name, and one as "the strange woman." Their familiar spirits are also set forth.

One was a widow, whose husband had died at the hand of the executioner for stealing. Her familiar spirit was "a deformed thing with many feet, black of colour, and rough with hair, the bigness of a cat, and the name of it unknown."

The next suspected person was her daughter, "a young woman agreeing with her mother in name and condition." Her spirit was "a cat, spotted with black, and named 'Inges.'" The third was a very old widow, reputed a witch for many years,—a repute which appears to have been hereditary in her family. Her spirit was "in the shape of a great black cat called Gibbe, which hath attended her above forty years."

The fourth was the daughter of the last named, "an obedient child and docile scholar of so skilful a parent." Her familiar was "in the shape of a bird, yellow of colour, about the bigness of a crow; the name of it Tewhit."

The next was daughter of a woman not long since dead, "notoriously famed for a witch, who had so powerful a hand over the wealthiest neighbours about her, that none of them refused to do anything that she required; yea, unbesought they provided her of fire, and meat from their own tables, and did what else they thought would please her."

---

* These ages do not correspond with the dates in the baptismal register of Fuystone parish. Helen was baptised May, 1605 A.D., and Elizabeth October, 1606 A.D.

Little is said of the sixth. The seventh was called "the strange woman." This *individuum vagum* "had a spirit in likeness of a white cat, which she calleth Ffillie; she had kept it twenty years."

"These," it is added, "do inhabit within the Forest of Knaresborough, in the parish of Fuystone, in which dwell many more suspected for witchcraft, so that the inhabitants complain much by secret murmurings of great losses sustained in their goods, especially in their kine, which should give milk; for help whereof their usual remedy is to go to those fools whom they call *wise men*. And the wizards teach them such wicked fopperies as to burn young calves alive, and the like, whereof I know that experiments have been made by the best sort of my neighbours, and thereby they have found help as they report. So little is the truth of the Christian religion known in this wild place and rude people, upon whose ignorance God have mercy!"

The victims of the delusion received almost daily visits from these accused women, and sometimes the apparitions were of the women *in propriæ personæ*, sometimes of their "familiars;" sometimes both were present at the same time; and frequently at these times—in the sufferer's presence—the apparitions of the witches were transformed into those of their familiars, and *vice versa*. At their approach, which they often foretold, the girls fell into a trance or ecstasy, and in this condition freely conversed with them in their different forms, argued with them, and often soundly rated them. They were invisible of course to any but the sufferers, and their utterances unheard except by them. The questions, replies, and conversation, however, of the latter were audible and intelligible to the bystanders, and by them were noted down at the time, and confirmed and explained by the girls upon recovery.

The first to come under the spell was the elder daughter, Helen. The power, viz., "a touch," to subject her to it, was supposed to have been gained by one of the women while "pinning her band" in the field some months previously. An attempt to obtain a like power over a neighbour on a subsequent occasion is thus described:—

"Thomas Forest, a young man, came riding late near the house of Margaret Wait, and there he was suddenly assaulted by many cats, so that he could hardly defend himself from them, but did ride away with all the speed he could, and so escaped, yet they followed him a great way; and it was told to the children afterward that the cats were witches, then assembled at the house of Wait's wife, who desired to have pulled Thomas Forest from his horse, that they might have got such a touch of him as they might have afterwards bewitched him."

The well-known use of images of the victims practised upon was also resorted to. In one of her trances Helen described the appearance of an old woman, who came in at the kitchen door, very wet with rain, and with her an "ill-favoured thing she could not describe. The woman stood behind it, and took forth of a poke and showed unto her some pictures (images) and a little creeping thing among them. The woman told her these were the pictures by which they bewitched folk. The picture of my daughter Helen was apparelled like her in her usual attire, with white hat, and locks of hair hanging at her ears; that of her sister was also attired in the child's holiday apparel; the rest were naked."

By means of such an image the death of an infant daughter (Ann Fairfax, baptized June 12th, buried October 9th, 1621 A.D.) was believed to have been brought about.

In "Pott's Discovery of Witchcraft" (Cheetham Society), the process is described on the confession of one of the Lancashire witches.

"The speediest way to take a man's life away by witchcraft is to make a picture of clay, like unto the shape of the person whom they mean to kill, and dry it thoroughly; and when they would have them to be ill in any one place more than in another, then take a thorne or pinne, and prick it in that part of the picture you would so have to be ill; and when you would have any part of the body to consume away, then take that part of the picture and burn it. And when they would have the whole body to consume away, then take the remnant of the said picture and burne it; and so thereupon by that means the body shall die."

In Middleton's "Witch of Edmonton" there is allusion to the same:—

Hecate. What death is t' you desire for Almachildes?
Duchess. A sudden and a subtile.
Hecate. Then I've fitted you.
Here be the gifts of both, sudden and subtile:
His picture made in wax, and gently molten
By a blue fire kindled with dead men's eyes,
Will waste him by degrees.—*Edition* 1778, p. 100.

The first entry in the diary is this,—

"Imprimis: — Upon Sunday, October 28th, 1621, my eldest daughter, Helen Fairfax, was sent into the parlour in my house at Newhall, a little before supper-time, to see that the fire did no hurt, and there she stayed for awhile, when William Fairfax, my eldest son, came into the place and found her laid along upon the floor in a deadly trance. . . . . We took her up, but could not recover her. . . . Nothing judged available was omitted to reduce her to some feeling; but our labour was unprofitable for divers hours, so that some gave her for dead; yet at last she respired, and shortly afterwards spake. Then we found, by her words, her imagination was that she was in the church at Leeds, hearing a sermon made by Mr. Cook, the preacher, and she told every one that spake to her. The next morning she was perfectly well again, but for some few days after she had many like trances, and in them supposed that she saw and talked with her brethren and sisters, who were dead long before."

Neither in the witches' caldron in "Macbeth," nor in "the charm" given in the following characteristic stanza of Ben Jonson, does a *penny* find place as an ingredient:—

A CHARM.

"The owl is abroad, the bat, and the toad,
And so is the cat-a-mountain,
The ant and the mole sit both in a hole,
And the frog peeps out o' the fountain;
The dogs they do bay, and the timbrels play,
The spindle is now a-turning;
The moon is red, and the stars are fled,
But all the sky is a-burning;
The ditch is made, and our nails the spade,
With pictures full, of wax and wool,
Their livers I stick with needles quick,
There lacks but the blood to make up the flood."

The story of a "charmed" penny, however, as related by Fairfax, is too rich to be omitted.

"On Friday, November 23rd, 1621, I was in the kitchen with many of my family, and there some speeches by chance were made of charms and lookers (as our rude people call them), and the names of many were reckoned up who were thought to be skilful therein; and it was said that such as go to these charmers carry and give them a single penny. The words gave occasion to my wife to remember and tell it, that she had a single penny given her amongst other money by Margaret Wait, sen., which she paid for corn. The woman desired her to keep the penny, for she would come for it again, which she did accordingly a few days after, and demanded it, affirming that she would not lack it for anything, for it kept her from dreaming. She said it had a hole in it, by which she did hang it about her neck in a thread, at which words such as were present laughed heartily. . . . She was very angry, and departed without her penny. At this relation I wished my wife to fetch the penny she had, ... and told her that if Wait's wife were a witch indeed, then if she went not presently the penny would be gone. She answered that it could not, for it was safely locked up in the desk in the parlour. . . . I arose and with my wife went to the desk, which was locked. We opened it, and sought the penny therein with all diligence, and left not a paper unopened, nor a place unsought, but the penny was not to be found; whereat we were a little amazed, for the place where the penny lay was upon a shelf in the desk easy to be seen, and the desk was securely locked when we came to it.

"On Sunday, the 25th of November, Helen went to church both before and after dinner, and in the evening Mr. Smithson, vicar of Fuyston, came to visit her, and tarried supper with us; and after supper, as we sat talking of these things in the parlour, especially of the penny, my daughter had occasion to open the desk, which stood by locked. She opened the lock and lifted up the cover, and presently both she and all who were present saw the penny lying upon the shelf in the desk, to the great marvel of us all, especially of myself who had so diligently sought for it before. Whereupon I took it and put brimstone upon it, and so thrust it into the midst of the fire, which was so vehement that it moved Mr. Smithson to say, "So I warrant you it will trouble you no more," and we all thought it to be molten and consumed; yet upon the Sunday following, the 2nd of December, the penny again lay in our sight before the fire, and was then taken up by Edward Fairfax, my son, a boy of ten years old. Then I took it, and with brimstone and fire dissolved it, and beat it to powder upon a stone."

Let us hope the penny was now completely got rid of.

About Christmas in the same year 1621 A.D. the second daughter, Elizabeth, was subjected to the evil influences of the sisterhood The manner in which one of them succeeded in touching her, and thus obtaining the power over her, is another interesting episode, over which, however, we must pass.

Witches were not free from sorrows and trials any more than other mortals (if mortals they were). On Friday, the 8th of March, 1622 A.D., Margaret Thorp, the fourth of the seven, appeared unto Helen in great trouble and weeping bitterly. She probably was feeling how deplorable was her condition.

> "I am shunned
> And hated like a sickness; made a scorn
> To all degrees and sexes."

She questioned her as to how she became a witch.

> "Call me witch!
> "What is the name? Where and by what art learn'd?
> What spells, what charms or invocations?
> May the thing called 'familiar' be purchased?"

The woman replied that one, in the appearance of a man of this world, met her upon the moor, and offered her money, which at first she refused, but afterwards sold herself to him body and soul.

"And he made her a lease back again of her life for forty years, which was now ended upon Shrove Tuesday last. The man did write their leases with their blood, and they likewise with their blood set their hands to them. . . . ' She said further that she knew forty witches, but there were only seven of their company. Helen said, 'I think thy sister at Timble is as evil as thou art, for she speaketh with black things in Timble Gill.' The woman said, 'Thou art a witch if thou canst tell that.' She replied, 'I am not a witch; . . . her own child told it.'"

The long-continued affliction in the family could not but attract the attention and excite the curiosity or sympathy of the surrounding neighbourhood.

"My uncle has of late become the sole
Discourse of all the country; for a man respected
As master of a governed family;
The house (as if the ridge were fixed below,
And ground-sills lifted up to make the roof)
All now's turned topsy turvy
In such a retrograde, preposterous way
As seldom hath been heard of, I think never.
* * * * * * * *
All in such rare disorder, that in some
As it breeds pity, and others wonder,
So in the most part laughter. It is thought
This comes by witchcraft."—*Heywood.*

It is noteworthy that whether pity, wonder, or laughter were bred toward the household, sympathy, at least of the more intelligent neighbours, seems to have been for the accused. In this case—

"'Twas not all one
To be a witch, and to be accounted one."

Fairfax complains several times somewhat bitterly that the vicar of Fuystone (Mr. Smithson), Mr. Henry Graver, and Mr. Jas. Robinson, of Swinsty Hall, favoured the women.

One neighbouring justice of the peace, however, appears to have been prevailed upon to make an examination into the charges against them. One of them (Margaret Thorp) was summoned to meet Helen Fairfax in his presence at Fuystone Church. After some preliminary inquiries the woman was subjected to the following test:—

"The same justice of the peace, also in the church at Fuystone, told me in private that he would try if Thorp's wife were a witch, by causing her to say the Lord's Prayer: for if she were a witch, he said that in the repetition of that prayer she could not say the words 'forgive us our trespasses.' I was silent and observed the trial. The woman being put to it, could not say those words by any means. At first she repeated the prayer and wholly omitted them, and then being admonished thereof, and urged to the point, she stood amazed, and finally could not at all utter them, of which many people were witnesses to their admiration."

If such tests only were applied to the women, their apparitions received occasionally somewhat rougher usage, as the following relations will show:—

"On the 3rd of May Jennet Dibb appeared unto Helen, and showed her an old silver spoon. She fell into the usual trance, but at last looked up and said to the woman, 'That is ours; that is our spoon.' And it appeared upon search that such an one was missing out of the locked desk."

"Helen still talked to the woman, and said, 'That is our spoon; thou shalt not carry it away; I will take it from thee.' Her uncle and the rest present saw nothing this while. At last she arose and went to the place where she saw the woman stand, and there the company saw her fight and strive with something. At last she said to the woman, 'Wilt thou go away with it, thou shalt not carry it away.' The servant shut the door and set her back against it. Helen still contended with the woman for the spoon, and her hand went apace, yet she did not touch either table or wall, but something which the company saw not. At last she drove the woman into a corner, and there got her down, and after some struggling she held the woman's hand with her left hand, and with the right she took the spoon from her, rose up, shook it at her, and said, 'How sayest thou now, Dibb's wife? I told thee I would take it from thee.' Then all that were present saw the spoon in her hand to their great amazement."

The servant left the door to look at the recovered spoon, and the woman "opened the door and ran away."

Again, on Sunday, the 11th of March, "the strange woman" appeared to the children in the kitchen, and threatened to kill the elder. But the girl got

"A rod, and starting up, beat the woman until she kneeled down and prayed her to forgive her. Then I took the rod and struck at the place where the children said the woman was, but they perceived it not, yet they saw the woman much troubled, and asked her 'what she ailed.' For she wept bitterly, that the tears ran down, and stirred from place to place to avoid the blows; and lastly told the children that I did strike at her, and she was afraid to be beaten. . . . . In this extremity her spirit at the instant came to help her, being then in likeness of a bird; it took her away, and both of them ran out of the door together."

These incidents are but specimens of such as happened, and are recorded, almost every day.

At the Spring Assizes at York (1622 A.D.), six of the unfortunate women were charged with witchcraft. Fairfax, his elder daughter, and Maud Jeffray were there and appeared against them. The younger daughter, Elizabeth, remained at home at Newhall.

The women fortunately were acquitted, though no remark or information on the subject is given — except indirectly—in the narrative. How, or on what grounds they escaped, therefore, on this occasion there is no record.

On Thursday, the 4th of April, two of them (Jennet Dibb and Margaret Thorp) returned to their homes. On the following morning these women with their spirits, the cat and the bird, appeared to the younger child at Newhall, and also on the following morning (Saturday), and told her that her father and sister were then at Tadcaster, on their way home, but "should hardly get home that night, for that they would go and meet them upon the moor." The apparition of one of these women also appeared on the Friday night to the two girls at Tadcaster, and in like manner warned them also "that she would meet them them again upon the moor."

The story of the journey home on this eventful Saturday is so inimitably told by the narrator that it must be given to our readers in his own words:—

"Item, on Saturday, the 6th of April, we departed from Tadcaster, and rode without any interruption till we came to Collingham or Clifford Moor, as some call it. There, the place being very fair, we alighted to walk on foot; myself and my daughter walked alone, and Richard England, my servant, led after us the horses upon which we rode; the rest of the company were before us about twelve score (yards). Jeffray's daughter said suddenly to those that were with her, that she saw the two women pass by them, and then 'the strange woman' went along the top of a bank which is cast up there for a great space together (the remains, as I take it, of the entrenchment of the rebels, 12th of Elizabeth), and she looked after them, and told them that they went towards Helen Fairfax, and stood round about her, and declared on which side of her each of them severally stood. At that instant I took my horse, not knowing anything of this matter, and my man offered to set my daughter up behind me, but she could not speak to him. I perceived that she was in trance and alighted again, and sat down with her upon the bank aforesaid, where she began to talk to Thorpe's wife and to the strange woman.

"Maud Jeffray also fell into the same condition. In which state we took them up, and carried them to the town of Collingham, where they came to themselves, and we rode on our journey very well till we came to the gate entering upon Harwood Moor, at which gate (as my daughter told me) Dibb's wife stood. All the company present passed the gate, and left the woman standing there, who stood in that place until Francis Pullein (a neighbour accompanying them) and Richard England came to the gate. . . . . . At their coming the women came with them from the place, and in their company all the three women overtook us. The two girls saw all they did, and laughed thereat, and reported it unto us, not being in any trance until they came all unto us; then they fell in trance, in which the women told them that Francis Pullein should go home on foot. Thereupon the women, sometimes one and sometimes another, were seen by the children to ride upon his horse behind him, which they talked of to the women, and by those words we understood what passed. The horse was suddenly so troubled, and unable to go forward, that the man was forced to alight; but then his case was worse, for two of the witches at once rode upon him (the horse) so that he could neither lead nor drive him but with much difficulty. Often he struck in the saddle, and where the wenches said the witches sat, at which time the women avoided the blows, and leaped from the horse, who as long as he was discharged of them, went on; but he found not much of that ease. Thus with much trouble we came to Harwood, to the house of Mr. Jackson, where they were presently well. . . . . From Harwood we departed, and rode on till we came again upon the moors above Stainburn, where they fell in trance again, and talked to the same women as before, and Francis Pullein's horse was used in the same manner again; so with much ado, we got home to my house about the setting of the sun.

"This accident concerning Pullein's horse is such as the greatest adversaries, I think, cannot say that he could be instructed to play his part so well in the imposture; for of this I am sure, he was very like to have died for many weeks after, but at last he recovered in some measure. Ridiculous are they that think the horse could combine in the practice, and wicked if they question the truth of this particular, which so many oaths hath confirmed."

Things resumed their usual course in the household. In a few days, certain eggs, pence, a shilling, and "two sugar cakes," mysteriously disappeared from locked desks, and the spirit of one of the women—perhaps to indemnify her against her expenses—was believed to have taken them. A remark, however, is made, which probably most readers will endorse :—

"These cakes, the two pence, and Jeffray's shilling were indeed gone and never seen more. The circumstances seem to prove that the woman herself, not her spirit, did these things. For I doubt how the rich usurers could keep their money in safety, if the devil had any such power to take it out of their chests."

Whether the witches were anxious to celebrate their victory at York with all *éclat* or otherwise, "the deponent sayeth not," but we find this record in the diary :—

"Item, on Thursday, the 10th of April, the children were both of them made blind by the black cat, and so continued till Friday at nine o'clock; then their sight was restored. They were told that all the witches had a *feast* at Timble Gill."

"'Tis now the very witching time of night,
When churchyards yawn, and hell itself breathes out
Contagion to this world."

"*Hamlet*," Act III., sc. ii.

"Their meat was wasted about midnight. At the upper end of the table sat their master, viz., the devil; at the lower end Dibbs, who provided for the feast and was the cook; and therefore she could not come to the children that day. It was true that the children that day saw her not."

At this time, one or other of the apparitions, sometimes several of them, appeared to the victims almost daily, and even more than once a day. The conversations and incidents of each occasion are minutely recorded, and the perusal of them, while sometimes provoking a smile, is frequently not without painful feelings of pity or regret at the credulity, or the wicked deceit they reveal.

The girls seem to have imagined, or believed, themselves to be more and more under the power of their supernatural tormentors. On two occasions it is stated of the elder that she was bodily borne away, against her will and her struggles, to some considerable distance by them.

"On Thursday, the 2nd of May, my daughter Helen was taken away (as she after reported) by Dibb's wife and Thorp's wife, who took her out of the entry, carried her to the river, and put her into it . . . but she got from them, and returning towards the house, in the way she fell in a deadly trance, in which I found her, and did marvel to see her clothes wet; so I caused her to be brought into the house, and she came to herself, and told us as aforesaid."

And again,—

"On Thursday, the 30th of May, being Ascension Day, Helen Fairfax, was suddenly taken away by Thorp's wife and the black cat, and carried out at the back door . . . over the water above Rowton Bridge, and over Ralph Holmes's ground, and then over the moor, and so through the fields again, and crossed Braime Lane above Caryer's house; then over the great hill there, and so crossed the fields on the north side of Slayter's house, and so the high moor, on that side upon a hill. There she saw many women together, amongst whom was Dibb's wife and the strange woman, who had a great fire there."

She was found here, and led to a neighbouring house (Jeffray's). "And," continues the narrative,—

"One came with all speed running to advertise me at my house of the accident, and found me, with others in much care, seeking the woods and waters for her, least she some way perished, and sorrowing for her loss. This news comforted us. I took some with me. . . . Then I brought her home, and by the way she showed me the way she had passed, which was over hedges and difficult places for the space of for more than a mile. The time also was so short betwixt her taking out of the house and her being found on the moors that it was not possible she could go thither in so short space."

There is one more story, that of a hare, which shall not be withheld from the reader, though probably he has already had enough of such, partly because Fairfax places considerable importance upon it as an evidence of supernatural intervention, and partly because it shows how the evidence, deemed by him unanswerable, could be easily explained.

"On Thursday, the 4th of April, my eldest son, William Fairfax, being in the field called Birkbanks, started a hare out of a bush and set a dog at her. Mr. Smithson, vicar of Fuystone, saw her also, and in like sort caused his dog to run at her, but they quickly lost the sight of her. That day, soon after, the child (Elizabeth, the younger daughter, the other being at this time with her father at York) was in trance, and the strange woman did appear to her, and told her that she was that hare which her brother and the vicar set their dogs at, and that she came over the water with her brother William, and that he should see *her again the next time that he went to that place,* which proved true.

"From the woman's report that she was that hare, the detractors and slanderous scoffers of this infant may be confounded, if they consider that the child foretold out of the woman's mouth that her brother should see the hare again, which he did indeed, in the same place, upon Tuesday, the 9th of April next following; which foretelling could be no imposture of the child, for her teachers, if they can suppose any such, could not themselves preface it so many days before. I cannot with silence pass over her saying, that being in that or the like shape she was senseless, for [as to] the transforming of shapes in this kind, the question deserveth to be written of in a whole volume; but it is far above my learning to resolve it; and books from which I might borrow any help, are (in this wilderness) as rare as civility is, or learning itself."

At the summer assizes in the same year the accused women were a second time placed on trial, and Fairfax with both his bewitched daughters, together with John Jeffray and his daughter, again attended to give evidence against them. A petition in favour of the accused from their neighbours—evidently promoted by Mr. Smithson, the Vicar, Henry Graver, and James Robinson—was presented. The grand jury, however, found a true bill, but, upon the trial in court, deception of some kind was suspected on the part of Jeffray and his daughter; the latter on being examined in a private room, is said to have confessed to an imposture, though it is added, if so, it was under undue threatening and pressure. The result was, that Jeffray was for a short time detained in custody, and the women again acquitted.

At the failure of these prosecutious Fairfax was evidently very much disappointed and annoyed. He says, "I am not aggrieved that they escaped death, which deservedly they might perchance have suffered; for the lives of so many ought to be very precious in the eyes of Christian charity. Notwithstanding, the proceedings which made the way easy for them to escape, I fear, were not fair. Either the hardness of hearts to believe, which made some of the best sort incredulous, or the openness of hands to give in some of the meaner, which waylaid justice, untying the fetters from their heels, and unloosing the halters from their necks, which so wise juries thought they had so well deserved. . . . . Upon myself was put an aspersion, not of dishonesty, but of simplicity; for it was given out that Jeffray and his family devised the practice, to which they drew my eldest daughter, and she the younger; and that I (like a good innocent) believed all which I heard or saw to be true, and not feigned. . . . . I thank them that they wrong not my integrity; and for putting the fool upon me, I could answer them, as Gregory did Mauritius the Emperor for calling him fool, and pray them to consider, that though they be so wise to think the children might deceive them, having seen them but once or twice in trance, and therefore could not collect much, yet all we who conversed with them day and night for the space of ten months, and observed all before written, and much more omitted,—it is impossible, I say, that all we, by children of their small capacity, be so long besotted that we could discover nothing to be feigned or counterfeited in so many occurrences."

The return of the family home on August 12th was followed by no cessation of the appearances of the apparitions—now of the women themselves, now of Inges the spotted cat, now of Gibbe the black one, now of Tewhit the yellow bird, or now of various "deformed things," their spirits or familiars—for two or three months.

There is an amusing account of the funeral of the husband of one of the women, and of her "familiar," the bird, being seen following it through the churchyard, and then perching upon the porch of the church until the procession issued from the edifice and then again joining it, and proceeding with it to the grave; but the incidents upon the whole were of much the same character as those of which the reader has already had a sufficient number of specimens. Helen, the elder daughter, was rendered deaf soon after the return, and remained so for some weeks. On the 19th of November there is this record with regard to her:—

"At this time my daughter Helen was perfectly well, but her memory was gone concerning the witches, and when her sister fell in trances she marvelled at it, and demanded what she ailed, and asked what disease she had. We told her that she was bewitched, and that she herself had been so, and questioned her of the black cat and other spirits; at which she laughed, and said, 'Jesus bless me! What tell you me of spirits and witches? I never saw a spirit.'"

After Christmas, 1622 A.D., the appearances to, and trances of, the younger girl became less frequent, and when the narrative ends, April 11th, 1622 A.D., the visitations were evidently gradually being withdrawn from her also.

In forming an opinion with regard to the incidents and events of this history, it must be borne in mind that they reflect the general feeling, mode of thinking, and manners of the day in which they are said to have happened. As to the origin of the hallucinations (if such they were) in the persons described, medical science could probably furnish much, in the way of explanation, which might save the young persons from a charge of deliberate imposture.

There can be no doubt the writer of "the discourse" was imposed upon, and that he conscientiously believed what he recorded. Before condemning his credulity, it may be well also to remember what Hartley Coleridge well says of him, in the "Northern Worthies,"—viz., "That in his belief in Dœmonology, Fairfax coincided with the spirit of his age and bowed to the wisdom of his ancestors. To have doubted of the existence of witches would have exposed him to the imputation of atheism, and as certain diseases were attributed to diabolical agency, an anxious parent might be excused for mistaking the symptoms in his own offspring."

The popular feeling in favour of such agency had been on the increase during the thirty years which had elapsed, since *Jewel, Bishop of Salisbury, preaching at St. Paul's Cross, before Queen Elizabeth*, used these words:—"It may please your Grace to understand that witches and sorcerers within these few years are marvellously increased within your Grace's realms. Your Grace's subjects pine away, even unto the death; their colour fadeth, their flesh rotteth, their speech is benumbed, their senses are bereft. I pray God they never practise further than upon the subject. . . . . *These eyes have seen* most evident and manifest marks of their wickedness."

And, may it not also be asked, in Fairfax's favour, whether we, of the latter half of the 19th century, with the advantages of all the advancements in science and in every branch of knowledge—in theology, "the higher criticism," and "the evolutions of the inner consciousness," —who yet have so many among us who believe in spirit-rapping, spiritualism, apparitions, and manifestations in *séances*, have much right to cast the first stone at the credulity of Edward Fairfax, in the beginning of the 17th century?

"Ah! from the old world let some one answer give;
'*Scorn* ye this world, their tears, their inward cares?
I say unto you, see that *your* souls live
A deeper life than theirs.'

* * * * * *

"'Children of men! not that your age excel
In pride of life the ages of your sires,
But that *you* think clear, feel deep, bear fruit well,
The Friend of man desires.'"

NOTES ON THE CHILDREN OF EDWARD FAIRFAX.

THE following notes may be of interest to the readers of the foregoing papers, on the family—many of whom are incidently mentioned therein,—of Edward Fairfax.

Four sons and three daughters survived him, and, at least one, a daughter, died in infancy. The sons appear to have gone out into the world, and all, or nearly all, records of them have been lost. The daughters soon after their father's death, married into local families.

William Fairfax, the eldest son, was B.A. of Corpus Christi College, Oxford—and a learned, but retiring, man. He was tutor in the family of Dr. Stanley, at Norwich, and the author of Notes on Euripides, and other classical works; and also of Notes on his father's Eclogues.

Thomas Fairfax—mentioned in the Dœmonology by Helen Fairfax, as her brother, was probably in the army or navy. "What was that which came to me," asks she of one of her tormentors, "Like my brother Thomas, all in gold lace?"

Edward Fairfax, bap. at Fewston in 1611 A.D., also mentioned in the Dœmonology.

Henry Fairfax, bap. at Fewston in 1619 A.D., said to have become a Jesuit priest.

Of the daughters the eldest was *Ellen, or Helen, Fairfax*, who occupies the prominent place in the aforegoing narrative. She was baptized at Fewston in 1605 A.D., and married in 1636 A.D. Christopher Yates. From the affidavits for marriage licenses at York in the above year, it would appear that a license to marry at either "Pateley Bridge or Fewston was granted to Christopher Yates, yeoman, of Pateley, and Ellen Fairfax, spinster, of the parish of Fewston." *(Paver's Index, Brit. Mus.)*

Christopher Yates—then of Padside—made his will in 1655 A.D., and it was proved in May, 1656 A.D. Therein he gives property to his wife Helen for life, and leaves her sole executrix. The children to whom legacies are given are, his eldest son Edward Yates, his second son John Yates, his third son Christopher Yates, and his two daughters Elizabeth and Magdalen Yates.

The family of Yates was a respectable one of good yeoman rank, and somewhat numerous in the parishes of Hampsthwaite (at Padside) and Pateley. They intermarried with the Days of Menwith, and other local families of note.

By the noncupative will of Dorothy, the widow of Edward Fairfax, in 1648 A.D., her daughter Helen Yates was left trustee for the portion of her niece Dorothy Richardson. Helen signs her name to this document by " her mark."

Elizabeth Fairfax, the second daughter of Edward Fairfax, was baptized at Fewston, Oct. 8th, 1608 A.D., and married after her father's death in 1635 A.D., *Phillip Richardson.* She was dead, however, before the making of the will of her mother in 1648 A.D., wherein her portion is left to her only child—then young—Dorothy Richardson.

Phillip Richardson married, secondly, Grace mother of John Beckwith of Bewerley, whose wife was Mary, daughter of Charles Fairfax, of Menston. Administration to the effects of Phillip Richardson at *Low Bishopside* was granted to his widow (Grace) and his daughter Dorothy Richardson, Aug. 17th, 1670 A.D.

In 1677 A.D. Abraham Pawson surrendered "a kiln belonging to a miln in Pateley Bridge," to the use of John Beckwith (son of Grace Richardson by her first husband) and Dorothy Richardson. *(Thornton and Bishopside Court Rolls.)*

Mary Fairfax, the next daughter married, in 1641 A.D. Lawrence Scarborough, of Carleton-in-Craven. The grant of the marriage license names Addingham as the place for the marriage, and gives the following particulars:—"Laurence Scarborough, parish of Carleton, aged 29 years, yeoman; and Mary Fairfax, spinster, aged 23 years, of the parish of Addingham." *(Paver's Index.)*

There are the following entries in Carleton Registers:—"1651 A.D., Ellen, daughter of Laurence Scarborough, baptized August 14th." "1653 A.D., William, son of Laurence Scarborough, baptized."

The fourth daughter, *Anne Fairfax*, was baptized at Fewston, June 12th, 1621 A.D., and buried there on Oct. 7th in the same year. She is the infant supposed to have died by the instrumentality of witchcraft.

The following is the will (non-cupative) before referred to, of the widow of Edward Fairfax:—

"The Eighteenth day of January 1648 A.D. Memorandum: that Dorothie ffairfax of Newhall in the Countie of Yorke, gentlewoman beinge sicke of bodye but perfect in minde and memorie did make her last will noncupative in these words, or to the like of this effect. ffirst her will and minde was that all the moneys due unto her should be divided into three parts, whereof shee did give her daughter Ellen Yeats, wife of Christopher Yeats one thirde parte, another thirde parte shee did give to Mary Scarborough her daughter wife of Lawrence Scarborough, and the other thirde parte shee did give to Dorothie Richardson her grandoughter doughter of Phillip Richardson; and further her will and minde was that the sayd thirde parte given to Dorothie Richardson should be payd to the said Ellen Yeats and remaine in her hands for the childe's use. (Signed)

Her
ELLIN X YEAITES.
mark.

MARY SKARBOUCK."

THE "BUSKY-DYKE" SCHOOL-ROOM, FEWSTON.

"Busky" or "Bosky" Dyke is a small dell formerly covered with bushes, hence its name. Across it runs the road from Fewston to Cragg Hall, near the northern margin of Fewston Reservoir. The spot has long had the character among the superstitious of being "haunted." In this place a Board school-room was erected in 1878 A.D.

THE Busky-Dyke, the Busky-Dyke,
Ah! tread its path with care;
With silent step haste through its shade,
For "Bargest" wanders there!

Since days when ev'ry wood and hill
By Pan or Bel, was crowned;
And ev'ry river, brook, and copse
Some heathen Goddess owned;

Since bright the Druid's altars blazed,
And lurid shadows shed
On Almas Cliff and Brandrith Rocks,
Where human victims bled;

Hag-witches oft, 'neath Bestham oaks,
Have secret revels kept;
And fairies danced in Clifton Field,
When men, unconscious, slept;

Dark sprite and ghost of every form—
No man e'er saw the like—
Have played their pranks at midnight hours,
In haunted Busky-Dyke.

There milk-white cats, with eyes of fire,
  Have guarded stile and gate;
And calves and dogs of wondrous shape
  Have met the trav'ler late.

And "Pad-foot" oft, in shaggy dress,
  With many a clanking chain,
Before the astonished rustic's eyes
  Has vanished in the drain.

On winter's eve, by bright wood fire,
  As winter winds do roar,
And heap the snow on casement higher
  Or beat against the door,

Long tales are told from sire to son,
  In many a forest ingle,
Of rushing sounds and fearful sights,
  In Busky-Dyke's dark dingle.

But lo, there now, as deftly reared,
  As if by magic wands,
In superstition's own domain,
  A village school-room stands!

Where thickest fell the gloom of night,
  And terror held its sway,
Now beams the rising sun of light,
  And intellectual day.

Before its beams, its warmth, its power,
  Let every phantom melt,
And children's gambols now be heard,
  Where "fearful bargest" dwelt.

Yet softly tread, with rev'rent step,
  Along the Busky shade;
There ghosts our fathers feared of old
  Will be for ever "laid."

GUY FAWKES AND THE OTHER CONSPIRATORS OF 1605 A.D.

"Treason doth never prosper; what's the reason?
Why, if it prosper, none dare call it treason."
Sir John Harrington.

ALTHOUGH direct proof of the connection of any of the conspirators in the Gunpowder Plot of November 5th, 1605 A.D., except Guy Fawkes, with the Forest of Knaresbrough, or its vicinity, is wanting, yet there are several striking incidents and coincidences, on which possibly more light may yet be thrown, but which even now are remarkable, and point to a strong probability of such a connection.

The originator of the plot was Robert Catesby, a wealthy country gentlemen, of Ashby St. Ledgard in Northamptonshire. In him foresters have no interest, but the first persons to whom he imparted his secret and enlisted in the plot were Thomas Winter, Thomas Percy, John Wright, and Guy Fawkes. All these are forest names, except that of Winter. But Winter and his two brothers, afterwards brought in, were the nephews of Sir William Ingilby of Ripley Castle, and so connected with the vicinity. Others were admitted afterwards to the plot, as their services on their money were needed. Among them were Robert and John Winter brothers of Thomas Winter, Christopher the brother of John Wright, Bates the servant of Catesby, Keyes, Garnet a priest, and also, it is said, one if not more of the name of Pulleine.

In the time of Henry III. there is mention of *Falcacius de Lyndeley*. In the year 1300 A.D., *Falkasius de Lyndeley* did homage to the Archbishop of York for possessions in Lindley. The same was repeated by *Faucus de Lindley* in

1318 A.D. In the Subsidy Roll of 2nd Richard II., we find, under the head "Villa de Ffarnelay," "*Johannes Ffaukes et ux ejus, Osteler, xiid,*" and also "*Willelmus Ffaukes et ux ejus iiij.d.*" In 1441 A.D., John Fawkes was one of the leaders of the forest men in the tumult, raised by them, against the tolls demanded in the markets at Ripon and Otley. Lindley is partly in the forest; and Farnley, on the southern border and adjoining Lindley, is still the seat of the influential and respected family of Fawkes.

There has been some doubt as to whether Guy Fawkes, the conspirator, was an off shoot from this family or not. He was born in York, and baptized, in the parish of St. Michael-le-Belfry there, on the 16th of April, 1570 A.D. The register is yet to be seen. His father was *Edward Fawkes*, registrar, and advocate in the Consistory Court of the Archbishop of that city, and died in 1578 A.D., when his son Guy would be about nine years of age. The wife of Edward, and mother of Guy and of his two sisters, Anne and Elizabeth, was named Edith, whose parentage and place of marriage are unknown.

The late Robert Davies, Esqr. F.R.S. of York, in a pamphlet published some years ago on "The Fawkes of York," and to which the present writer is chiefly indebted for the information contained in this paper, gives the descent, and the supposed descent from the Fawkes of Farnley, of this family, as follows.

The head of the House at Farnley, in the latter portion of the 15th century, was John Fawkes, Esq., holding under the Crown, the office of Steward of Knaresborough Forest. He died intestate in 1496 A.D., administration to his effects being granted, in the Prerogative Court at York, on the 4th of November in that year, to his eldest son, Nicholas Fawkes. He left three sons, viz.,

(1). NICHOLAS, who succeeded him at Farnley.

(2). WILLIAM, who died,—while residing in the family of Mr. Richard Laton, notary and advocate of York,—unmarried, or leaving no issue.

(3). HENRY, who was established in business as a

merchant in York, and admitted to the freedom of the city in 1504 A.D. In 1522 A.D. he was also sword-bearer to the city.

This Henry Fawkes had, at least, one son named Reginald. He was admitted to the freedom of the city in 1548 A.D., and is described in the city register as, "Reginaldus Fawkes filius Henrici Fawkes, de Ebor. Gent."

Reginald Fawkes succeeded his father in his municipal offices. In 1576 A.D. he married Alice Bilbowe, of Coney Street, and died, in 1591 A.D., leaving issue, with whom, however, we are not concerned.

At the same period as Reginald Fawkes lived, there was also living in York a Mr. William Fawkes. He was settled in 1530 A.D. in the parish of St. Michael-le-Belfry, as a Notary and Proctor in the Ecclesiastical Courts. Mr. Davies supposes that he was a second son of Henry Fawkes and brother of Reginald,—but the *proof* that he was so is wanting; and this is the missing link, which may yet be supplied, to connect Guy Fawkes with the ancient and honourable house of Farnley. Seeing that he was of the same christian name, William, was residing in the same parish, and following the same profession as William the brother of Henry, and at the very time that Henry's son Reginald, was occupying civil offices in the city,—the coincidences are very remarkable, and seem to establish a presumption, little as possible short of proof, that he (William) was, as well as Reginald, a son of Henry Fawkes, merchant.

William married Ellen, daughter of William Harrington, merchant, sheriff, and Lord Mayor (1531-6 A.D.). He was made registrar of the Exchequer Court in 1541 A.D., was living in 1558 A.D., and had, at least four children.

(1). Thomas, a merchant, who died without issue, in 1581 A.D.
(2). Edith married John Foster.
(3). —married Humphrey Ellis.
(4). Edward.

The last followed the honourable profession of his father

—a notary and advocate in the Ecclesiastical Courts. He married a lady whose christian name was Edith, but whose father's name and residence are undiscovered. They had four children baptized and registered in the parish of St. Michael-le-Belfry.

ANNE in 1568 A.D., and died the same year.

GUY in 1570 A.D., baptized April 16th

ANNE in 1572 A.D.

ELIZABETH in 1575 A.D.

The grandmother of these children, Ellen, widow of William Fawkes, died in 1575 A.D., and among other bequests of her will is the following to her little grandson —the future conspirator—"Item: I give to Guye Fawkes my beste whistle, and one ould angell of gould."

Edward Fawkes, the father, died shortly afterwards, in 1578 A.D.; thus leaving his wife, Edith, and three surviving children, of whom Guye, then about nine years of age, was the eldest.

One thing should be noted here, viz., that the children of Edward and Edith Fawkes were all baptised in the Church of England, and also that, from entries in the parish books, both the parents were regular communicants at the church of St. Michael-le-Belfry. In his boyhood's days Guye attended the Free School in "le Horse Fayre," where he had, according to statements of Fuller and Strype, among his school companions, Thomas Morton afterwards Bishop of Durham, and Thomas eldest son of Sir Henry Cheke. It may also be noted that the master of this school at this time was John Pulleyn, B.A. He was appointed in 1575 A.D., and held the mastership until his death in 1590 A.D.

In 1581 A.D. Thomas Fawkes, the eldest brother of Edward Fawkes, and uncle of Guy, died, leaving his property to his two neices, Anne and Elizabeth, to the exclusion of his nephew. Their father, Edward, had died intestate, hence his real property would all be inherited by Guy, as the heir; which may well account for his uncle's will in favour of the sisters.

These sisters of the conspirator have not been traced

after this time, nor has any mention of them been found.

The uncle's will contains, however, the following: "to Guye Fawkes, my nephewe, my golde ringe, and my bedde and my paire of shetes, with the appurtenances."

About—or perhaps a little before—this time (1581 A.D.), an event had taken place which exercised most important influence upon the future of the young boy. It brought him, at the age of 12 or 13 years, to a home on the boundaries of our forest, and into contact with some—if not several—of those who were his companions in the plot five and twenty years afterwards. This event was the marriage of his mother, Edith, widow of Edward Fawkes, with Dionis Baynebridge or Bainbrigg, of Scotton.

Scotton is now, as it was then, a small, pleasant hamlet, by the road leading from Knaresborough to Ripley, on the northern bank of the river Nidd, and separated from the forest by that river alone. It is supposed to derive its name, so says Hargrove, from early settlers from Scotland. "This village became," says the same historian, "the residence of the Percys and the Pulleynes, whose mansions still remaining are converted into farm-houses. Percys' is now the property of William Roundell, Esq., and retains many marks of antiquity about it. . . . . The house where the Pulleyns resided is the property of Sir T. T. Slingsby, Bart. It is a very large building, but hath undergone so thorough a repair, that scarce any marks of antiquity remain upon it."

This was the place at which the young Guy Fawkes and his two sisters became the inmates of their step-father's, Dionis Bainbridge's, house. Assuming that this branch of the Fawkes's of York was descended from the Farnley family, there was already a connection by marriage between them and the Bainbridges.

Anthony Fawkes, the eldest son of John of Farnley, in the earlier part of the 16th century, married Frances, daughter of — Vavasour, of Weston, and died, before his father, at York, in 1551 A.D. Frances, his widow, married for her second husband, Peter Bainbridge, of Scotton, and their only son was the Dionis, or Dennis Bainbridge, who now married Edith, widow of Edward Fawkes, of York. Peter Bainbridge dying early, his widow, the mother of Dennis, then married for her third husband, Walter Pulleine, Esq., of Scotton (2nd wife).

Thus we have closely connected, or residing in the same village at the time referred to, the three influential families of Percy, Pulleine, and Bainbridge.

One of the family of the latter appears at one time to have possessed property, and resided, near Fewston, where a farm and farm-house, until lately owned by the Wright family of Beckwith, is still named Bainbridge Gate and Bainbridge House. A Captain Bainbridge resided at Moor Park, near Harrogate, within the last forty years.

The Pulleines of Scotton, whether the original stem or an elder branch, were one of the three great parts of the clan of that name inhabiting the forest and its vicinity. There is a tradition that the name is derived from an early ancestor being master, or keeper, of the colts or young (pulli) horses belonging to the King in Knaresborough Forest. The crest of the Scotton branch was "a colt's head erased sable, bridled or." The other branches resided chiefly in the parish of Fewston and at Killinghall, both within the Forest. The crest used by that at Fewston, however, was a pelican feeding its young from its breast. A square of glass bearing this remained in the window of their old residence, near Fewston Church, until removed at the demolition of the house about the year 1876 A.D. It is now in the possession of Mr. B. B. Kent of Menwith Hill. Walter Pulleine at the time of our story represented the family at Scotton. He was a Romanist, and one, if not more of his sons and grandsons, were Romish priests.

The Percys of Scotton were an off-shoot of the great family of the name—Earls of Northumberland. Spofforth, which had formerly been a chief residence of the house, but dismantled after the Battle of Towton, was only a few miles to the south: while Topliffe, a favourite residence of the Dukes until a short time before, was only a like distance to the north.

There is no direct proof that Thomas Percy, a leading spirit in the plot, was of the Scotton branch. But Francis Percy, the head of the house in 1585 A.D., who had also married a Vavasour of Weston, had, among his five sons, one named Thomas, who is unaccounted for in the pedigrees of 1612 A.D. Considering, therefore, that Guy Fawkes was brought up with this family here, and that the two names are so closely associated afterwards, the coincidence is, at least, significant. The family were zealous Roman Catholics. The wife of Thomas Percy, the conspirator, was sister of the brothers John and Christopher Wright, also conspirators. They are said to have sprung from Welwick, in Holderness, and to have been Protestants, but that both they and their sister were won over to the Romish faith by Percy.

Thus it is seen, that the marriage of Edith, widow of Edward Fawkes of York, transplanted her and her children into a hotbed of Romanism at Scotton, and, also, into close connection with important Romanist families bearing the same names as several of the future co-partners with her son in the conspiracy of 1605 A.D. And we are not surprised, from their surroundings, to find that the mother adopted the faith of her second husband, and that her son —the son of the Protestant Edward Fawkes of York,— did the same with all the fanaticism of a pervert.

Here it was that, asssuming Thomas Percy to be of the Scotton family, the young Guy would first make his acquaintance, and that of Percy's brothers-in-law, the Wrights. He would also probably have the opportunity of doing the same with Thomas, Robert, and John Winter. Their father was Robert Winter, of Caudwell in Worcestershire, but their mother was Jane, daughter of Sir William Ingilby of Ripley, and their mother's aunt was Frances (*neé* Ingilby), wife of James Pulleyne, Esq., of Killinghall. Ripley, where it may well be supposed the nephews of Sir William would often be visitors, is but a short walk from Scotton, and the families, being all related, would, no doubt, be more or less associated on terms of considerable intimacy.

These facts and probabilities, incidents and coincidences, taken together shew, without much doubt, that Knaresborough foresters had, at one period, as their neighbours or visitors, a considerable number of that band of misguided, though sincere and conscientious men, who by "the Gunpowder Plot of the 5th of November, 1605 A.D.," placed a landmark and blot, which will ever remain, in our national history.

In 1591 A.D. Guy Fawkes attained the age of 21 years, and soon afterwards he is found disposing of the small property, inherited from his father, in the neighbourhood of York. His seal on one of the deeds of sale—yet in existence—bears, what appears to be, a falcon. A Falcon is the crest of the Farnley family.

A tradition exists in the neighbourhood that he was, for a time, parish clerk at Spofforth. The writer has, however, seen no evidence to support the tradition, or to point to the probability of its truth.

In 1593 or 4 A.D., having disposed of his small inheritance, he left England to seek his fortune in the armies of the Continent; and ultimately was engaged with those of Spain. His being so may explain the habit he had, afterwards, of writing his name, according to the Spanish form, "Guido" instead of Guy.

In 1604 A.D., when Robert Catesby conceived his diabolical plan for the destruction of the King and Parliament, he communicated it first to Thomas Winter, the younger of the three brothers above mentioned, and sent him to sound the Spanish Ambassador in the Low Countries as to the project.

At Ostend Thomas Winter met with his probably former acquaintance, Guy Fawkes, and induced him to return with him to England. There Catesby, John Wright, Thos. Percy (to whom Catesby had opened the matter), and Thomas Winter, explained the project to him and enlisted him in it.

It is not necessary to enter into the well-known history, and to repeat, how the plot was laid,—discovered—the conspirators seized,—Guy in the very act of examining, in the dark vault, on that ever historical morning of November 5th, 1605 A.D., the trains of powder which he was to explode as soon as the intended victims were assembled.

Guy Fawkes and Thomas Winter, who also was taken in London, were at once sent to the Tower. Fawkes was frequently examined—and, under torture, urged in vain to reveal the names of his companions. On the 31st of January, 1606 A.D., the two were drawn from the Tower to the Old Palace at Westminster, "over against the Parliament House," and there beheaded. Robert Winter, and others, also died on the scaffold. Catesby, Percy, John and Christopher Wright, with others, had shut themselves up in Holbeach House in Worcestershire, where they were beseiged by the sheriff of that county. They were, ultimately, driven out by fire being set to the doors, &c., and all fell mortally wounded, in endeavouring to escape, in the court yard.

Nothing could possibly justify the crime in which these men were engaged, and in which they perished. Yet few persons will fail to admire the constancy and firmness, with which Fawkes, at least, met the just reward of his deeds. When asked, "If he was not sorry for what he had intended to do?" he replied, "I was moved only by conscience and reason, and I am sorry for nothing but that the act was not performed." No torture of the rack could wring from him a betrayal of his friends. "Notwithstanding," wrote Lord Salisbury, "he confesseth all things of himself, and denieth not to have some partners in this particular practice, yet could no threatening of torture draw from him any other language than this, that he is ready to die and rather wished ten thousand deaths, than willingly accuse his master or any other."

When men of position and education like Percy, Fawkes, the Wrights, the Winters, and others of the same stamp—not ruffians and cut-throats as they have been too frequently represented,—engaged in a scheme, such as theirs, to murder the King and the whole legislature of the country, it could only have been possible, from their having been driven to despair by the spirit of the legislation to which they were subjected. Romanists they were, but also men—and educated Englishmen—and that they should, even for a moment, entertain such a hellish design is only to be explained by this, and by the penal laws enacted against them, their co-religionists and their religion, having been prssed upon them beyond human endurance.

The sooner, therefore, the memory of the whole matter, as one of recrimination or party triumph between Englishmen, is relegated to the regions of the past, the better it will be for the credit of all the parties immediately concerned in it, and the more it will speak for the progress of the common Christian forbearance, and charity, of our own, or any future, age.

SONNET.

SUMMER.

IN warmth and conscious strength, full-blown, free,
Life throbs through ev'ry vein of nature fair;
With busy forms and sounds it fills the air:
Robes dark and rich are cast o'er shrub and tree,
And deep new instincts breathe in gnat and bee.
With joys parental full mute are the birds;
In satisfaction stand, replete, the herds
In cooling streams of crystal Wharfe or Dee.
On every flower and fast-maturing seed,
On every waving crop, ay, every clod,
Is force and beauty writ; in all we read
The power of nature, nay, of nature's God!
Man, basking in the sunshine of that power,
Rests, till autumn fruits on him it shower.

THE FAMILY OF FRANKLAND, OF BLUBERHOUSES.

"Libera terra; liberque animus."
(Frank land; Frank mind.)

The family motto.

THE township and manor of Bluberhouses, which, for three hundred years, have belonged to the honourable family of Frankland, were originally a portion of the Forest. In the reign of King John, William de Stuteville was Lord of Knaresborough and alienated this portion of his charge, no doubt with the King's consent, to Robert-le-Forester.*

By the family of Robert-le-Forester, the manor and lands were given to the Priory of Bridlington, and the gift was confirmed, and the lands "disafforested" in 1226 A.D., by Richard, Earl of Poicton and Cornwall, who was, at that time, Lord of Knaresborough. The Prior and Brethren of Bridlington,—after sundry contests and law-suits, about the rights of common pasture on the moors, with their brethren of Bolton Priory, and regarding a portion of the township with Brian de Insula, and Robert de Percy lords of the two Timbles (Timble Brian and Timble Percy)—

* In the Register of Archbishop Grey, of York (1216-1255 A.D.), there is frequent mention of the name "Forestarius," in connection with grants of lands and of wardships in the neighbourhood. This family would seem to have been tenants on the Archbishop's manor of Otley, and as the part of that manor most connected with the forest was the township of Little Timble, they probably resided there, and may possibly be the same as the "del woods" of later times.

held the manor and estate of Bluberhouse until the dissolution of the monasteries in the reign of Henry VIII. Among the list of their possession surrendered to the king at that time is,

"Blauverhouse, land and manor—value (annual) £10."

In the 5th year of Elizabeth's reign, 1562 A.D., the lordship of Bluberhouses, with "the scite and mansion of the Hall," was granted by the Crown to Thomas Wood, Gentleman, and William Frankland of the Ryes, in the County of Hereford, and his heirs.

William Frankland, thus first brought into contact with the Forest, would seem to have belonged to the Guild of Clothworkers in the City of London, and though described as of the Ryes, to have been a member of an ancient Yorkshire family, which appears, in the earliest records, as settled at Thornton-Bishopside in Nidderdale.

It is impossible to give anything like a full pedigree of the several branches of this family, within the compass of one of these forest "leaves," but the following outline of that of the forest branch will be of interest to foresters.

The name "Franklyn," or "Frankland," points to Saxon times, and to an honourable source, for its origin.

In the *computus* of the Bursar of Fountains Abbey in 1457-8 A.D., there is mention of John Franklan as connected with that foundation.

I. In the Subsidy Roll for the Wapentake of Claro 16th Edward IV. (1475 A.D.), John Franklyn, and Roger Franklyn appear as of Thornton-Bishopside.

II. In 1504 A.D., Robert Frankland of Linton-in-Craven made his will, and directed his body to be buried in the Church of St. Michael there, on the north side ; and gave bequests "to the fabric at Bolton," "to the kirk work at Ripon," to the Abbot of Coverham "to pray for my soul," to his brother William and his son John ; to his *brother Roger* and sons, *William and John* ; and appointed his wife to be executrix.

By the *Valor Ecclesiasticus* (26 Henry VIII.), it appears, that the Abbot and Brethren of Fountains had property at

Linton; and there can be little doubt but that Robert Frankland was their tenant at that place.

III. John Frankland de Lynton, grandson of the above Robert, made his will in 1544 A.D., and describing himself as of Grassington *i.e.* in the parish of Linton, shews his connection with the John and Roger Franklyn of Thornton, in 1574 A.D., by referring to "my lands in Bishopside held of the Archbishop." He also mentions Thomas Frankland, son of his brother Richard Frankland; Elizabeth his daughter, wife of John Pearte; Jennet his sister, wife of Christopher Oldfield; and he leaves the sum of 3s. 4d. for the vestures or ornaments about the altar in the church at Lynton, and to the repair at Lynton Bridge.

IV. William Frankland of Thurley, in Bedfordshire, is stated in the pedigrees to have been a brother of the above John de Lynton, and son of William de Lynton.

V. The children of William Frankland of Thurley are given as, (1) John—the ancestor of the Franklands of Thurley: (2) Thomas: (3) Richard: and, by some authorities, (4) William, born 1490 A.D., and who became Rector of Houghton-le-Spring, in county of Durham, in 1522 A.D., Chancellor to Bishops Ruthal, Wolsey, and Tunstall; and, in 1538 A.D., Dean of Windsor and Rector of Chalfont, in the County of Bucks, where he died in 1557 A.D. Dean Frankland was one of the prominent and remarkable men of the stirring times in which he lived. His will, a copy of which cannot now be found, was the subject of considerable litigation in the 5th of Elizabeth, on account of some bequests therein to "superstitious uses." His place in the family pedigree is somewhat uncertain, as there are some reasons which seem to point to his having been the son, not the brother, of Richard Frankland of Nelsing.

VI. Richard Frankland, the third son of the above William Frankland of Thurley, resided at Nelsing or Nealsing, a farm in the parish of Giggleswick, and at no great distance from his ancestors' home in the parish of Linton. He was at Nelsing as early as the 23rd Henry VII. (1507 A.D.)—for the Abbot of Salley sued "Richard

Frankelyn nuper de Nelesing" in that year in the matter of a debt. (*Recovery Rolls, 23 Henry VII.*) His will is dated April 10th, 1532 A.D., and was proved in July of that year.

The sons of Richard Frankland of Nelsing were, (1) Hugh of Nelsing, from whom descended (son) *Richard Frankland*, of York, and (grandson) Sir Henry Frankland, of Aldwark, near that city, also *William Frankland*, of Houghton-le-Spring, and *two*, if *not three, other sons*; (2) William Frankland of the Ryes, in the County of Herts, to whom the grant of Bluberhouse was made in 1562 A.D., and who died in 1577 A.D. (3) Richard Frankland, of Bluberhouses; and two daughters.

VII. William Frankland of the Ryes had only one grandson, who was a minor in 1583 A.D., and probably died under age without issue. By his will, dated August 19th, 1574 A.D., he (William of the Ryes) gave to his brother Richard and his son Hugh "the Manor of Bluberhouses, and all his lands there and at Fuiston," and, also, he gave to the master and wardens of the Guild or Fraternity of Clothworkers in London, two tenements in Thames Street, upon the condition to pay 20s. a year for purposes mentioned, and also £3 a year to the poor of Somerscales, Hazelwood, and Storiths, in the parish of Skipton, when any of them should demand it.

From this will, it will be seen that there was property, probably a portion of the Crown grant, in the township of *Fewston*, as well as in that of Bluberhouses.

VIII. Richard Frankland, of Fewston, brother to the above William, succeeded under his brother's will, to the estate there. His sons were:—

(1) Hugh Frankland, of Thirkleby and Roche Abbey, born at Fewston. The will of this Hugh is dated 20th January, 1606 A.D., and was proved November, 1607 A.D He was cousin to William Frankland, of Houghton-le-Spring—(whose will at Durham date 1589 A.D., see)—thus proving his father, Richard, and his uncle William of the Ryes, to have been brothers of Hugh of Nelsing, whose

son William, of Houghton-le-Spring, was. He married, but left no issue, and appears to have been the first of the name at Thirkleby, which has since his time been the principal seat of the family.

(2) The second son of Richard Frankland was Ralph Frankland of Fewston, who was aged 60 years in 1607 A.D., and succeeded his brother Hugh, in that year, in the family estates. A servant of "Ralph Frankland" is mentioned in Fairfax's Dæmonology in 1620 A.D. He was buried at Fewston, 21st February, 1630 A.D.

(3) The third son was John Frankland, whose children were *Richard* of Thirkleby and Roche Abbey; *John*, baptized at Fewston, 1599 A.D.; and *Mary*, baptized September 9th, 1628 A.D. He (John) died August, 1656 A.D. A wife (1st) predeceased him, and was buried at Fewston, June 11th, 1620 A.D.

Besides the above three sons, Richard Frankland had four daughters, viz :—Ann, wife of John Jeffray (m. 1594 A.D.), will dated 30th May, 1633 A.D., described as of Clifton Hamlet. His Daughter, Maud, is mentioned in Fairfax's Dæmonology; ——— wife of —— Gill; Mary, wife of William Curtis (m. 1608 A.D.); and ——— wife of Holmes.

IX. Hugh Frankland, of Thirkleby, eldest son of Richard, as above, by his will dated 26th September, 1599 A.D., left to his wife Johanna the Thirkleby estate for life, Richard, the son of his brother John, to succeed her; to his brothers Ralph and John, his "monasteries" of Roche Abbey; to Richard, his brother Ralph's son, £10; to William, his brother Ralph's son, his property at Ryes; to the poor of the parish of Fewston, "where I was born," £6 13s. 4d.; and to his sister, Ann Carlisle, 40s.

X. Ralph Frankland of Fewston, 2nd son of Richard had sons. (1) William Frankland of Thirkleby. (2) Richard Frankland of Fewston, who appears to have been married and had a daughter, Joan, who married (about 1638 A.D.) Thomas Palliser of Newby Wiske (*see Dugdale's Visitation*) and whose second son, William Palliser (born 1643 A.D.) became Archbishop of Cashel. (3) Ralph Frankland, buried at Fewston June 22nd, 1629 A.D., and (4) a daughter, Frances, married Hugh Bethel. Ralph Frankland was himself buried, as before stated, February 21st, 1630 A.D.

By a copy of Court Roll still extant, dated 7th June, 1638 A.D., William Frankland of Thirkleby, Henry Frankland, Knight, his son and heir apparent, and Richard Frankland "de ffuiston" gentlemen, surrendered in the Forest Court at Knaresbrough a messuage and 30 acres of land (easily identified as Cragg Hall and the land of which the estate originally consisted) to the use of Henry Fairfax of Newton Kyme, clerk, and his heirs.

From a survey of the Forest in 1613 A.D., it appears that Mr. John Frankland's copyhold land in Fewston "lay south of Meagill." This is the situation of Cragg Hall with regard to that hamlet. It is thus gathered that Cragg Hall was the property continually referred to as "in Fewston," and parted with, as above, in 1638 A.D., after which no such property is mentioned. The "Hall" is a late Elizabethan, or early Jacobean, erection, and may possibly have been built by William Frankland of Ryes, or his brother, Richard Frankland, who succeeded him, and who is described as of Fewston.

One peculiarity, regarding Cragg Hall estate, was that the tithe, arising therefrom, was a separate property from the other tithes of the parish, and was frequently dealt with apart from them, and apart from the estate at this period.

XI. William Frankland of Thirkleby, eldest son of Ralph Frankland of Fewston, married Lucy, daughter of Sir Henry Botler of Hatfield-Woodhouse, county of Herts, and was elected to represent Thirsk, in Parliament, in 1628 A.D., and again in 1640 A.D.

XII. His son, Sir Henry Frankland, knight, succeeded him to Thirkleby and Bluberhouses.

XIII. Sir William Frankland, knight, born in 1638 A.D., succeeded his father Sir Henry, and married Arabella, daughter of Henry Bellasis, eldest son of Lord Fauconberg. He was created a baronet by Charles II., in 1660 A.D., and died in 1687 A.D. Five children survived him, of whom

XIV Sir Thomas Frankland, Bart., was his successor, and married Elizabeth, daughter of Sir John Russell, Bart., of Chippenham, in the county of Cambridge, and grandaughter of Oliver Cromwell. He had seven sons and three daughters. Sir Thomas the eldest, Henry of Mattersea, in the county of Notts, and Governor of Fort William, in the Presidency of Bengal, in India. Frederick, who twice represented Thirsk in Parliament; and Robert, murdered with other Europeans at Jeddo, on the Persian Gulf. One daughter, Frances, married Roger Talbot, Esq., of Wood End, and another, Mary, married Thomas Worsley, Esq., of Hovingham.

XV. Sir Thomas Frankland, the 3rd baronet, was much employed in the service of the State, and four times represented Thirsk in the House of Commons. His wife was Dinah, daughter of Francis Topham, Esq., of Oglethorpe, by whom he had two daughters. One of them (a descendant of Oliver Cromwell) married the Earl of Lichfield, who was a descendant of Charles I., and so united these once discordant lines. Sir Thomas, leaving no surviving son, was followed in the baronetcy and estates by

XVI. Charles Henry Frankland, his nephew, and son of Henry Frankland of Mattersea. Charles Henry Frankland, born in 1706 A.D., was for many years (from 1738 A.D.) before succeeding to the family honours and property, and also after doing so, collector of customs at Boston in America, and afterwards Consul General to Lisbon. While in Boston he was visited in 1742 A.D. by his brother, and successor to the title, Thomas Frankland, who at that time was captain of H.M. frigate *Rose*. While there he fell in love with, and married (on a second visit), Sarah, the daughter of Judge Rhett of South Carolina. The following complimentary lines to him on the occasion of his visit were published in the *Boston Evening Post* at that time.—

"To Captain Frankland, Commander of His Majesty's Ship Rose, now in Boston."

"From peaceful solitude and calm retreat,
I now and then look out upon the great;
Praise where 'tis due I'll give; no servile tool
Of honourable knave, or reverend fool;
Surplice or red-coat, both alike to me;
Let him that wears them great and worthy be,—
Whether a coward in the camp or post,
Traitor in want, or traitor in the court,
Alike reward their cowardice deserves;
Alike their treachery, he who eats or starves,
Or brave by land, or hero on the main,
Alike respect their courage should sustain.
Then let me lisp thy name, thy praise rehearse,
Though in weak numbers and in feeble verse.
Though faint the whisper when the thunder roars,
And speak thee great through all Hispania's shores,
Still safe in port the red-coat chief may scare,
Dread of the boys, and favourite of the fair,
Still shudder at the dangers of the deep;
To arms an enemy, but a friend to sleep.
We see thee, *Frankland*, dreadful o'er the main,
Not terrible to children, but to Spain.
With thee, thy dawning beams of glory play,
And triumph in the prospect of the day.
O, let the kindling spark, the glowing fire
Your generous soul inflame, as once your sire,*
With him the schemes of tyranny oppose,
And love your country as you hate her foes."

The engagement and ultimate marriage of Sir Charles Henry Frankland, the collector at Boston, with Agnes Surriage of Marblehead—a village in Massachusetts, U.S.—have been the subject of much romance. A full account of the matter was published in a learned and pleasant volume of 130 pages from the pen of Elias Nason, at Albany, U.S. America, in 1865 A.D., and previously it had formed the subject of O. Wendell Holmes's ballad of Agnes. Sir C. H. Frankland died at Bath 1768 A.D. without issue.

* His great grandfather Oliver Cromwell.

XVII. The successor of Sir Charles Henry Frankland in the family honours and estates was his brother, Sir Thomas Frankland, who, as is before mentioned, married Sarah Rhett of South Carolina. He was successively Admiral of the Red, then of the White, in the King's fleet. He died, also at Bath, November 21st, 1784 A.D., leaving a large family of sons and daughters.

XVIII. His eldest son, another Sir Thomas Frankland, Bart., succeeded. He married Dorothy, daughter of Wm. Smelt, Esq., of the Leases,—represented Thirsk in Parliament, was High Sheriff of Yorkshire in 1792 A.D., and died in 1831 A.D.—only one out of five children surviving him, viz.,—

XIX. Sir Robert Frankland Bart., was his successor. Sir Robert was born in 1784 A.D., married, in 1815 A.D., Louisa Anne, third daughter of Lord George Murray, Bishop of St. David's. In 1836 A.D., he assumed the name of Russell. He was M.P. for Thirsk from 1815 A.D., to 1834 A.D.; High Sheriff of Yorkshire in 1838 A.D., and died March 11th, 1849 A.D., leaving five daughters, but no male issue.

His widow, the late Lady Frankland Russell, built and endowed, in 1856 A.D., the pretty rural church on the old family estate at Bluberhouses; and also the Hall there, now used by Lord Walsingham as a shooting box. It is a curious coincidence that Lady Frankland Russel, the widow of the last of the Franklands of Bluberhouses, unconscious of the connection, caused many of the architectural details for the Hall she erected there, to be copied from those at Cragg Hall, which, in all probability, was erected by William Frankland, Esq., to whom the estate three hundred years before was originally granted, or by Richard Frankland, Esq., his brother, and successor. The Baronetcy, on the death of Sir Robert Frankland Russell, descended to the heir male, his cousin, Frederick Frankland, who thus became Sir Frederick Frankland, and was succeeded by his son, Sir William Frankland, Bart., in 1880 A.D. The family estates, however, did not accompany the title, and the present Baronet has, therefore, now no connection with the forest.

The youngest of the five daughters of Sir Robert Frankland Russell, Rosalind Alicia, married, in 1854 A.D. Francis Le Strange Astley, Esq., nephew of Lord Hastings; Julia Roberta, the fourth daughter, in 1845 A.D. married Ralph Neville, Esq.. M.P., son of the Dean of Windsor and nephew of the second Lord Braybrooke; Emily Ann, the third, married in 1874 A.D. Sir William Payne Galwey (who died December 1881 A.D.), and inherited the estate and hall at Thirkleby; the second daughter, Caroline Agnes, died unmarried in 1846 A.D. Augusta Louisa, the eldest, married, in 1842 A.D., Thomas, fifth Lord Walsingham of Merton Hall, Norfolk, and to her only son, the Right Honourable Thomas, sixth Lord Walsingham, the present owner—who succeeded to the title on his father's death in 1871 A.D.—descended the old family property of the Franklands at Bluberhouses, and also that at Aldwark near York. Lord Walsingham occasionally makes the Hall at Bluberhouses his residence, and enjoys, among other pleasures of this beautiful spot, the unequalled grouse shooting* on the blue hills and moors from which the village receives its name.

* In 1872 A.D. his Lordship made in one day of 14 hours, with his own gun, on Bluberhouses Moor, the hitherto unequalled bag of 423 brace of grouse.

THE ROMANCE OF SIR CHARLES HENRY FRANKLAND AND THE MAIDEN OF MARBLEHEAD.

DR. OLIVER WENDELL HOLMES'S BALLAD OF "AGNES."

THE circumstances of this romance, alluded to in a previous page, were as follow:—Charles Henry Frankland, Esq., heir apparent of the Franklands, was in 1738 A.D., appointed collector of customs at Boston in America, and soon after saw, and fell in love with, Agnes Surriage then a village maiden at Marblehead a few miles from Boston. He had her taken to that city, and there educated in all lady-like learning and accomplishments. Her beauty, refinement, and gentle manners, won the hearts of all with whom she came in contact. But the patron-lover seems to have feared to make her his wife, and, ultimately, a sinful relationship was entered into between them. Fleeing from Boston society, he purchased a large property in Hopkinton —a place 25 miles from that city,—and there, in 1751 A.D., on a beautiful and romantic site, built a large mansion —furnished and embellished it with all that wealth could procure,—and there resided for several years. In 1747 A.D., he had succeeded, by the death of his uncle, to the Baronetcy and estates at Thirkleby and Bluberhouses; and in 1754 A.D., a law suit with his uncle's widow, with reference to her husband's will, called him over to Europe. He came, accompanied by Agnes, and the law matter settled, they went on a tour on the continent. November 1755 A.D. found them at Lisbon. On the 1st of that month occurred the terrible earthquake, by which the city was laid in ruins, and 50,000 of its inhabitants swallowed up. Sir Charles Henry Frankland was buried beneath a portion of the ruins of the cathedral. Agnes rushed from her lodgings, regardless of the still falling houses, in search of him. Clambering over a heap of ruins she heard moans from beneath, and then a voice which she recognized as that of him of whom she was in search. He was extricated, and, though at death's door, he ultimately recovered. His first act on recovery was to repair, so far as possible, the injury he had done his faithful deliverer, by an immediate marriage. And thus Agnes Surriage became Lady Frankland.

This is the story—very briefly stated—as related by Elias Mason in his book entitled, "Sir Charles Henry Frankland, or Boston in Colonial times." It is the subject of the beautiful ballad of "Agnes" by Oliver Wendell Holmes. The whole poem is too long to find a place here, but it is so pretty, that the desire to enrol, at least, the leading parts of it, among the Lays of the Forest is irresistible.

PART I.

"The tale I tell is gospel true,
As all the bookmen know,
And pilgrims who have strayed to view
The wrecks still left to show.

The old, old story,—fair, and young,
And fond—and not too wise—
That matrons tell, with sharpened tongue
To maids with downcast eyes.

* * * * * *

'Tis like some poet's pictured trance
His idle rhymes recite,—
This old New-England born romance
Of Agnes and the Knight.

Yet, known to all the country round,
  Their home is standing still,
Between Wachuset's lonely mound
  And Shawmut's threefold hill.

One hour we rumble on the rail,
  One half-hour guide the rein,
We reach at last, o'er hill and dale,
  The village on the plain.

With blackening walls and mossy roof,
  With stained and warping floor,
A stately mansion stands aloof,
  And bars its haughty door.

This lowlier portal may be tried,
  That breaks the gabled wall;
And lo! with arches opening wide,
  Sir Harry Frankland's hall!

'Twas in the Second George's day,
  They sought the forest shade,
The knotted trunks they cleared away,
  The massive beams they laid.

They piled the rock-hewn chimney tall,
  They smoothed the terrace-ground,
They reared the marble-pillared hall,
  That fenced the mansion round.

Far stretched beyond the village bound,
  The master's broad domain;
With page and valet, horse and hound,
  He kept a goodly train.

*   *   *   *   *   *

PART III.

*   *   *   *   *   *

Her place is at the master's board,
  Where none disputes her claim,
She walks besides the mansion's lord,
  His bride in all but name.

The busy tongues have ceased to talk,
Or speak in softened tone,
So gracious is her daily walk
The angel light has shown.

No want that kindness may relieve
Assails her heart in vain,
The lifting of a ragged sleeve
Will check her palfrey's rein.

A thoughtful calm, a quiet grace,
In every movement shown,
Reveal her moulded for the place,
She may not call her own.

And, save that on her youthful brow
There broods a shadowy care,
No matron, sealed with holy vow,
In all the land so fair.

PART IV.

A ship comes foaming up the bay,
Along the pier she glides;
Before her furrow melts away,
A courier mounts and rides.

"Haste, Haste, Post Haste!" the letters bear;
"Sir Harry Frankland, these."
Sad news to tell the loving pair!
The Knight must cross the seas.

"Alas, we part!"—the lips that spoke,
Lost all their rosy red,
As when a crystal cup is broke,
And all its wine is shed.

"Nay, droop not thus—where'er," he says,
"I go by land or sea,
My love, my life, my joy, my pride,
Thy place is still by me!"

Through town and city, far and wide,
  Their wandering feet have strayed,
From Alpine lake to ocean tide,
  And cold Sierra's shade.

At length they see the waters gleam,
  Amid the fragrant bowers,
Where Lisbon mirrors in the stream
  Her belt of ancient towers.

Red is the orange on its bough,
  To-morrow's sun shall fling
O'er Cintra's hazel-shaded brow,
  The flush of April's wing.

The streets are loud with noisy mirth,
  They dance on every green;
The morning's dial marks the birth
  Of proud Braganza's queen.

* * * * * *

Ah! Lisbon dreams not of the day—
  Pleased with her painted scenes—
When all her towers shall slide away
  As now these canvas screens!

The spring has passed, the summer fled,
  And yet they linger still,
Though autumn's rustling leaves have spread,
  The flank of Cintra's hill.

The town has learned their Saxon name,
  And touched their English gold,
Nor tale of doubt, nor hint of blame
  From over sea, is told.

Three hours, the first November dawn
  Has climbed with feeble ray
Through mists, like heavy curtains drawn,
  Before the darkened day.

How still the muffled echoes sleep!
  Hark! hark! a hollow sound,—
A noise like chariots rumbling deep,
  Beneath the solid ground.

The channel lifts, the water slides,
  And bares its bar of sand,
Anon a mountain billow strides
  And crashes o'er the land.

The turrets lean, the steeples reel,
  Like masts on ocean's swell,
And clash a long discordant peal,
  The death-doomed city's knell.

The pavement bursts, the earth upheaves,
  Beneath the staggering town!
The turrets crack,—the castle cleaves—
  The spires come rushing down.

Around, the lurid mountains glow,
  With strange, unearthly, gleams;
While black abysses gape below,
  Then close in jagged seams.

The earth has folded like a wave,
  And thrice a thousand score,
Clasped, shroudless, in their closing grave,
  The sun shall see no more!

And all is over. Street and square
  In ruined heaps are piled;
Ah! where is she, so frail, so fair,
  Amid the tumult wild?

Unscathed, she treads the wreck-piled street,
  Whose narrow gaps afford,
A pathway for her bleeding feet,
  To seek her absent lord.

A temple's broken walls arrest,
  Her wild and wandering eyes;
Beneath its shattered portal pressed,
  Her lord unconscious lies.

The power that living hearts obey,
  Shall lifeless blocks withstand?
Love led her footsteps where he lay,—
  Love nerves her woman hand.

One cry,—the marble shafts she grasps,—
  Upheaves the ponderous stone;—
He breathes;—her fainting form he clasps,—
  Her life has bought his own.

PART V.

How dark the starless night of death,
  Our being's brief eclipse,
When faltering heart and failing breath,
  Have bleached the fading lips!

She lives! What guerdon shall repay
  His debt of ransomed life?
One word can charm all wrongs away,—
  The sacred name of *wife*?

The love that won her girlish charms
  Must shield her matron fame,
And write beneath the Frankland arms
  The village beauty's name.

Go, call the priest! no vain delay
  Shall dim the sacred ring!
Who knows what change the passing day,
  The fleeting hour may bring?

Before the holy altar bent,
  There kneels a goodly pair;
A stately man, of high descent,
  A woman, passing fair.

No jewel lends the blinding sheen
 The meaner beauty needs
But on her bosom heaves unseen,
 A string of golden beads.

The vow is spoke,—the prayer is said,—
 And with a gentle pride,
The lady Agnes lifts her head,
 Sir Harry Frankland's bride."

* * * * * * *

Sir Charles Henry Frankland and his wife returned to Boston, and to their country residence at Hopkinton. He was afterwards twice Consul General at Lisbon. In 1767 A.D. they came again to England and resided at Bath, where as before stated, he died in 1768 A.D. In Weston Church, in the suburbs of that city, there is the following inscription.

"To the memory of Sir Charles Henry Frankland of Thirkleby in the County of York, Baronet, Consul General for many years at Lisbon, from whence he came in hopes of recovery from a bad state of health to Bath, where after a tedious and painful illness which he sustained with patience and resignation becoming a Christian, he died 11th January, 1768 A.D., in the 52 year of his life, without issue, and at his own desire, lies buried in this church. This monument is erected by his affectionate widow, Agnes, Lady Frankland."

"Hard by the terraced hillside town,
 Where healing streamlets run,
Still sparkling with their old renown,—
 The "waters of the sun,"—

The Lady Agnes raised the stone
 That marks his honoured grave,
And there Sir Harry sleeps alone
 By Wiltshire Avon's wave.

The home of early love was dear;
 She sought its peaceful shade,
And kept her state for many a year
 With none to make afraid.

At last the evil days were come,
  That saw the red cross fall;
She hears the rebels rattling drum,—
  Farewell to Frankland Hall."

As thus stated, the widow returned to their former home at Hopkinton near Boston, and there resided until the breaking out of the War of Independence. She then finally left the country and came to England, residing with her husband's relations at Thirkleby, until 1782 A.D., when she married as her second husband John Drew, Esq., a banker of Chichester, and, in that city, in the following year, she died aged 57 years—and there she is buried.

The following is the conclusion of the ballad:—

"I tell you, as my tale began,
  The Hall is standing still;
And you kind listener, maid or man,
  May see it if you will.

The box is glistening huge and green,
  Like trees the lilacs grow,
Three elms, high-arching, still are seen,
  And one lies stretched below.

The hangings, rough with velvet flowers,
  Flap on the latticed wall;
And o'er the mossy ridge-pole towers
  The rock-hewn chimney tall.

The doors on mighty hinges clash,
  With massive bolt and bar,
The heavy English moulded sash,
  Scarce can the night-winds jar.

Behold the chosen room he sought
  Alone, to fast and pray,
Each year, as chill November brought
  The dismal earthquake day.

There hung the rapier blade he wore,
  Bent in its flattened sheath;
The coat the shrieking woman tore*
  Caught in her clenching teeth.

The coat with tarnished silver lace
  She snapped at as she slid,
And down upon her death-like face
  Crashed the huge coffin's lid.

A graded terrace yet remains;
  If on its turf you stand
And look along the wooded plains,
  That stretch on either hand,

The broken forest walls define
  A dim receding view,
Where, on the far horizon's line,
  He cut his vista through.

If further story you shall crave,
  Or ask for living proof,
Go see old Julia, born a slave
  Beneath Sir Harry's roof.

She told me half that I have told,
  And she remembers well
The mansion as it looked of old,
  Before its glories fell.

The box, when round the terrace square
  Its glossy wall was drawn;
The climbing vines, the snow-balls fair,
  The roses on the lawn.

And Julia says, with truthful look
  Stamped on her wrinkled face,
That in her own black hands she took
  The coat with silver lace;

*** A woman buried with Sir C. H. Frankland in the falling ruins at Lisbon, caught the sleeve of his coat with her teeth, and in her agony bit a piece therefrom.**

And you may hold the story light,
  Or, if you like, believe;
But there it was, the woman's bite,
  A mouthful from the sleeve.

Now go your ways; I need not tell
  The moral of my rhyme;
But youths and maidens, ponder well
  This tale of olden time."

The poem was published about 1861 A.D. In the edition published by Sampson, Low and Co., London, in 1881 A.D., the author has added this note :—

"It is greatly to be regretted that the Frankland mansion no longer exists. It was accidentally burned on the 23rd of January, 1858 A.D., a year or two after the first sketch of this ballad was written. A visit to it was like stepping out of the century into the years before the Revolution. A new house, similar in plan and arrangements to the old one, has been built upon its site, and the terraces, the clump of box, and the lilacs, doubtless remain to bear witness to the truth of this story."

JANE LISTER: A CHILD OF CRAVEN IN WESTMINSTER ABBEY.

"A little slab of marble also, graven
With these two words, spelt anciently, 'Deare Childe,'
These and no more."

—*Rev. S. J. Stone.*

THE shortest, and yet one of the most touchingly eloquent, monumental inscription in England's great national mausoleum—Westminster Abbey—is to be found in one of the cloisters. It is this—

"Jane Lister—Deare Childe.
October 7th, 1688."

The words are cut in a plain marble slab, inserted in the wall, and devoid of any symbol or ornament whatever. There stands this simple monument to the memory of a child—eloquent in its brevity and simplicity; and thrice eloquent when seen by the side of those elaborate tombs, with which the Abbey is filled, to the memory of England's greatest sons!

"Storied urn and animated bust,"

telling of deeds of arms on land and sea, of eminence in the Senate, in literature, or in commerce; and epitaphs, which have taxed the learning of scholars and the genius of poets to pay a tribute to the worth of departed great ones, are in vivid contrast with these two words, after the almost unknown name of Jane Lister, "Deare Childe."

As we stand and read, and re-read them, how many emotions are stirred within the breast! Truly "One touch of nature makes the whole world kin." Dear child! Dear to some parents' hearts two hundred years ago—dear to brothers and sisters—all now long passed away! What doth their "deare" one here? On every side

> "The ancient, venerable dead;
> Sages who wrote, and warriors who bled,"

and a little child in the midst of them! Does not the mind instinctively turn to a far-off day in the far-off fields of the Holy Land, when the Divine Teacher, moved by the contentions of His disciples as to who should be the greatest, took a child and set him in the midst of them, and taught them,—that lesson hard for all men to learn—the lesson of humility; and on another occasion reminded them that "of such (little children) is the kingdom of heaven."

The Rev. S. J. Stone has made the words of this epitaph the text for one of his sweetest idylls. But he says he first saw them on a tablet in 1861 A.D., in the wall of a country church in Buckinghamshire, "and it was the remembrance of them that, in 1864 A.D., suggested the title of the poem; but several years afterwards a reviewer pointed out the fact that a tablet similarly inscribed is to be seen in the cloisters of Westminster Abbey." It was these words, therefore, though first seen in another place, that inspired the poet's pen. Yet what he beautifully wrote of one careless wanderer's steps arrested by them, in the country churchyard, has no doubt been true of thousands of such when wandering through the sacred precincts of the great Abbey.

> "And yet he lingered here;
> He who had wandered with me and scanned
> With heedless eyes that cared to rest on none,
> The carved annals of a score of tombs.
> He, who had laughed at this, and sneered at that,
> Nor gave elsewhere a reverent word for one—
> Yet lingered here, and lingered on, until
> I moved away to test him; still he stayed.

. . . .

As I turned, I saw
The face was wholly changed, the open brow
Thrid as with pain or thought, the careless eyes
Filmed with a mist of tears, and the strong lips
Set closer, as prepared against a sense
Of quivering weakness. Facing round again
Upon the little monument, he said
'Tell me of him or her.'"

It is little that can be told of "Jane Lister—Deare Childe." But some account of the parents who, when they laid her body to rest among the dust of a nation's great ones, lovingly placed this unpretending slab, and inscribed these two words, "Deare Childe," to her memory may be of interest, and what little is known of the child shall be woven into the narrative.*

The beautiful Susan Temple, Maid of Honour to Anne of Denmark,—a former "Sea King's daughter from over the sea,"—Queen of James I., married for her first husband Sir Giffard Thornhurst. Their only daughter, Frances, married Richard Jennings, and became the mother of Sarah the well-known Duchess of Marlborough. For her second husband, Lady Thornhurst was united to Sir Martin Lister of Barwell in Lincolnshire — an offshoot of the ancient family of that name in Craven. The sole issue of this marriage was a son, born in 1638 A.D.—Martin Lister, the father of the "Deare childe."

Martin Lister was educated at St. John's College Cambridge, and adopted the medical profession, and became famous both as a physician and a naturalist. He was one of the earliest members of the Royal Society, and a frequent and valued contributor to its proceedings; the intimate friend also of Ray, Evelyn, Thoresby, and most of the *literati* and men of science of his day. He frequently paid visits to his relations in Craven, and on some of these visits made the acquaintance of a lady there, whom, in 1668 A.D., he married—Anna, the elder of the two

* The author is much indebted for his information to a paper by the late Mr. Davis, of York, in the Yorkshire Archæological Society's Reports.

daughters and co-heiresssses of Mr. Thomas Parkinson, of Carlton Hall.

For the two following years (1669-70 A.D)., Dr. Lister appears to have resided at his father-in-law's house at Carlton. The baptism of his first child is thus recorded in the register of that parish—

1670. Susanna, the daughter of Martin Lister and Anna his wife, was baptised on the 9th of June, in the year 1670.

In the following year his father-in-law died, and by his will, dated April, 1671 A.D., after dividing his property to his wife and two daughters, he gave a legacy of twenty shillings to the nurse of "Dr. Lister's child, then at his house." He also directed, among other matters, that the following words should be cut upon his tomb—"Felix iter a seculo ad cœlum hic ero sanus."—remarkable as being afterwards, (1691 A.D.), the dying words of Richard Baxter. A slab still exists (covered by the tiles) in the chancel of Carleton Church, with the inscription, probably from the pen of Dr. Lister—

Lector
Si quæris animam,
Recessit in Cœlum;
Si Corpus
Thomæ Parkinson
hic in spe Ressurrectionis invenit
Requiem tertio die Maii.
Anno Domini 1671.
Felix iter a seculo ad cœlum hic ero sanus.

Carleton Hall now became, in right of his wife, the elder of the two co-heiresses, the property of Dr. Lister, who, however, never appears to have occupied it, and it was sold by his son to Lord Bingley.

Dr. Lister took up his residence in York, and practised there as a physician.

While resident in York (1671-1683 A.D.) he carried on an active correspondence with many men eminent in science and learning, and himself issued during the time several valuable scientific works.

In 1683 A.D., or 1684 A.D., he removed, with his family to the metropolis; and shortly after this date he is known to have been residing in the Old Palace Yard, Westminster. Either at this place or at York, immediately previous to his removal, was born the "deare childe." She was baptised in the adjoining church, St. Margaret's Westminster, on December 26th 1683 A.D. . Here, in their home under the shadow of the great Abbey, she spent the five years of her brief life—often, no doubt, with her elder brothers and sisters played and prattled in the sacred cloisters where now for nearly two hundred years she has rested.

About this time—viz., from 1683 A.D., to 1691 A.D., Dr. Lister was engaged upon the publication of his greatest work, "Historia sive Synopsis Methodica Conchyliorum." This work includes etchings, on copper-plate, of more than a thousand figures of shells from drawings by the author's two elder daughters, Susannah and Anna, and done with a fidelity and spirit which bear strong testimony to the extraordinary talent and industry of the girls, who could only at that time have been from 15 to 20 years of age. In quick succession several other works, on natural history and medicine issued, from his pen, and also, "A journey to Paris in 1698 A.D.," written, as he states, "chiefly to satisfy my own curiosity, and to delight myself with the memory of what I have seen."

In 1695 A.D., Dr. Lister lost his wife, the mother of the "deare childe," and of his other children. She was interred in the Parish Church of Clapham, in Surrey, near to which, to a country house, he about this time removed. The bereaved husband there erected a monument to her memory, remarkable as applying to the wife a similar epithet to that already applied to the child. The inscription was this—

Hannah Lister—Deare wife;
died 1695.
And left six children in tears
For a most indulgent mother.

She was the daughter and heir of
Thomas Parkinson of Carleton-in-Craven.

Three years afterwards, in 1698 A.D., he married as his second wife, Jane Cullen, of St. Mildred, Poultry. On the accession of Queen Anne, in 1702 A.D., to the throne, Dr. Lister, probably through the influence of his niece, the imperious Sarah, Duchess of Marlborough, was sworn in one of the four Court physicians.

In public life and in his profession he appears to have been a man of the *genus irritabile*. His books and papers show him to have been almost always engaged in controversy, and exposed to "the envenomed shafts" of many sharp critiques, notably some of a Dr. King. It can hardly, however, be supposed that his irritability of temper, and love of controversy, were carried into private and domestic life. The little glimpses which we now and then obtain of his home all point to the contrary; and there certainly was a kindliness of disposition about him, which won for him the abiding esteem, and friendship, of those who had the privilege of intimate personal acquaintance. The gentle Evelyn, and Ray the botanist, were his life-long friends. Thoresby speaks of him as "my father's friend, the learned Dr. Lister." And in 1708 A.D., the esteemed and aged Rector of Barwick-in-Elmet, George Plaxton, wrote to Thoresby, then in London, "I would have you visit my old friend Dr. Martin Lister; tell him I am still alive, and have the same value for him that I had in 1672 A.D.—for so long have I known him."

On February 2nd, 1711-12 A.D., Dr. Lister died at his house at Epsom, and by his will directed that his body should be interred by that of his first wife in Clapham Church. There, in the same grave with her, he was laid. A plain marble slab, placed side by side with that which he had placed to her memory, was erected to his own, and bore the following record:—

Near this place lies the body of
Martin Lister,
Doctor of Physic and Member of the Royal Society,
And one of Queen Anne's Physicians,
Who departed this life the Second
day of February, 1711-12.

Both these monuments have been, the writer understands, destroyed or removed. May it not be, therefore, that Dr. Martin Lister, the uncle of the Duchess of Marlborough, the naturalist, and philosopher, and Court physician, will live less vividly, in the world's memory, as the possessor of these distinctions, than as the parent who wrote upon his child's tomb (which has already survived his own), in the Abbey of Westminster, that brief, simple, touching record, and epitaph — "Jane Lister — Deare Childe"?

SONNET.

AUTUMN.

AUTUMN! realization's tranquil hour!
Thou com'st with spoils of spring and summer strown,
And yet of nature's life in both, the crown,—
The season rich of fruit, and not of flower!
Orchard and coppice witness to thy power,
Beneath their loads of red or russet-brown;
While fields of ripened grain, in weakness sown,
Into thy lap their varied treasures pour.
By reaping-hook or scythe no longer won,
The last rich sheaf in harvest-home is borne.
From forest monarch, as from berried thorn,
The yellow leaves are whirled. The work is done;
And now creation sinks to winter's rest,
In thankful trust on her Creator's breast.

LEAVES FROM THE NOTE-BOOK OF A FORESTER OF OLDEN TIMES.

THE following brief leaves, or notes, commencing two hundred years ago, and extending over nearly seventy years, are from a manuscript book, in vellum cover, now in the possession of the writer, and may be of interest to some readers.

The book originally belonged to a person named Parke, probably the Rev. Henry Parke, incumbent (1690 A.D. to 1704 A.D.) of Wentworth in South Yorkshire, or his brother George Parke, and afterwards passed into the hands of Thomas Parkinson* of Denton, the brother-in-law of Parke, and then into those of his son, Stephen Parkinson* of Denton, and Cragg Hall in the forest. (b. 1680 A.D., d. 1763 A.D.)

The earlier pages are occupied by two long, and one short, Latin poems, "Ad Amicum, A.—B." and "Elegia," &c., of no special interest, and subscribed "G. Parke."

* Son and grandson of Peter Parkinson of Denton, who was son of William Parkinson of Kildwick Grange, and elder brother of Thomas Parkinson of Carleton Hall in Craven.

Peter Parkinson married in 1630 A.D. Ellen daughter of — Parker and having acquired, either before or by his marriage, a property at Denton near Otley settled there.

In 1670 A.D. he is found holding land, as tenant, under Lord Fairfax of that place. A lease granted to him and others of "the Warren" at Denton, by the 3rd Lord Fairfax, in the above year, is now in the writer's possession.

The uppermost two or three lines, of many of the subsequent pages, are taken up with brief memoranda, chiefly in Latin, in the same hand writing as the poems. There are also a few short accounts at the end of the book, and in the same hand. These appear to have been the work of Henry, or George, Parke, and to have been all, which the book contained, when it passed to its next owner, who, with his son its third owner, utilized the unoccupied space for ordinary business accounts, interspersing them, however, with notes and memoranda on other matters.

A selection from the latter is given below in chronological order. The authorship of the different extracts will be readily gathered. Some will be found of limited and local interest in Wharfedale and at Fewston; a few of a little genealogical value; and several appealing to the attention of a wider circle of readers, as showing the value of agricultural produce, in the neighbourhood, in the early part of the last century.

"May 15th, An. D. 1683. Hac nocte mors Mtri: Hudson (1) est mihi nunciata.

Cum senibus juvenes tumulo conduntur in uno,
  Et cum matre sua filia chara jacet.
Fortia quid nobis morituris corpora prosunt!
  Quid mortis lucta forma superba valet.
Quem mundi vis magna petit nec pellere posset
  Hunc juvenem mortis pallida tæla premunt.
Quid veneri prodest Cynara tenuisse creatum;
  Horrida mors a pro sævior inde rapit.
Heu cadit in silva fabris aptissima quercus,
  Fronde carens tenera cum vitiosa manet.

Fructi feris verni flores carpuntur inhortis
  Cum neglecta nimis ætera turba cadat."

"An. 83 (1683) Nov. 9mo. obiit, S. Wharfe.—
Nunc hunc, nunc illam rapit inclementia mortis
Conjux jam sequitur, fœmina chara præit."

---

(1) "1678 A.D. Mr. William Hudson of Ffewston and Mistress Jane Banister, widdow, were lawfully married by virtue of a license from the Court of York."—*Hampsthwaite Parish Register.*

"An. D. 83 (1683) Feb. 15to. nunciata est mihi mors Franciscæ Dominæ Fairfax." (1)

"An. D. 83 (1683) Feb. 25to. Sepultus fuit Dom: Gualterus Hawksworth, (2) cujus vitæ fila sororibus fatalibus—sunt contorta."

"October 28th 83. fuit sepulta Lydia Hollins.
Natas heu video lugentes funera matru.
Sed matre natæ funera triste sequi,
Naturæ cursum fera mors mutare videtur,
Ordine nec certo currere fata sinit."

"An. Dom. 1683 Junij. die 25to.
Ad medicinales aquas (3) prope Knaresbrough profectus sum."

"Junij. 29mo. St. Petri die. Copgraviam ubi fons St. Mungonis (4) nomine honoratur adij hic bis terve meipsem imersi. Deinde Julij 1mo redij.

"Stephen Parkinson his book, and my age was 24 years when my father died, that was in the year 1703."

---

(1) Wife of Henry fourth Lord Fairfax, and daughter and heiress of Sir Robert Barwick of Toulston. Buried at Denton. Tombstone there.

(2) The following inscription is on a tomb under the Holy Table in Guiseley Church :—

"Here lyeth interr'd the body
Of Sr. Walter Hawksworth of
Hawksworth, Bart., who was
born the 22nd day of Novr.
1660. And he departed this
life of a consumption the
——day of February 1693.
He married Ann the seventh
daughter of Sir Robert Markham of Sedgebrook in the
County of Lincoln Bart. He
had issue by her at one birth
a daughter and a son."

Slater's History of Guiseley.

(3) The Spas at Harrogate, or possibly those in Forest Lane between Harrogate and Knaresborough.

(4) St. Mungo's Well, at Copgrove near Knaresborough, is a spring of very cold water formerly of great repute for its healing virtues, but now neglected and almost forgotten.

"*Memorandum.*—Mr. Humferes* preached my father's funeral sermon. He did take for his text in the Book of Isaiah at the 40th chapter and the 6th verse. "The voice said, Cry. And I said, What shall I cry? All flesh is grass, and all the goodliness thereof is as the flower of the field."

Memorandum.—"Mr. Omferes received his wages on the 28th of September in the year 1701 A.D.,—the sum is 14 shillings and 7d. for the whole yeare."

The same memorandum is repeated yearly until,

"On the 18th day of December in the year 1705 A.D. againe I paid to Mr. Humferes all his wages and he did leave us on the 4th day of June in the year 1708 A.D."

"For a memorandum. May the 28th day 1709 A.D., I Stephen Parkinson of Denton bought two closes of Marmaduke Foster of Denton. By condition of bargain for sessments and lays, I am pay thus: for land-sess one shilling and 2 pence in the quarter, in the whole year 4 shillings and 8 pence; for the Tithes I am to pay 7 shillings in the yeare; for lays I pay 3 shillings and 3 farthings at a lay. The two closes are called 7 acres of land, cost me the summe of 7 score pounds."

"A memorandum. February the first day, 1714 A.D. being the yeare 1715 A.D. The Lady Day following there was the greatest wind that ever was in man's time living. Then it tooke almost all the thake of the tanhouse and of the——house and the over barne. It did blow downe many trees and many barnes, and some dwelling houses. This is set down by me Stephen Parkinson."

"Memorandum. In the yeare 1714 A.D. my sister Ann was married to Christopher Hird, (1) the son of Thomas Hird of

---

* Mr. Humferes was, in all probability, a curate schoolmaster at Denton, residing in the house of the writer,—and teaching the children of the household and of the neighbours. The items of "wages" would be the tutorial fees. In 1708 A.D. the Rev. Henry Humphrey became vicar of Otley—the parish in which Denton is situated—and continued vicar until his death in 1744 A.D.

(1) The family of Hird of Rawdon, that of Clapham of Denton and Stephen Parkinson, the writer of the memorandum, were all previously connected by marriages with the family of Day of Day Ash. John Hird uncle, of the above Christopher, was married to Jane daughter of Francis Day. He died 1751 A.D. she 1750 A.D. Stephen Parkinson the writer had married Hannah Day, sister of Jane, in 1706 A.D. Richard Hird of this family founded the Low Moor Ironworks

Rawdon, and I paid to the said Christopher Hird, in part, my sister's portion the summe of £30 0s. 0d. This done on the 10th of June."

"April the 10th 1716 A.D., I accounted with my brother (1) Day for hides. I had from him, and for the sessments he had paid for (2) Hannah's land and all other things. The sum of 7 shillings balance was paid. Soe at this time we are straight."

"Denton May the 18th 1716 A.D.

Memorial. My Lord ffairfax sold his estate, at (3) Denton and Askwith, to one James Ibbotson of Leeds; and a place near York called Bilborough to sixe men,—Captain ffairfax, Barnard Banks, Nathaniel Hird, one Smithe, one Markes, and one Roodman of York. They took possession on the day and yeare above written.

This day above written James Ibbotson tooke possession and all set there hands to a paper and paid sixpence. All the tenants paid sixpence, as before mentioned, to Mr. James Ibbotson of Leeds."

"*Memorandum.* In the year 1716 A.D. I, Stephen Parkinson bought of Edward Robinson of Swinsty, the Cragg House being the 12th day of November, and on the 17th we did article for it.

---

about 1790 A.D. He left two daughters, one of whom married the Rev. Lamplough Wickham from whom the Wickhams of Bradford are descended. The other (Christiana) married in 1801 A D. Sir Charles Des Vœux of Indeville Queens County Ireland.

(1) John Day of Day Ash, another brother was Francis Day, rector of Topliffe, 1713 A.D. to 1763 A.D.

(2) Hannah, neè Day, wife of the diarist.

(3) The sixth Lord Fairfax. Markham in his life of the 3rd Lord Fairfax attributes the sale of Denton entirely to Lady Fairfax widow of the fifth Lord. But her son, the 6th Lord b. 1690 A.D. would then be 25 years of age. He emigrated to America, and died there in 1782 A.D. The following is the reference by Markham to this transaction. "The fifth Lord was elected M.P. for Yorkshire in 1688 A.D. to succeed his father, and sat till 1707 A.D. (Died 1710 A.D.) His wife Catherine was daughter and heiress of Thomas Lord Culpepper, on whose death she succeeded to Leeds Castle in Kent, to the proprietary right of the northern neck of Virginia, and to an estate of 300,000 acres in the Shenandoah valley. Her mother was Margaret de Hesse. Lady Fairfax sold Denton, and all the Yorkshire property, to pay off the debts on her estates in Kent. She did this so recklessly that the price given for Denton was covered by the value of the timber. It was bought by a Leeds merchant of the name of Ibbotson, whose successors built a great modern house, and there is not now a vestige of the old Fairfax House." p 409.

The purchase is 600 pounds—200 to be paid at May Day, and 400 at Martinmas next (1).

At the bargain meeting I spent 1 shilling, at the articling one shilling and sixpence, and I paid Mr. Robinson five shillings, and to Harper (2) for taking enterance of all the land 15 shillings."

"October — day 1718 A.D. a memoriall.

The first hides that were tanned at Cragg (3) I sould (five) to Edward Hudson of Fuiston att the rate of 16 shillings and 6 pence a hide. The sum is 4 pounds 2 shillings and six pence."

"ffor a memorandum 1718 A.D. I laid the garret chamber; the boardes I bought of Allne Smith of Denton being 39 inch boardes, and 18 half inch boardes, which cost me one pound two shillings and six pence, this being att Cragg in the Forest in 1718 A.D."

The following extracts will probably be of interest to agriculturists.

"Memorandum. The first year at Cragg (1717 A.D.) I solde sheepe and woole at the sume of one pound five shilllings (each). The second year, sold sheepe and woole at the summe of one pound 5 shillings (each). The third yeare, sold sheep and woole at the sum of 2 pounds (each)."

"ffeb. 8th day 1723 A.D. Sold to Abraham Huddleston of Burley a bay mare coming four year olde, and he came for her to my house at Cragg on the 13th day of ffeb. and had her 'livered to him, he is to pay for her at Easter after; the price being five pounds five shillings; but I am to give him one shilling and sixpence again when he pays for her. (later). "All paid for."

---

(1) This purchase included the house — variously designated Over and Upper Cragg House, and Cragg Hall, with about 30 acres of land adjoining, and was, therefore, only the nucleus around which the larger estate afterwards gathered. The house is of the time of Elizabeth, and had belonged in succession to the Franklands, the Rev. Henry Fairfax (whom see), and others.

(2) William Harper was the tenant under Edward Robinson, and had to give way to the new owner.

(3) The Diarist seems to have joined the business of a tanner to his occupation as a yeoman while at Denton, and to have commenced, at Cragg Hall, what afterwards—in the latter part of the last century and early part of this,—became a very extensive but unfortunate business. The large tan-yard begun by him, some distance below the house in the valley, was removed in 1850 A.D.

"In the yeare 1719 A.D. I had barley (1) in the Low Trough (2) being all the close barley. I had 7 quarters 12 strokes. The 7 quarters sold to William Gott att one pound 1 shilling and 6 pence a quarter."

"In the yeare 1720 A.D. I had the Green Field (3) all barley, and sould it to William Gott for one pound one shilling and 6 pence a quarter. I had 6 pence of earnest money. There were about 6 quarters and one stroke, which comes to 5 pounds 18 shillings and three pence, (but I had 6d. of earnest)."

"In the year 1721 A.D. I had barley, one acre, in the Delf Close; wee had three quarters of it."

"In the yeare 1723 A.D. all the Low Trough was barley; we had nine quarters 3 strokes of itt—the old measure."

"In the year 1724 A.D. all Great Delf Close (4) barley, and sould it on the ii day of December to Robert Harrison of Addingham for one pound one shilling and 6 pence a quarter. There were about six quarters on itt."

"Memorandum. In the year 1723 A.D.—it being a very dry summer—wee had the Great Delf Close wheat, beinge three dayes worke (3 cutting). Wee had on itt 21 loads of wheat. I sold as much wheat as I took tenn pounds 8 shillings and 4 pence for."

"August 4th 1724 A.D. I bought of Francis Jeffery of the Browne Bank two dayes mowing of grasse (i.e. as much as would take one man for two days to cut), and I am to give one pound 17 shillings and sixpence for it. But hee had paid for mowing itt, and he had made half of it into hay, soe wee did get the rest of it up into hay the day I bought it as above mentioned. And wee got the last part of this hay on the 15th day of August 1724 A.D."

"Feb. 20 day 1727-8 A.D. Sold at Bradford one steire (steer, ox) that was four years old, for 10 pounds. I did breed him at Cragg. He would have been 5 years old next June. He was sold to Halifax."

---

(1) It should be borne in mind that the land, and climate, of the district are unsuitable to the profitable growth of barley or any other grain—except perhaps oats. Though much land was under arable cultivation up to thirty years ago, now the whole—or very nearly so,—is grass.

(2) Area: 2a. 2r. 14p.

(3) Area: 2a. 1r. 19p.

(4) Area: 2a. 2r. 27p.

"December 22 day 1727. I paid John Harrison 10 shillings for five yeares now last past of that tythe belonging to Mr. Barker for my lands at Denton, which is two shillings in the yeare due to Mr. Barker. I paide it in Otley, in Cordelay's, John Cordelay beinge by."

"Memorandum for the year 1726. We did build the Oven House. (1) What I paid for building itt: first, I pay'd on the 16th day of May to Jane Irish for Masons' table 10 shillings." (No further items follow).

"February 7th day 1725-6 Francis (2) did go to learn with Mr. Atkinson att Hampstwait. I am to pay one shilling and 6d. a week for his table att Thomas Randall's and 5 shillings to Mr. Atkinson."

A like entry occurs frequently until 1729, when there is the following :—

"May first day 1729, I paid widow Randall for Francis's table 19 shillings and six pence beinge in full of all accounts. And this day above written I paid Mr. Atkinson for his learning tenn shillings being in full of all accounts, and so farewell. I paid for Francis learning and table the sum of 12 pounds 7 shillings and 6 pence."

"Memorandum. In the yeare 1730 I sett 20 apple trees, and three cherry trees; and in 1731 I sett 13 apple trees; and February 16th day I cut up a thorn hedge in the middle of the orchard. (3) This done at Cragg in the Forest by me Stephen Parkinson."

"For a memorandum. April 25th day. Att night happened a fire at Denton Hall (4) which burnt all down. This was in the yeare 1734. One Samuel Ibbotson bought it, and lived in itt at this time. It was the finest hall that was within the dale. This is sett down by Stephen Parkinson at Cragg Hall in the Forrest.

"June 28th day 1740. My son Thomas was married with Mary Pullyen (5) of Timble."

---

(1) The out building now standing to the east of the northern wing of Cragg Hall.

(2) His third son who died October 6th 1732 A.D.

(3) The orchard thus planted, or rather re-planted, remained until 1842 A.D. when the trees, having become old and barren, were uprooted.

(4) This was the Hall in which the Fairfaxes had so long resided, and which came to them through marriage with the heiress of the Thwaites.

(5) This ancient Forest family was seated at Timble and Fewston from very early times. In the Poll Tax Roll A.D. 1378, mention is made of Isabel Polayn residing here with two servants. This is earlier than the family is found at either Scotton or Killinghall. The connec-

"Memorandum. The 20th day of ffebruary in the year one thousand seven hundred and forty one my sonne Thomas had a girl born by his wife at Timble. When she was christened they called her (1) Mary."

"Memorandum. The 3rd day of January 1743 I went with Stephen, my sonne, to Robert Wilks about making up a match

---

tion of the three branches has not been discovered, the prevailing christian names, however, were the same, and the same coat of arms was used by all, namely, "Azure, on a bend between six lozenges or, each charged with an escallop sable, five escallops of the first."

Crest. A pelican feeding its young from its breast.
(Fewston and Killinghall branches):—

The Scotton branch however used for their crest, "a colt's head erased sable, bridled or."—

The seat of the Fewston branch was New Hall. George Pulleyne of Newhall near Fewston made his will on June 5th 1557 A.D. and gave to "my brother Sir John Pulleyne vycar of Fuston my lease of Newhall and of other lands which I have of the grant of Mayster William Pulleyne." "Sir John Pulleyne" was vicar of Fewston from 1545 A.D. to 1583 A.D. and Henry Pulleyne, clerk, who succeeded him, from 1583 A.D. to 1591 A.D. Before the end of the 16th century Newhall had been acquired by the Fairfax family. In 1599 A.D. Sir Thomas Fairfax of Denton disposed of it, by his will of that date, to Edward Fairfax, the poet, who shortly after made it his residence.

The chief branch of the Pulleynes still resided in the township of Timble, and in the early part of the 18th century was represented by Anthony Pulleyne Esq., of that place. He died in 1728 A.D. leaving three daughters co-heiresses. Of these, Elizabeth, the eldest, born 1710 A.D. married William Simpson Esq. of Fellisclifie in 1735 A.D. and died 1741 A.D. Mary, the second married Thomas Parkinson of Cragg Hall, and was the great grandmother of the present writer. Elizabeth, the youngest, married 1st Edward Yates of Padside, and 2ndly Stephen Parkinson of Hardisty Hill, (his second wife) brother of her sister's husband. The crest of the Pulleyne family of this part of the Forest and of Killinghall, (a pelican feeding its young with blood from its own breast) remained in stained glass, in one of the windows of New Hall until removed preparatory to the house being taken down, in 1867 A.D. when the reservoir was formed which now washes over its site. The glass is now (1882 A.D.) in the possession of Mr. Bramley B. Kent of Menwith Hill.

(1) This "girl" Mary married, on 10th January 1763 A.D., John Blesárd Esq. of Guiseley, whose daughter and only surviving child Elizabeth, became the wife of her cousin the late Robert Blesard Esq. of Blenheim Terrace, Leeds. She and their only surviving child, Phœbe late wife of Thomas Tennant Esq., were among the most munificent benefactors to the churches and charities of Leeds in this century.

with his daughter Anna, beinge his youngest daughter. He has three daughters, the eldest Elizabeth; the second Mary; and the youngest Anna. The 10th day of January Stephen went to York for license to marry Anna, but got none, because she was under age. But he got license the next day at Harewood and was married the 19th day of January, 1743-4 A.D.

"Memorandum. May 9th day 1744 A.D. my sister Elizabeth Day died att Menwith Hill, and was buried at Hampsthwait the 12th day of May."

"Memorandum. This 14th day of July 1744 A.D was the House (1) reared at Hardisty Hill. There was at the rearing, Thomas Tiplady, John Parker, Samuel Stubbs, Christopher Watson, Joshua Yeadon, Benjamin Swain, Joseph Watson. The masons were Thomas Snell, Anthony Snell, George Hudson, Simeon Moorhouse. The wrights were James Graham, Francis Graham, William Croft."

"Memorandum. My brother John Day died at Menwith Hill on the 29th day of July 1745 A.D. at 6 o'clock in the evening, and he was buried at Hampsthwaite on Lammas Day being the first of August, 1745 A.D."

"Memorandum. This 23rd day of December 1745 A.D. Edward Yates of Padside married one Betty (2) (Elizabeth) Pullyen of

---

(1) This house was erected by the diarist for his recently married (see preceding memorandum) son, Stephen, in the family of whose descendants it remained until 1848 A.D. when it was sold by the Trustees of Stephen Parkinson, Esq. of Newington Place near York, to the late Mr. Carr of Bolton Bridge who resided in it until his death some twenty years ago. It is now the residence of Mr. John Bramley whose wife is the grandaughter of Mr. Carr. In the latter part of the former half of this centuary (19th) there was erected on the estate, to meet the demand for houses caused by the factory of Messrs. Coldbeck Ellis & Co. at West House, sixteen cottages and other buildings. Twelve of these, which stood on the south side of the Skipton and Knaresbrough road, at its junction with the Hardisty Hill road, were purchased by the Leeds Corporation, and two years ago, were removed and the material utilized for the boundary walls of the reservoirs.

(2) The youngest co-heiress of Anthony Pullyene Esq. and sister of Mary, wife of Thomas Parkinson second son of the diarist. She afterwards married, for her second husband, Stephen Parkinson of Hardisty Hill, the diarist's 4th son.

Timble. It was a very windy day—but no rain: so I sett this down for a memorandum."

"Memorandum. April 19 day 1737 A.D. my partener Thomas Stubbs buried at Pannell Church. Mr. Simison preached a sermon. The text was 19th chapter and 26th verse of Job: "And though after my skinne wormes destroy this body, yet in my flesh shall I see God."

With this memorandum this heap of stray leaves must be crowned. Others there are in the book but of insufficient interest to be brought forth for addition to the pile. The writer of them died, in 1763 A.D., at the patriarchal age of 81 years, and his wife in 1766 A.D. at the still greater age of 86 years. Their tombstone is yet to be seen, at the east end of the chancel, in the churchyard at Fewston. Besides the sons already mentioned they left two daughters, one of whom, Jane, died unmarried, and the other, Hannah, married 1st the Rev. James Rayer, curate of Guiseley, and 2nd, in 1759 A.D. James Hulbert Esq., a London physician, who ultimately settled with his wife at the Old Vicarage at Bingley, and from whom is descended the writer's aged relative and friend Miss Ann Hulbert—the last of her race.

THE FAMILY OF WOOD OF SWINSTY.

SWINSTY Hall, the largest, and by far the most important and interesting, of the several 16th century "Halls" in the forest and its neighbourhood, stands in the Township of Little Timble, an outlying part of the manor and parish of Otley, and adjoining, on the south, the townships of Fewston and Norwood. In the latest survey (1767 A.D.) of the forest of Knaresborough, before its enclosure in 1770 A.D., the township of Little Timble is included, as within the forest. In other surveys, however, it does not seem to have been included.

At the time of the Doomsday survey, it was a "Berewick" of the Archbishop of York's manor of Otley, to which it has continued to belong to the present time. In the 31st Edward I. (1302 A.D.,) it was returned as representing the twelfth portion of a Knight's fee.

The history of the Hall, its legends, its peculiarities, its owners (the Wood, Robinson, and Bramley families) have all been so fully investigated and so well described by Mr. William Grainge,* that to speak of them again, in this "leaf," would be merely to repeat what he has already so ably and pleasantly written. The hall and its surroundings are, therefore, referred to here, only, for the purpose of identifying them as the place, whence originated the surname of *Wood*.

* **"An Historical and descriptive Account of Swinsty Hall, by William Grainge 1857 A.D." Also "Swinsty Hall and its Legends" in the *Harrogate Herald*, May 18th, 1881 A.D.**

In the 13th and 14th centuries surnames were gradually coming into use; and such names were frequently taken, or rather perhaps *given*, from the surroundings of the place at which the persons, indicated by the name, resided. Such was the case with the surname of "Wood," and other instances will be found referred to in these "leaves."

Early in the reign of King John, the portion of the Forest now known as Bluberhouses was alienated to *Robert-le-Forester*. In the Register of Archbishop Grey of York (1216 A.D. to 1255 A.D.) there is frequent mention, in connection with the Manor of Otley, of the name *Forestarius*. A grant of land, in 1238 A.D., from Robert de Lelay to the Archbishop is witnessed by, among others, "Ysaak de Tymbel" and "Ada (or Adam) Forestario de Ottley."

Perhaps it would be too much to say that this, probably an official name, might be that of the same family as we shortly after meet with denominated "de Sale" *i.e.* "of the Forest or Wood;" but there is some possibility that such was the case.

We come now, however, to more certain ground.

In the Register (1) of Archbishop Corbridge (1300-1304 A.D.) we learn that, in 1302 A.D., there was residing, then, and for two generations earlier, on his Grace's Manor at Tymbel, a family then known by the name of "de la Sale;" *i.e.* "of the forest" or "of the wood." (*Saltus*, a forest, or wooded valley.) The wardship and power to give in marriage, of "John (who must then have been a minor,) the son of Richard, the son of Robert de la Sale de Tymbel," was granted, in the above year, by the Archbishop to "William le Sarjaunt de Bloberhous."

A little later, viz. in 1371 A.D., the "de la Sale" had been contracted, and partly anglicized, into "del Wode." In that year, Walter, the son of "John del Wode," did homage to the Archbishop for lands that he held of the Manor of Otley at Timble (2).

---

(1) Surtees Society's publications vol. 49.
(2) Register of Archbishop Greenfield, Ibid.

In the Subsidy Roll (1) of 1379 A.D., printed elsewhere in these "leaves," the same person is described as "Walterus del Wode and ux ejus—capenter vj.d."

The "de" or "del" in this, as in so many other instances, was soon omitted, and thus the name became simply that of "Wode" or "Wood."

From the Herald's visitations of Yorkshire, edited and published by Foster, we learn that, "——— daughter of ——— Wood of Swinsty" married John Pulleine of Scotton (2). There is no date given, but this marriage was a very early one.

Again, Walter Wood of Little Tymble married Agnes daughter of William Clapham of Beamsley (3).

In 1504 A.D. Walter Wood Esquire was a witness, on behalf of Sir Robert Plumpton, in a suit at law regarding the forest. *(See Antè p. 31.)*

Seven generations later than the previous marriage with the Pulleine family, Ralph (William ?) Wood of Swinsty Hall married (about 1523 A.D.) Ann Pulleine of Scotton (4).

A Richard Wood, in his will dated May 12th 1523 A.D., is described as "Richard Wode of Tymyll, Gentleman," and he directs that his body be buried in the churchyard of St. Michael's Church at Fewston, gives his best beast to Otley Church as a mortuary, and mentions "Agnes, his wife," *William* his son, and his younger children. John Jeffray and Christopher Lindley are appointed feoffees of all his lands in the Forest of Knaresborough;—and also

---

(1) As the short list in this Roll of the persons taxed in Little Timble, is accidentally omitted in the Roll as printed at the beginning of this book, it may be given here;

"TIMBLE.

"Walterus del Wode and his wife—capenter (?)	vj.d.
Richard Paytson and his wife	iiij.d.
Willemus Milner and his wife	iiij.d.
Robertus Wrightson and his wife	iiij.d.
Agnes Paytson	iiij.d.
Agnes filia Willelmi Milner	iiij.d.

Summa ij.s. ij.d."

(2) Pulleine of Scotton Pedigree.

(3) The Clapham of Beamsley Pedigree.

(4) Pulleine Pedigree.

refers to "the agreement between me and Mr. Ralph Pullande concerning the marriage between my son and his daughter." Among the executors named are the two feoffees and "Giles Wod my brother." The witnesses to the will are John Graver, John Jeffray, Brian Wod, John Hearfield, and Thomas Pullan. The Giles Wood mentioned in this will as the brother of the Testator, was Giles Wood of Pickering. He is so given in Foster's Yorkshire Pedigrees.*

An inquisition post mortem on the goods of Richard Wood of Pickering, son of Giles Wood of that place, was held in 1567-8 A.D., wherein mention is made of his lands at Pickering, Copmanthorpe and several other places, and also of "a messuage called the Bakehouse, three oxgangs and divers other lands in the *Forest of Knaresborough.*"

Giles (Egid) Wod was admitted a member of the Corpus Christi Guild at York in 1495 A.D., and "Richard Wood" (probably the son) in 1543 A.D. On the former, the Editor of the Surtees Society's list of members, adds a note—"Probably Giles Wood of Pickering, yeoman, brother of Richard Wood of Timble in the parish of Fewston. His son Richard Wood of Pickering, gentleman, died in 1568 A.D., leaving, with other issue, a younger son, Anthony, who settled at Copmanthorpe, and was grandfather of John Wood, Lord Mayor of York in 1682 A.D., from whom the Woods of Hollin Hall near Ripon are descended."

In 1575 A.D. the owner of Swinsty Hall was Ralph Wood; and in the marriage settlement, (given in full by Mr. Grainge), made in that year, of his son Francis Wood with Ellen, or Helene, daughter of Henry Sothill of North Grange, there is an undertaking to erect, what now constitutes the principal, and more modern, portion of the Hall. It seems, however, never to have been quite finished, and remains so still. Francis Wood, for whom the more modern part was thus built, was the last of his family to reside at it. In 1590 A.D. it passed from him, in consideration of a mortgage upon it for £2,000, to Henry Robinson of the Old

* Pedigree of Wood of Hollin Hall.

Laund in Lancashire. Francis Wood afterwards resided at the Grange at Arthington, and some of the family settled at Stainburn, in the parish of Kirkby Overblow. At a subsequent date, it would seem that he, or his widow, returned to the neighbourhood of the old home. In 10th Charles I. (1635 A.D.) Helene Wood, *widow*, surrendered in the Forest Court at Knaresborough a messuage house, building, and lands in the hamlet and "ville" of Timble, to the use of "William Ratcliffe de Skales" his heirs and assigns. In the same year the will of Helene Wood, widow, was proved at Knaresbro' by William Ratcliffe of Skales and Ann his wife. There is also, among the records of the Forest Court, the will and an inventory of the goods of William Ratcliffe and Ann his wife, "*daughter of the late Helene Wood*, widow."

The name yet survives at Timble and the vicinity.

In 1639 A.D. the woods at, and around, Swinsty were still sufficiently large and important to be separately mentioned, along with other property. *An inquisition post mortem*, held in that year, as to the goods of Henry Robinson, then lately deceased, of Swinsty Hall, there is recited "a mansion house with pertinents," five other messuages and various parcels of meadow and pasture land, and then "a large pasture commonly known as *Swinsty Wood*, and common of pasture for sheep and cattle on the forest of Knaresbro."

From this account, it appears, then, pretty certain, that this family name, as borne by, at least some of the families designated by it in Yorkshire, had its origin in the forest glades, and well timbered forest valley, in the neighbourhood of Swinsty. And this interesting fact augments the regret of foresters, antiquarians, and others interested in historical and genealogical studies, that it should have been found necessary for the extensive woods of fine timber, possibly part of the forest primeval, stretching down from the Hall to the river on the east and south-east, to be, within the last few years, entirely swept away, in the construction of the large reservoir of the Leeds Corporation. But such has been the case; and now the cradle, and early home, of the "Woods" is doubly *Woodless*.

WILLIAM MAKEPEACE THACKERAY.

"O gentle censor of our age!
Prime master of our ampler tongue!
Whose word of wit, and generous page,
Were never wrath except with wrong,—

Fielding—without the manner's dross,
Scott—with a spirit's larger room,
What Prelate deems thy grave his loss?
What Halifax erects thy tomb?

But, may be, he,—who so could draw
The hidden great,—the humble wise,
Yielding with them to God's good law,
Makes the Pantheon where he lies."

—*Lord Houghton in Cornhill Magazine.*

ON the southern banks of the Washburn, about half a mile above Fewston, there stood, until lately, a substantial farm-house bearing the name of "Thackeray" or "Thackray." Four years ago it was entirely removed to make way for the upper reservoir of the Leeds Corporation, the waters of which now completely cover the site. The situation was at the western end of a large flat holm, which occupied the bottom of the valley, and not more than one hundred yards from the river. To the west of the house, and at about the same distance, ran a large brook, descending to the Washburn from the high moorlands, and named "Thackeray Beck."

The house, lately removed, was comparatively a modern one, but, there can be no doubt, it occupied the place of one, or more, of antient date.

In the Subsidy Rolls of the second year of Richard II., (1378-9 A.D.) already given among these "Leaves," under "Wapentake of Claro," and "Villa de Tymble," occurs probably the first-known mention of the name,—"*William de Thackwra*," and in "Villa de Clynt," there are found the names "Willelmus de Thackray et uxor ejus," and "Johannes de Thakray."

In 1666 A.D., again mention is made of the place, as "Thackera Holme," in connection with a surrender, in the Forest Court at Knaresborough, of lands at Low Cragg.

The word is thus distinctly a "*place*" name, and, therefore, given by the place, as a surname, to the family, and not imparted to the place by the family. It may however have originated as a *place* name in the *trade* name of the person resident at it. Possibly the derivation of the word is from "*thec*" or "*thack*" meaning thatch; which would be "*theccer*" or "*thacker*" when applied to a man using the thatch; and "*ey*," an isle, or island. In which case the meaning would be "the isle of the thatcher." A similar etymology is found in the name Bardsey—"Bards-"ey," or the Bards' Island.

The more probable derivation, however, is from "*thec*" or "*thecker*," and "*ea*," a water or mere,—and thus the meaning of the word, "*the thatch*, or *thatcher's*, *water* or *mere*." Thackeray Holme might well, at no very distant time, have suited the requirements of either explanation. As a mere, or shallow lake, its banks, or the whole of it, would produce in abundance the reeds, rushes, &c., frequently used for the purpose of thatching.

From the place, the family residing near it would receive its name as a surname, with—as usual—the prefix "de," "de Thackeray"; the "de" however being soon, as in innumerable such cases, dropped.

As a family name few have been subject to a greater variety in spelling. The following modes are from the registers of two parishes (Hampsthwaite and Kirkby-Malzeard) alone. Tackerey; Theccoray; Theccorey; Theccory; Theccerey; Thecceray; Thackeray; Thackrey; Thackray; Thackurey; Thackwray; Thaqueray; Thackura; Thaccura; Thackrey; Thackaray, &c. Two or three branches of the family have come down to the present time, and are still found, in the parish of Fewston. In the adjoining one of Hampsthwaite it has been, until recently, numerous, and from thence it is that the members of it known to fame have gone forth.

Walter Thackeray was resident at Hampsthwaite, at the beginning of the 17th century. His wife Margaret was interred there in 1609 A.D. One of his numerous grandchildren was Thomas Thackeray, born in 1628 A.D., and married, Mary (probably Brown) whom he left a widow with a large family in 1670 A.D. The second surviving son was Timothy Thackeray, and the third Elias Thackeray, born 1665 A.D. Elias must have developed, in youth, a more than usual aptitude for learning, since,—and probably as an encouragement to him therein—Elizabeth Day, widow of John Day of Hartwith, who, by will dated June 25th 1681 A.D., left several legacies for educational purposes, among the rest, left one of twenty shillings to "Elias Thackeray son of Mary Thackeray widow of Hampsthwaite."

Elias, thus encouraged, persevered in his studies, and was the first of the family to rise above their yeoman rank. He became Rector of Hauxwell in the North Riding, where he died a bachelor in 1737 A.D. Having no family of his own he was free to take an interest in the numerous family of his brother at Hampsthwaite. This brother, Timothy Thackeray, had meanwhile become the parish clerk of his native village,—an office which passed on to four, if not five, of his descendants, and was held by the last of them up to very recent times.

The eldest son of Timothy Thackeray, named after his grandfather, Thomas, was put forward by his worthy uncle, the Rector of Hawkswell. Born in 1693 A.D., he successively became Head Master of Harrow School, Doctor of Divinity, and Archdeacon of Surrey, and died in 1760 A.D.

From Archdeacon Thackeray's family of sixteen children, has come a long list of names of men eminent alike in the Church, in the Army, and in Literature. They cannot here be even enumerated. The youngest son—the 16th—was William Makepeace Thackeray, afterwards of the India Civil Service, and who died at Hadley in 1815 A.D. His grandson, bearing the same somewhat peculiar Christian name, was Willliam Makepeace Thackeray, the subject of this paper,—the author, satirist, and novelist.

No adequate biography of this eminent man has yet been given to the public, and but gleanings only, from the great field of his life and works, can be given here.

He was born in 1811 A.D., at Calcutta, where his father, Richmond Thackeray, who also was in the India service, resided. In 1816 A.D. his father died, and he, the only child, was brought home by his mother, and placed at Charter House. From thence he proceeded to Trinity College Cambridge, in 1829 A.D., where he manifested his predilection for literature, by taking a foremost part in one or two humorous publications in the University. He left Cambridge before the time for proceeding to a degree; and afterwards studied at Weimar, and, especially painting, at Paris.

On coming of age in 1832 A.D., he inherited a fortune of about £500 a year,—much of which, both principal and interest, was, soon afterwards, sunk and lost in literary ventures, and some by a bank failure.

Thus thrown upon his resources, he tried one or two precarious means of livelihood, but ultimately, about 1836 A.D., settled down to literature as a profession. The "Times," "Frazer's Magazine," and "Punch,"—especially the latter,—had the benefit of his contributions for many years. The great fame of Punch, some years ago, was due to the contributions of Thackeray and Leech. During this time he also published several books of sufficient note to establish his name before the public. In 1846 A.D., he commenced the publication of "Vanity Fair," and when it was finished, in 1848 A.D., its author held a foremost position in the ranks of literary men, and a reputation which will live long as the English language survives.

At intervals of two years each—in 1850 A.D.—1852 A.D., and 1854 A.D., "Vanity Fair" was followed by "Pendennis," "Esmond," and "The Newcomes." In 1856 A.D. he prepared and delivered—in that and the following years,—his Lectures on "The Humourists of the 18th century," followed by a second series on "The four Georges." "The Virginians" was published in 1857 A.D., and in 1859 A.D., he undertook the last great work of his life,—the editorship of the then projected Cornhill Magazine. The Magazine proved an enormous success. Therein appeared "The four Georges," the incomparable "Roundabout Papers," and "The Adventures of Philip."

Thackeray had married, in 1837 A.D., and three daughters,—one of whom alone survives,—were the fruit of the marriage. They were very dear to him, and his closest companions. In one of his ballads—"The White Squall," he thus speaks of them;

> "I thought, as day was breaking,
> My little girls were waking,
> And smiling, and making
> A prayer at home for me."

In the height of his fame and prosperity he did not forget the old family nest in the forest, but on one—if not more than one occasion—he sought it out and did his *devoir* at the shrine of his ancestors. His daughters accompanied him. The one now left—herself occupying a place in the world of literature not unworthy her illustrious father, says of one of these visits,—in a letter to the present writer, "I was with my father when he made a journey to Hampsthwaite; and we saw the place where the home had once stood on the slope of the hill, and from which his progenitors had set out on their journies * * * This little expedition with my father is one of the happiest recollections of my old life."

On December 24th 1863 A.D., Thackeray died suddenly, at the large house, he had recently erected for himself, at Palace Green, Bayswater, in the 53rd year of his age, and was interred at Kensal Green. An excellent bust to his memory is placed in the great national mausoleum, Westminster Abbey, where Lord Houghton, and many other of his friends, thought the remains themselves ought to have rested.

Thackeray was not without serious faults. As a writer he certainly looked too much upon the worse side of human nature and the world. Satire, concealed or open, seems to run through all his works, and the reader, while fascinated by them, rises from the perusal of them, in anything but good humour with his race.

Personally, Thackeray is said to have been one of the kindest, most generous, and gentle of men. Whatever, therefore, of cynicism, or satire, finds a place in his writings, was not the offspring of his own nature, but must have arisen from an unfortunate experience, or undue estimate, of the evil in the men and women of Society.

Shirley Brooks, in an "In Memoriam" in Punch, speaks beautifully—and probably hits the truth—when he writes,

"He was a cynic! By his life all wrought
  Of generous acts, mild words and gentle ways;
His heart wide open to all kindly thought,
  His hand so quick to give, his tongue to praise!

He was a cynic! You might read it writ
  In that broad brow, crowned with its silver hair;
In those blue eyes, with childlike candour lit,
  In that sweet smile his lips were wont to wear!

He was a cynic! By the love that clung
  About him from his children, friends, and kin;
By the sharp pain, light pen, and gossip tongue
  Wrought in him, chafing the soft heart within!"

SAVING THE COLOURS OF THE 24TH REGIMENT AT ISANDHLWANA, FEB. 14TH, 1879 A.D.

How sleep the brave who sink to rest,
By all their country's wishes bless'd!

By fairy hands their knell is rung;
By forms unseen their dirge is sung;
There honour comes, a pilgrim gray,
To bless the turf that wraps their clay;
And Freedom shall awhile repair,
To dwell a weeping hermit there."

—*Collins.*

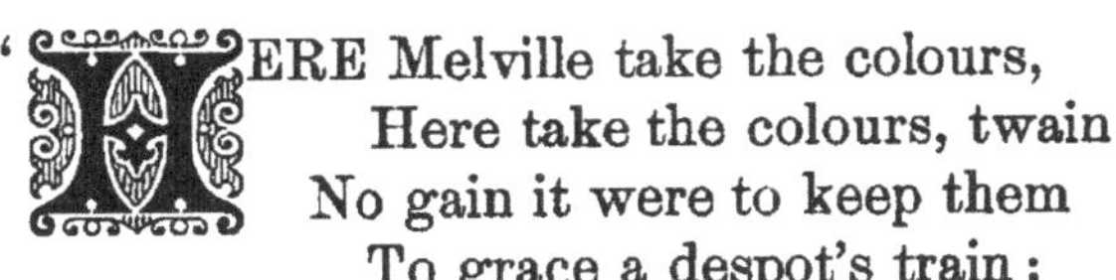

"HERE Melville take the colours,
Here take the colours, twain;
No gain it were to keep them
To grace a despot's train;

"Make way o'er drift and brushwood,—
Make way as best you can,
The Zulus now surround us,
We must perish to a man!"

"Men of the Twenty Fourth!
Our colours back I send,
But we are here, and here we stand
And fight it to the end;

"Our colours saved with honour,
Will lead men on again,
When long our life-blood's watered
This fatal Afric plain!"

Thus spake the gallant Colonel,*
  When the camp was all but lost,
And closer round was closing,
  The untold Zulu host.

Then turned, and foremost fighting,
  As ever in the van, (1)
He fell, and there, around him,
  Fell nigh every man.

Young Melville took the colours,
  With Coghill (2) at his side,
And nobly thus they bore them,
  Through the darkly surging tide. (3)

---

* Lieutenant Colonel Pulleine, who at first commanded the camp at Isandhlwana, on the fatal morning of its destruction by the Zulus, was the son of the late Rev. Robert Pulleine rector of Kirkby Wiske. The family are believed to be descended from that branch of the forest family, of the name, seated at Killinghall.

"When the loss of the camp seemed quite certain, Colonel Pulleine called Lieutenant Melville, and said, "Lieutenant Melville, you and your senior Lieutenant will take the colours and make the best of your way." He shook hands with him, and then turned round and said, "Men of the 24th we are here, and here we stand and fight it out to the end." He was quite cool and collected. These were probably his last words, for he fell early in the fight." *The Kaffrarian Watchman.*

(1) "Lieutenant Colonel Pulleine started for the front bright and happy. At last he had his wish. He had always said, "When the bell rings I shall be there." *Letter from South Africa.*

(2) Lieutenant Coghill was the eldest son of Sir John Jocelyn Coghill of Glen Barrahane, County Cork in Ireland. The following account of the family, connecting Lieut. Coghill with Knaresbrough, and taken from a history of the family compiled by Mr. James Henry Coghill, of New York, will be of interest.

A John Cockhill gent. of Cockhill in Co. York was living in reign of Richard II and Henry IV. His son Thomas Coghill married Marjory daughter of John Slingsby of Scriven, and was father of Thomas Coghill the younger, whose son Marmaduke Coghill married Maude, daughter of John Pulleine of Killinghall. He rebuilt Coghill Hall in 1555 A.D. This house continued the seat of the family until sold by Sir John Thomas Coghill Bart. to the Countess Conyngham in 1796 A.D. Since then it has gone by the name of Conyingham Hall and is now the seat of Basil Thomas Woodd, Esq.

The above Marmaduke Coghill was the father of Thomas Coghill, whose son, Thomas, was the father of John Coghill baptized at

They braved the living ocean,
  Of fiends that round them press'd,
As vessel braves the billow
  That bears it on its crest.

They sped o'er rock and brushwood,—
  The swift pursued by swift,—
Adown the rapid torrent bed,
  And by the famèd Drift;

Till 'fore them rolled the river,
  And 'hind the foemen press'd,
When Melville took the colours
  And wound them round his breast.

Then like the noble Romans, (1)
  They swam the swollen flood,
As flew the deadly assegai,
  And waters blushed with blood.

The further bank they gained,—
  Pursuèd, bleeding, spent,—
Then to the shelt'ring ravine,
  Their painful footsteps bent.

Knaresborough March 11th, 1615 A.D. and who married Lucy, daughter of Thomas Tancred of Whixley Hall. They had issue an only son, John Coghill, a master in Chancery—who was knighted in 1686 A.D. He died in 1699 A.D. and was the ancestor in the female line, of Sir John Joceyln Coghill Bart. of Glen Barrahane. Sir John by paternal descent is a Cramer, his grandfather Sir John Cramer assumed the name of Coghill in compliance with the will of his cousin, Hester, Countess of Charleville.

Hargrove, in his history of Knaresbrough and its Forest, states that the arms of both Coghill and Cramer were, when he wrote, to be seen on the front of Coghill Hall.

(3) "On looking back, I saw our men completely surrounded, firm as a rock, falling rapidly but fighting to the last. The loud yell of the Zulus filled the air. There was no other noise, except the demoniac shrieks, as the awful work was done with the short stabbing assegai. I saw Lieutenant Coghill trying to fight his way through, as also Adjutant Melville, who had seized the colours, and was vainly trying to carry them through." *Narrative of Mr. Young.*

(1) Horatius, Lartius and Herminius.

With back to rock together,
  They turned to die, or slay;
Side by side and foot by foot,
  They, as lions, stood at bay.

In face of clam'ring hundreds,
  Their charge unflinching kept,
'Till o'er it flowed their life-blood,
  And in its folds they slept. (1)

Now long as hearts of Britons
  Are warm, and true, and bold,
And long as deeds of daring
  And feats of arms are told,

And long as duty's pathway
  Is held more dear than life,
And name of "God and country,"
  Stands foremost in the strife,

Let Britain point her children,
  To the far Afric land,
When duty calls them, boldly,
  To do, and dare and stand,

And with a mother's memory,
  And all a mother's pride,
Bid them to die for duty,
  As these, her heroes, died."

---

(1) The bodies of Lieutenant Adjutant Melville and Lieutenant Coghill were found by the side of a precipitous path, about half a mile from the Buffalo river. The bodies of a number of Zulus were laid at a short distance from them, showing that they had sold their lives dearly, while *beneath their bodies were found the colours of the Regiment.* The Queen's colours were discovered, little injured, on the side of the river about 400 yards below the crossing place. They might have been wrenched from the hands of the brave custodians by the flood in crossing; but more probably they had been taken from their dead bodies by some of their pursuers, and afterwards cast where they were found,—their value not being known.

THE REV. ROBERT COLLYER: A FOREST BOY; THE POET PREACHER OF AMERICA.

ABOUT sixty years ago there resided, at West Houses near Bluberhouses, in one of a row of cottages almost adjoining the large factory of Messrs. Coldbeck, Wilks, and Ellis, a worthy, skilled blacksmith, or mechanic, named Samuel Collyer, with his equally estimable wife. They had been atttracted to this busy hive of industry—then in the zenith of its prosperity—in the forest, from the sunny south; Samuel Collyer from London,—his wife from Norwich.

"My father," writes the son—the subject of this leaf,—"was one of the most healthful men I ever knew, and my mother one of the most healthful women. My father's eyes were dark and soft, my mother's were blue blended with grey, and could snap fire and make things boom. * * * * My father was as good a smith as ever stood at an anvil, and that was all. He had no other faculty, except that of striking a tune in the little meeting house, and you were not sure what the tune was going to be until he got to the end of the first line. But my mother was a woman of such a faculty, though she could hardly read or write, that, I believe, if she had been ordered to take charge of a 70 gun ship, and to carry it through a battle, give her time to learn the ropes, and she would do it. She had in her, also, wells of poesy and humour, and laughter so shaking, that the tears would stream down her face, and a deep abiding, tenderness like that of the saints."

Robert, one of several children of this estimable couple, is the subject of this memoir.

He was born in the early part of the year 1824 A.D.; but not in the forest home of his parents.

"Robert," says his mother, "was born at Keighley, though our home, before and after, was at Blubberhouses. My husband had a difference with his employer about wages and went away to Keighley, where Robert was born, but he was only nine days old when his employer sent for my husband again, and we went back to Blubberhouses, where my son was christened, and which is the only early home he remembers."

At four years old, Robert was sent to a school at Fewston—two miles away—kept by Willie Hardy. Willie was a cripple, having been deprived, in infancy, by illness, of the use of his legs. His establishment was a thoroughly characteristic country school of the first half of this century, yet one of which many, who are men and women now, once pupils in it, have kindly and pleasant recollections.

The school-room was also the living-room of the family. On the hearth stood the small round table for the family meals, flanked, in each corner, by the usual high-backed chair. Three or four benches, or "forms,"—as they were called,—for the younger scholars, occupied the centre of the room. Along one side, by the window, stood *the desk*, accommodating ten or a dozen of the head scholars—face to face; and at the end, in his comfortable arm chair, during school hours sat the master. Each pupil "came up" to him, in turn, "to read," or repeat his lesson. On a table at the master's right hand rested the end of a long, tough, hazel rod—not unlike the instrument which worthy Dr. Johnson described as, "a long stick with a hook and worm at one end and a fool at the other." The small end of this rod was placed in a loop, hanging from the ceiling, above the heads of the youngsters. When necessity required, it was easily unlooped, to be brought with a thwack on the head, or shoulders, of any luckless offender in however distant a part of the room. Intellectual progress, we may be sure, was not very rapid—and the three R's, with a little mensuration for the more advanced pupils, was the extent of the learning contemplated.

Willie Hardie continued his school up to his death, in 1879 A.D., which, curiously enough, was almost co-incident with the opening of the Board School in the village.

He served his generation and then—his work being done—fell asleep.

> "The master is dead, and the schoolmates are fled,
> Wand'ring the wild world o'er;
> Some sleep in the grave, and some over the wave,
> Whose faces we see no more."

This school was the only one that Robert Collyer ever attended—and this only from four to eight years of age.

No merciful legislation, at that time, protected those who could not protect themselves; and at the age of eight years Robert was put to work at the factory. There were no half-timers, and no half holidays, in those days, but from six o'clock in the morning to eight at night, it was work, work, work, for young children, tender women, and strong men alike.

At this employment the child remained for six years, evidently, in spite of circumstances, not unhappy years. Home influences, and the buoyant spirits of childhood, could sweeten even ceaseless labour. The following sketch of his early home is from his own pen.

"But in those brave old days, while the first fifteen years were passing, which do so much for us all, there we were altogether in one of the sweetest cottage homes that ever nestled under green leaves in a green valley. There was a plum tree, and a rose tree, and wealth of ivy, and a bit of greensward, outside; and inside, one room on the floor, and two above; a floor of flags scoured white, so that you might eat your dinner on it, and no harm done except to the floor; walls whitewashed to look like driven snow, with pictures of great Bible figures hung where there was room; and, in their own places, kept as bright as to be so many dusky mirrors, the great mahogany chest of drawers and high-cased clock, polished elm chairs, and corner cupboard for the china which was only got out at high festivals; a bright, open, sea-coal fire, always alight, winter and summer; with all sorts of common things for common use stowed away snug and tight in their own corners, like the goods and chattels of Ed'ard

Cuttle, mariner. That was the home in the day of small things, when the world was young and the glory of life was in its spring."

At 15 years of age Robert passed out of this home to a very different one.

There resided at Ilkley—over the moors,—in Wharfedale, a man, John Birch, of the same trade as Samuel Collyer and who, in early days, had befriended him in some way. Birch had also married Frances, or "Frankie" Robinson of Bluberhouses, which may have led to the continuance of his acquaintance with the Collyers. To this man, Robert was apprenticed to learn the trade of a blacksmith, and took up his abode in his master's house at Ilkley. Here he continued to reside from this time, 1839 A.D., until he married, and emigrated to the United States. And while here, under most adverse circumstances, he built up the edifice of the wide knowledge of books, of men, and things, manifested in his after life. With his working tool in one hand and a book in the other, he diligently used both. We are told of him, that while working at the anvil, or standing by the forge, he had a book, held open by scraps of iron, on a shelf by his side. He, and three or four other youths, united together, in their leisure hours, for mutual instruction and self culture; their money was clubbed to obtain good books, and,—in the summer time, retiring to the fields and hill sides, and in the long winter evenings by the light of a common candle,—they pored over their treasures together. The passion for reading, which, in childhood's days in the forest, devoured "The Pilgrim's Progress," and "Robinson Crusoe," was now turned to mastering such works as the "Encyclopœdia Britannica," the best English Reviews and Macauley's Essays.

Thus employed years passed away. In 1844 A.D., Samuel Collyer, the father, died, very suddenly, as he stood at his anvil, and the old home at West Houses was broken up.

To his trade, and his studies, Robert added, about 1848 A.D., the work of a local preacher among the Methodists;

and this led him to visit, and ever since take an interest in, many of the neighbouring villages and dales.

The impulse, which has moved so many of his fellow-countrymen to seek a home and position, in the New World, became too strong to be resisted in Collyer; and in 1850 A.D. he married, and immediately afterwards quitted the shores of old England for those of the United States of America. He settled near Philadelphia, and for eight or nine years, there followed his trade of a blacksmith; on Sundays still going forth as a local Methodist preacher. But during this time, his continued assiduous self culture, education, and mental and moral force of character, were steadily bringing him to the fore among men. His religious views, seem, however, to have drifted away from the old creed of John Wesley, and John Wesley's dearly loved Mother Church, and a separation ensued. Unfortunately he found the ranks of Unitarianism to afford him a more congenial sphere, and removed to the quickly rising city of Chicago, where for some time he was employed as a missionary among the poor, and the young men, of the city.

In 1859 A.D. he was ordained to the pastorate of the, then lately formed, congregation known as Unity Church. His ministry in this charge from that time, until he quitted it in 1879 A.D. for that of the church of the Messiah in New York, seems to have been one of the most popular in the United States. As a preacher his fame spread to the old world, as through the new. He was sought to occupy important pastorates in other cities but declined to remove. In 1869 A.D. a very magnificent edifice was erected for him by the congregation at the cost of 210,000 dollars. At its opening, on the 20th of June in that year, the offertory amounted to 57,000 dollars (£11,500), which is said to have been the largest offertory ever made in America, and probably, in the world. Two years later, that is in 1871 A.D., occurred the disastrous fire in Chicago which reduced the principal portion of the city to ashes, and among other of its stately edifices, Unity Church. This was a heavy blow to its pastor. His own home was consumed, and almost every member of his congregation suffered great loss. An appreciative chronicler says, "It (Unity Church) had not merely been built for him but built by him, and was his pride and joy. When further effort was hopeless, that great stricken poet preacher was led away, blind, and nearly distracted, from excess of exertion and exposure to smoke and dust. He recovered his sight, however, and on the following Sunday he gathered his people around him in the open air, and preached on the sorrow that had befallen them all, comforting and exhorting them all to a good courage. He ended his sermon by a brief reference to his own position. He would stay by his people, he said. He did not think they could find a cheaper parson, he had preached one year for 75 cents and could do it again if necessary. He could support himself, for the present, by lecturing, and, as a last resource, he could make as good a horse-shoe as any blacksmith in Chicago."

It was some similar allusion to his olden life, that led the students, of one of the rising Universities of the west, to commission Collyer to forge for them a horse-shoe, at 1,050 dollars, which they raised among themselves. He accepted the commission and did the work, and the shoe now figures among the treasured objects of the Academic Museum.

From all parts of the States, and from England, offerings came flowing in to repair the loss, and a second Unity Church, more capacious than the former, but less costly and magnifical, arose without the pastor having to resort to his old trade, "and the pulpit of that church is to this day one of the noblest and mightiest civilizing powers in the great west."

Two volumes of sermons,—"Nature and life," and "The Life that now is," and a pleasant little book, "Simple truth," are the best known, but form only a portion of his many sermons, lectures, and essays, which have found their way to the general public both in England and

America. These have gone through several editions, one of them, "Nature and Life" was in its 10th edition in 1876 A.D. The sermons are brim full of the poetry of the sorrows, trials, joys, aspirations, and hopes of humanity. All the beautiful fragments of the broken Divine Image in man are admirably delineated. The wellings up of a large, generous, manly heart are manifest on every page. But, as might be expected, there is, to an English churchman, the lack of the restoring, binding dogma of the Church's creed. Without this a churchman must regard all teaching as incomplete. In these volumes, truth is presented like fair, lovely, and loving woman, beautiful and noble in herself, but incomplete without the force, the power, the hard muscle and firm bone of man, on which to lean. There is, throughout them, the poetry of the Divine Fatherhood, and of manhood, wanting the uniting bond of the God-man, with the certainty, and stay, of definite Divine Revelation to rest upon. But this must necessarily be the case, from the position the worthy author has taken up in Theology, and what to us seem to be the defects of his doctrine, probably are to him its greatest attractions.

However this may be, these volumes are deserving of the notice they have attracted. As a preacher, and lecturer, none is more sought after than their author, and none more popular throughout the length and breadth of his adopted country. The highest literary and intellectual society is open to him, while his name is a household word in America, and not unknown on this side of the water—certainly not unknown in the forest.

How the factory boy, from the forest in the old country, has become one of the first preachers, literary, and intellectual men, of the great new one in the west, must ever be a leaf from the forest's history, instructive, as it is romantic! Two stanzas from a poem, "Saxon grit," by Collyer, perhaps bear upon the origin of the romance.

"Then rising afar in the western sea,
A new world stood in the morn of day,
Ready to welcome the brave and free,
Who could wrench out the heart and march away
From the narrow, contracted, dear old land,
Where the poor are held by a cruel bit,
To ample spaces for heart and hand,
And here was a chance for the Saxon grit.

* * * * * *

Then slow and sure, as the oaks have grown,
From the acorns that fell on that old dim day,
To this new manhood in city and town,
To a nobler stature shall grow alway;
Winning by inches, holding by clinches,
Slow to contention, and slower to quit,
Now and then failing, but never once quailing;
Let us thank God for the Saxon grit."

The Rev. Robert Collyer is now (1881 A.D.) pastor of the church of the Messiah in New York, a charge to which he was reluctantly induced to remove, from his first love in Chicago, in 1879 A.D.

In 1865 A.D., and 1871 A.D., and again in 1878 A.D., he visited the old country, and his forest home, to which he clings with an affection characteristic of his strong, tender nature. Views of it, and of the surrounding scenery, adorn his rooms in New York. On his last visit, he delivered a lecture, in the New School-room at Fewston, on an interesting episode in the village history two hundred and sixty years ago. And his Archæological and Historical knowledge of the neighbourhood—and especially of Ilkley and its surroundings,—is almost unequalled, while his collection of Yorkshire books is perhaps the largest in America.

The following anecdote related in Harper's Magazine some years ago, together with two or three reminiscences of his childhood's forest home, from his own tongue or pen, will aptly close this notice of Robert Collyer.

"The smithy" (in which Collyer had worked at Ilkley) "was drawing near to its day of disappearance. But before that day arrived, a gentleman appeared at the door and inspected, with some interest, an anvil standing in the centre of the shop.

'How long has that anvil been here?' he asked of the blacksmith?

'Why,' said the workman, 'it must have been here thirty or forty year.'

'Well,' said the gentleman, 'I will give you twice as much for that anvil as will buy you a new one.'

'Certainly,' replied the puzzled smith; 'but I would like to know what you want with this anvil.'

'I will tell you. There was formerly an apprentice in this shop who used to work at it. That boy has now become a great man. Thousands love and honour him as a friend and a teacher, and I wish to carry back this anvil, to America, as a memorial of the humble beginning of his life.'

The bargain was completed, and the anvil is now in Chicago."—

Harper's Magazine.

In a speech delivered in London, June 3rd, 1871 A.D. Collyer, said: "There has never been a moment, in the 21 years that I have been absent from this land, when it has not been one of my proudest recollections, that I came of this grand old English stock, that my grandfather fought with Nelson at Trafalgar; and my father was an Englishman, and my mother an Englishwoman, and that so far as I can trace my descent back and back,—and that is just as far as my grandfather—we are all English, every one of us. Well, there is not a day when I stand on the lake shore that I do not see the moors, that are lifted up about my old habitation, and a little stone cottage nestling in among the greenery, and the glancing waters, and the lift of the lark with his song up into heaven until you cannot see him, and a hundred other things besides that belong to this blessed place of my birth and breeding."

—*The Inquirer, June 3rd,* 1871 A.D.

"There was an old well at which I used to drink when I was a boy. I thought there was no well like it in the world,—clear, brown water distilled from the moors. I longed to drink again of that well through all the years I lived in this new world, as David longed to drink of the well at Bethlehem. I went back at last, and drank deep of it; but the water did not taste quite so sweet as I expected. I went again, and just put my lips to the water for love of the old memories. I went again last summer but one. An old peasant woman was filling her pitcher there. I began to ask her about the life which was one with mine once, and has passed away. She was a living chronicle,—told me a wealth of things I longed to know,—of life and death, sorrow and joy, shadow and shine, touching and pathetic some of them beyond imagination,—

took up her pitcher and went home; and I went my way with wet tears, and was ever so far from the old well before I bethought me that I had not even wet my lips this time. I did not care any more for the sweet, hazel-brown, water. I had been seeing visions of the soul's life."—*Sermon-Unity Pulpit, Boston, Feb.* 1881 *A.D.*

"Again," he writes, "I want to tell, what one of my children used to call, a true story."

"It came to me one day when I went on a pilgrimage to a huge old factory, in the valley of the Washburn in Yorkshire, in the summer of 1865 A.D. The handful of people left there then were at work among the wheels and spindles, watching me between whiles; for strangers seldom came to that remote place, and I was clearly a stranger; and then my dress was not what they were used to, especially my American "wide-awake." They were as strange to me, as I was to them. There was not a face I knew, no not one. And yet this was where I was once as well-known to everybody as the child is to its mother, and where I knew everybody as I knew my own kinsfolk; for it was here that I began life, and lived it for a space that now seems a lifetime all to itself. And this brings me to my dream.

I saw in one of the great dusty rooms of the factory, a little fellow about eight years old, but big enough to pass for ten, working away from six o'clock in the morning till eight at night, tired almost sometimes to death, and then again not tired at all, rushing out when work was over, and, if it was winter, home to some treasure of a book. There was "Robinson Crusoe," and "Bunyan's Pilgrim," and "Goldsmith's Histories of England and Rome," and the first volume of "Sandford and Merton," and one or two more that had something to do with theology. . . . . .

One of these books, that used to lead all boys captive in those good old days, this boy, I saw in my dream, would hug up close to his bowl of porridge, and eat and read; and then would read after he had done eating, while ever the careful house-mother would allow a candle or a coal. But, if it was summer time, the books would be neglected, and the rush would be out into the elds and lanes, hunting, in the early summer, for birds' nests the tender and holy home canon would never permit to be robbed, and it was always obeyed; or, in the later summer, seeing whether the sloes were turning ever so little from green to black, or whether the crabs (of the wood, not the water) were vulnerable to a boy's sharp and resolute teeth, and when the hazel-nuts would be out of that milky state at which it would be of any use to pluck them, and what was the prospect for hips and haws.

The men who profess to know just how we are made, as a watchmaker knows a watch, tell us that once in seven years we get a brand new body; and that old things become new. I wonder sometimes if it is not so with our life. Is *that* new as well as the frame? There I was that day, a grey-haired minister from a city which had been born and had come to its great place, since the small lad began to work in the old mill as I saw him at the end of a vista of four and thirty years!

I watched him with a most pathetic interest. 'Dear little chap,' I said, 'you had a hard time; but then it was a good time too,—wasn't it, now?' How good bread and butter did taste, to be sure, when half a pound of butter a week had to be divided among eight of us, and white wheaten bread saved for Sunday! Did ever a flower in this world beside smell as good as the primrose, or prima donna sing like the skylark and throstle? Money cannot buy such a Christmas pudding, or tears, or prayers, such a Christmas-tide as the mother made, and the Lord gave, when you and the world were young. Seven years you stuck to the old mill, and then you were only fifteen; and then, just when they were crowning the Queen, you know, you had to give it up, and to give the home up with it, and to go out, and never return to stay. And so I lost sight of you out of that hard but blessed life in and out of the factory, and have never set eyes on you until to-day,—you dear little other-one, that was dead and is alive again, was lost and is found!

This is my story, and I tell it as a word of encouragement to many who may need such a word, about the way of life which I have travelled many miles since I set out, not knowing whither I went, to the pulpit and pastorate of Unity Church."

"*The Simple Truth*"—"*Looking back.*" 1878 *A.D*

He *now* would say "this is my story of the way which I have travelled, many miles since I set out, not knowing whither I went, to the pulpit and pastorate of the Church of the Messiah at New-York, and to the primacy of the Unitarian Church in the United States."

The following "Story in Rhyme," as he calls it, is from Collyer's pen, and may fitly find a place among "Lays and Leaves of the Forest."

UNDER THE SNOW.

It was Christmas eve in the year 'fourteen,
  And, as ancient dalesmen used to tell,
The wildest winter they ever had seen,—
  With the snow lying deep on moor and fell.

When waggoner John got out his team,—
  Smiler, and Whitefoot, Duke and Gray,
With the light in his eyes of the young man's dream;
  As he thought of his wedding on New Year's day,

To Ruth, the maid of the bonnie brown hair,
  And eyes of the deepest blue,—
Modest and winsome and wondrous fair;
  And true to her troth, for her heart was true.

"Thou's surely not going?" shouted mine host;
  "Thou'll be lost in the drift as sure as thou's born;
Thy lass winnot want to wed wi' a ghost,—
  And that's what thou'll be on Christmas morn.

It's eleven long miles from Skipton toon,
  To Blueberg hooses and Washburn dale,
Thou had better turn back and sit thee doon,
  And comfort thy heart wi' a drop o' good ale."

Turn the swallows flying south!
  Turn the vines against the sun!
Herds from rivers in the drouth!
  Men must dare or nothing's done.

So what cares the lover for storm or drift,
  Or, peril of death on the haggard way,
He sings to himself like a lark in the lift,
  And the joy in his heart turns December to May.

But the wind from the north brings its deadly chill
  Creeping into his heart, and the drifts are deep;
Where the thick of the storm strikes Blueberg hill,
  He is weary, and falls, in a pleasant sleep;

And dreams he is walking by Washburn side,—
  Walking with Ruth on a summer's day,—
Singing that song to his bonnie bride,—
  His own wife now for ever and aye.

Now read me this riddle. How Ruth should hear
  That song of a heart, in the clutch of doom?
It stole on her ear, distinct and clear,
  As if her lover was in the room.

And read me this riddle. How Ruth should know,
  As she bounds to throw open the heavy door,
That her lover is lost in the drifting snow,—
  Dying, or dead, on the great wild moor?

"Help! Help!" "Lost! Lost!"
Rings through the night as she rushes away,
Stumbling, blinded, and tempest-tossed,—
Straight to the drift where her lover lay.

And swift they leap after her into the night,—
Into the drifts by Bluberg hill,—
Pullan, Ward, Robinson, each with his light,
To find her there, holding him, white and still!

"He was dead in the drift, then?"
I hear them say,
As I listen in wonder,—
Forgetting to play,
Fifty years since come Christmas day.

"Nay, nay, they were wed," the dalesman cried,
"By parson Carmalt o' New Year's day;
Bonnie Ruth were me great-great-grandsire's bride,
And Maister Frankland gave her away."

"But, how did she find him under the snow?"
They cried with a laughter touched with tears.
"Nay, lads," he said softly, "we never can know,
No, not if we live a hundred years."

"There's a sight o' things gan'
To the making o' man."
Then I rushed to my play,
With a whoop and away,
Fifty years syne come Christmas day.

A FORESTER'S RETURN.

"The free fair homes of England!
Long, long, in hut and hall,
May hearts of native proof be reared
To guard each hallowed wall!
And green for ever be the groves,
And bright the flowery sod,
Where first the child's glad spirit loves
Its country and its God."
—*Mrs. Hemans.*

OF Switzerland's dark rocks, I'm told, and mountains capp'd with snow,
Of fountains and of famed lakes, in deep green vales below;
Of fair Italia's sunny skies, with Lombard's fruitful plain,
Of purple vineyards in France; and German's golden grain;
Of Norway's pine-clad hills, with streams of silver foaming down;
Of orange groves in sunny Spain, whose fruits the gods might own;
Of scenes of glory bright, I'm told, in ancient East the best;
Of prairies, mountains, forests grand, far in the glowing West.
To none of these affection turns,
For none of these the exile yearns.

On Snowdon's hoary top I've stood, and looked o'er lovely Wales;
From foot to head I've wandered through the beauteous Yorkshire dales;
Killarney's emerald glades I've seen, and eke her silvery flood,
Scotia's "mountains stern and wild, brown heath and shaggy wood;"
In cities' tinsel glare new scenes, new joys, and friends, I've met;
Friends whose love, and loving care, no time will e'er forget;
And in the world's wide Senate House some honours I have won,
In halls of rich and great have stood, when wit and beauty shone.
Yet not to these does memory cling,
Nor yet of these the poet sing.

The home of youth in forest glen—its green or rocky nooks;
Ancestral woods resounding loud, with caw of clam'rous rooks,
The grand old trees beneath whose shade, in noontide heat I played,
The heath-dyed burn on whose green banks, a truant boy, I strayed;
The fields, and braes, and wide brown moors, or deep thick-wooded dell,
Where first I plucked the primrose pale, the crow-foot, or hare-bell;
The grey crag tall by which I built my mimic house, or huts,
The coppice grove where free I sought spring nests, or autumn nuts.
To these it is that memory clings,
And 'tis of these the poet sings.

Schoolmates too with whom full oft the rock's high crest I scaled,
Or, wandering on the Pleasant Mount, by well-known signals hailed;
The village maidens, brown and bright, with eyes of mirth and truth,
That, like the sun of morning, lit the erôsian blush of youth;
A father's care, and guiding hand laid gently on my head,
The sense of watchful love and rest, a mother's smile can shed;
The church whose time-worn turret grey just peeping through the trees;
The dulcet peal of Sabbath bells as borne on evening breeze.
To these it is affection turns,
For these it is a wanderer yearns.

World-weary and storm-tossed I seek, where them I found of yore,
Alas; to find that there, for me, they now exist no more;
The home, which deep in memory dwells, is far, though seems so nigh;
And ev'ry well-known object round wakes but a plaintive sigh.
I look around. The tree yet stands, and children love its shade;
And *there* the fields; and *there* the crag with marks long since I made;
And *there* the burn, and *there* the flowers, the lane, the wood, the wold,
And children gambol there to-day, as we gamboll'd of old!
And still to these affection clings,
And 'tis of these the poet sings.

The playmates who with me were joined, in sports in heat or snow,
Now know not him they knew so well ere furrows marked his brow,
And though I pass their daily haunts, they raise no kenning eye,
To me, once of themselves, but *now*, "a stranger passing by!"
And many, O *how* many, with whom the path of youth I trod,
Have lived, and loved, and sleep now deep beneath the green, green sod!
From where, at noon or eve, we met, in places then our homes,
I'm bid to seek and con their names, writ on the mouldering tombs!
To these the lamps of memory burn,
For these the exile's feet return.

And gone the dearest ones of all, who hailed with joy my birth,
Whose love and care once made their home, the home to me on earth;
That home beloved, of them bereft, has lost its dearest ties,
And now exists but where they rest—at home—beyond the skies.
Yet 'tis with tears, dear home of youth, and sorrow quick with pain,
That after exile, sorrow, toil, I look on thee again.
Unchanged! yet deepest scars of change, on every side are seen!
Unchanged! so changed thou ne'er canst be, to me, what thou hast been!
Yet long to such affection clings,
And 'tis of these the poet sings.

God's House yet stands, and points on high, as it hath done of old,
While generations long have passed, and ages slowly rolled;
There by One Spirit, in one faith, God's children still upraise,
With heart and voice, the earnest prayer, and anthem, loud, of praise.
Faint type of that Rock-founded Church, which ne'er can pass away.
But stands, unchanging, and unchanged, through the eternal day,
Beneath thy shade, O lay me down when here my work is done,
There let me sleep, with dear ones left, and those whose crown is won;
And let the fragrance from the spot, where stood the forest home,
By summer's breath, or autumn winds, be wafted o'er our tomb!
The exile home for this returns,
It is to this hope brightly burns.

THE REV. CANON STUBBS, D.D.

FOREMOST among the men, who have sprung from forest-ancestry, stands the Rev. William Stubbs D.D., Canon of St. Paul's London, and Regius Professor of Modern History in the University of Oxford. By universal consent he is accorded a high place among the living Historians of this country.

In the Lay-Subsidy Roll (given elsewhere among these leaves) of the 2nd year of Richard II. (1378-9 A.D.),—under the heading "Wappentachium de Clarrowe, villa de Clynt,"—occurs the entry "Willelmus Stubbe et uxor ejus."

The home of "William Stubbe and his wife," was at Birstwith, then included in "Villa de Clint." Surnames were only, at that period, coming into general use, and this William was probably the first who bore that of Stubbe. Even in his grandson's time, fifty years later, the name seems scarcely to have become fixed, as a family one, but was still "de" Stubbe, or Stubbes. The derivation is most probably from "stob," or "stub," the root end of a broken tree. Such an object, or objects, may have existed in the vicinity of the family residence, hence the members would receive the designation "*de*," *i.e.* "of," Stubb, or Stubbs.*

* "About 1350 A.D. flourished Thomas de Stoubbes or Stubs, who was born at York, or at least in Yorkshire, and entered the Order of Black Friars at York, and became Master of Theology. He was remarkable for ecclesiastical learning, and regular life. He was ordained Priest December 20th 1343 A.D. in Durham Cathedral, but the date of his death is unknown. From his learned pen fourteen valuable works proceeded."—*Yorkshire Archæological Society's Journal part xxiii.*

William Stubbe of 1379 A.D. had a son, also named William, and his son John de Stubbes, in 1430 A.D. was an officer—"*the Grave*"—of the Forest of Knaresborough.

John de Stubbes's son, William Stubbes, resided at Ripon, but John de Stubbes's property at Birstwith descended, in 1442 A.D., to William's son, Thomas.

This Thomas Stubbs of Ripon, was followed, in the succession, by his son, also named Thomas, a little before 1490 A.D. The second Thomas was also "*Grave*" of the Forest,—and, therefore, had probably returned to residence at Birstwith,—in 1498 A.D. His brother, William Stubbs, was chaplain, in 1516 A.D., to the Shepherd Lord Clifford of Skipton and Barden, and may have had something to do —let us hope not,—with that scape-grace son, the "Madcap Harry," of whom the father writes so despairingly in 1512 or 1513 A.D.

Thomas Stubbs died in 1535 A.D., and his son and successor, Miles Stubbs, died in 1555 A.D. Miles left two sons. William, the elder, married Alice Bilton, and went to reside at Felliscliffe. John, the other brother, also resided at the same place.

William of Fellliscliffe died in 1575 A.D. His third son was Thomas Stubbs, who resided at Whitewall and died there, in 1648 A.D., aged 75 years.

Thomas, the son of Thomas of Whitewall, was connected by marriage with the Atkinsons, who held one of the principal farms, under the Ingilby family of Ripley, at Håverah Park, and, between 1664 A.D. and 1672 A.D., he succeeded Thomas Atkinson there as tenant.

His son Thomas Stubbs of Haverah Park, born 1650 A.D., married Alice Simpson of Clint, and died in 1716 A.D.

Though tenants of the farm in Haverah Park, the family was of substantial yeoman rank, owning considerable property in the neighbourhood. The eldest son of Thomas, and his successor in the farm, was John Stubbs; whose granddaughter Ann Stubbs—only child of his son also named John Stubbs of Haverah Park—married in 1774 A.D., Thomas Parkinson of Cragg Hall, and was grandmother of the present writer. As the sole heiress of her father she brought considerable landed, and other property, to the family.

The fourth son of the last Thomas of Haverah Park was Joseph Stubbs, who broke away from the family home, and resided at Greystone plain, in Fellliscliffe. He had three sons. (1) Thomas; (2) Joseph; and (3) William who resided in London, and from whom is descended the Rev. Stewart Dixon Stubbs, vicar of St. James's, Pentonville.

Thomas Stubbs, the eldest son, born in 1735 A.D., removed to Ripley, and thence, he, or his descendants, successively, to Boroughbridge and Knaresborough, where, in the last generation, the family occupied the position of wine merchants, bankers and solicitors.

At Knaresborough, in 1825 A.D., the great-grandson of Thomas Stubbs of Ripley was born—William Stubbs, the subject of this article.

He was educated at Knaresborough and at the Grammar School at Ripon, and thence proceeded, under the ptronage of Bishop Longley, to Christ Church Oxford, where he took the degree of B.A. in 1848 A.D., with first-class honours; and was in the same year ordained Deacon, by the Bishop of Oxford, and Priest in 1850 A.D. He was Fellow of Trinity College in Oxford from 1848 A.D. to 1851 A.D., and in the latter year, took his M.A.

From 1850 A.D. to 1867 A.D. he held the College Living of Navestock in Essex. In 1858 A.D. he published "Registrum Sacrum Anglicanum," a work alone sufficient to hand down the name of its author, as a man of learning, untiring research, and accuracy of statement, to future ages. The late Archbishop of Canterbury, in 1862 A.D., appointed Mr. Stubbs, librarian and keeper of the manuscripts, of the Archiepiscopal Library at Lambeth Palace, —an office which he resigned in 1867 A.D.

In the preceding year he had been nominated to the Regius Professorship of Modern History in his University, and he again took up residence in Oxford. He is Honorary Student of Christ Church, Curator of the Bodleian Library and of the Taylor Institute, Delegate of the Press, member of the Hebdomadal Council, and also of many Royal and other, British and Foreign, learned societies.

Since his return to Oxford, one valuable historical work after another has been edited by him, or has flowed forth from his deep, and accurate researches, and facile pen. The greatest of these works is, undoubtedly, the "Constitutional History of England," in three volumes, from the earliest times to the accession of the first of the Tudors. It is devoutly to be hoped, that opportunity, in the midst of his many labours, may be given to enable him to continue this most valuable and exhaustive work, through, at least, the important epochs of the Tudors and Stuarts.

This "leaf" shall conclude with the testimony of two, from among that of many scholars and writers of note, to Dr. Stubbs's work and position as a Historian. The following is by Edward A. Freeman Esq., F.S.A., given in a lecture on "*Points in Early Northumberland History*," delivered at Hull, and afterwards published in *Macmillan's Magazine*, for September 1876 :—

"On later times I will not enter ; I need not read in your ears the long bede-roll of the worthies of your shire. Among the honoured names of Northern England I will name but one, the latest, but not the least. It is by no unfitting cycle that the list of the great historians of England, which began with a man of Bernicia, ends, as yet, with a man of Deira. The line which began with Beeda goes on, through Simeon of Durham and Roger of Howden and other worthy names, till, in our own day, the same Northern land has sent forth, in Professor Stubbs, the most life-life portrait painter of English kings, and the most profound expounder of the English constitution. From one, who lived at Jarrow and who sleeps at Durham, the torch has been handed on to one, who has come forth from Knaresborough and Ripon, to make the form of the second Henry stand before us as a living man, to make the legislation of the first Edward stand before us as a living thing."

The next is from an account of "*The Constitutional History of England*," by a writer in the *Quarterly Review*, January—April 1879 A.D.

"We have intimated that, in respect to the main flow of the English constitution, there has been little left for Mr. Stubbs's erudition to discover. But in those numerous details of the current, which form most important episodes of our History, Mr. Stubbs is ever increasing our knowledge, not only from the stores of his investigation, in which he has no superior, past or present, but from that profound insight, which makes old, and well known, facts luminous with new ideas. These important volumes will make English History a new study, and a new pleasure, for this generation. We only wish Mr. Stubbs may be induced to continue his work, into the later reigns. Such a guide in the Stuart period, for instance, would be invaluable.

"We cannot but express our great satisfaction, that the eminent services, which Mr. Stubbs has thus rendered to the cause of sound learning, have at length received due recognition and encouragement. His recent appointment to a Canonry in St. Paul's Cathedral, is one of the most conspicuous instances of the justice and discernment, with which the ecclesiastical patronage of the Crown, has of late been generally administered. Upon no one could the post have been more worthily bestowed, and such a nomination confers honour upon the Prime Minister, as well as Mr. Stubbs."

It was in 1879 A.D. that the late Earl of Beaconsfield, then Prime Minister, nominated, on behalf of the Crown, Professor Stubbs to the Canonry, vacated by the promotion of Dr. Lightfoot to the See of Durham, in the Cathedral Church of St. Paul, London. His University on the occasion, conferred on him the degree of Doctor of Divinity, and on the same day he was made honorary LL.D. at Cambridge. The graceful act, on the part of the Premier, was received, by all parties, with much favour, as the recognition of great erudition, and untiring industry, and merited the encomium of the Reviewer as being equally to the honour "of him who gave and him who took."

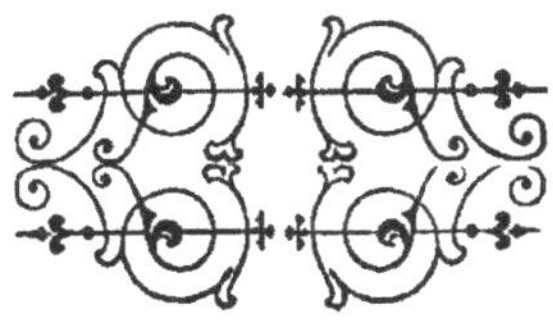

THE INSCRIPTIONS ON THE BELLS.

The two bells of St. Michael's Church, North Otterington, bear the following inscriptions: the smaller bell, "Holiness to the Lord, A.D. 1658." The other, "Jehove sanctitatem consonemus soror parvula: A.D. 1689."

YES! wide our notes of invitation fling
On Sabbath morn, with song and sunshine round,
And hallow the very breezes with the sound,
By which God's servants to His House we ring.
O, little sister, ever thus let us chime with one accord,
O'er lea, and hill, and hamlet, "Holiness to the Lord."

And when again we hail the bridal day,
And beating hearts, in youthful ardour light,
Their holy vows before our altar plight,
As with glad step they start on life's brief way;
O, little sister, let us sweetly ring with high accord,
To bridegroom, and to bride, "Holiness to the Lord."

But when, around, the scene is one of woe,
And forth we send the sad funereal knell,
To breasts that full, with anguish, sink and swell,
And burning tears of dark bereavement flow;
O, little sister, let us toll, alone, or in accord,
O'er fatherless and widow, "Holiness to the Lord."

O, spare us time! O, spoiler's hand pass by!
Still let our notes resound, nor make us cease
To bear our message of eternal peace,
Till saints of earth, with angel-hosts on high,
Take up, O little sister, *there*, our song with glad accord,
And through eternal ages sing, "Holiness to the Lord."

WILLIAM GRAINGE; THE HISTORIAN OF THE FOREST.

"If there's a hole in a' your coats,
I rede ye tent it;
A chiel's amang ye takin' notes,
And, faith, he'll prent it."
—*Burns.*

SOME fifteen or twenty years ago, the curiosity of the dwellers in every part of the forest, was exercised by the visits, at intervals, of a kindly, pleasant, enquiring visitor. At that time visitors there were few. He made his way to the remote farm-houses; an old bank, or earthwork, was to him a special delight; the ancient halls and houses of the yeomen-foresters of the present, or bygone times, were carefully scanned, and their inhabitants questioned about their *fore-elders*, and about any old documents they possessed, likely to elucidate those mysteries of the past, to which the memories of the oldest could offer no clue. The parsons also received several visits; the churches were objects of great attention; and over those queer, old, parchment-covered books — the parish registers—it was said "he spent hours together."

In spite of some native suspicion, the visitor made many friends. The clergy, and other intelligent inhabitants, were glad to see him, and to open their old oak desks and deed boxes, or parish registers, freely to his scrutiny.

Soon interesting columns began to appear in the local newspapers. There were accounts given of old halls, and of worthy fore-elders, and descriptions of pleasant walks, and of charming nooks and corners in the forest, none of which had ever been written about before.

The foresters discovered that they had a history: and that they, and their fathers, and their forest homes, had a place in the annals of the great county of York, and of England. Kings had even been visitors to the forest; generals, and poets, and men of renown in literature, and other things, had really sprung from among themselves!

A few years later, and the writer of these things new and old, published them all in a book, which took its place among the best of the local histories of the county.

This enquirer and writer was *William Grainge*—the painstaking, worthy, and respected historian of the forest. Though not by birth "a forester," his great interest in, and love for, the forest; the service he has done it by his admirable history, together with a residence for many years within its bounds, will plead for a forester claiming him as one of the most worthy of the brotherhood, and giving in these "Leaves" some account of him and of his works.

For the following sketch of the early life of William Grainge, the writer is indebted to "*The Biograph*" for March, 1881 A.D.

He was born on the 25th of January, 1818 A.D., and brought up on his father's farm, called Castiles, in the parish of Kirkby Malzeard, about eight miles west of Ripon, just on the verge of the western moorlands. This farm had been in the possession of the family for nearly three centuries. William was the youngest survivor of several children. The place was quiet and lonely, the scenery around was beautiful, and some of it wild and romantic. The remains of an old British circle, or fort, were situated near the house, and the contemplation, of this mysterious series of earthworks and trenches, in his youthful days, may, in some measure, account for his early love for antiquarian pursuits. The school education he received was at Kirkby Malzeard; it was merely rudimentary, and did not extend much beyond his twelfth year; hence he may be classed among self-educated writers. From his youth he was remarkably fond of reading, and as soon as he had the opportunity of becoming acquainted with them, "Dove's English Classics" became his especial favourites; being small pocket volumes they were well adapted for his purpose, and were his constant companions when at work—for he shared in all the labours of his father's farm—and at noon, or other times, while others rested or slept, he read. In his youth he was fond of rambling into wild and lonely places, where the hand of man had done nothing to mend, or mar, the beauties of nature. Alone he explored all the valleys, woods, glens, and ravines within half a dozen miles of his home, and thus acquired a love of wild natural scenery, geology, and botany, which has stuck to him through life. And, even yet, such rambles among woods, rocks, and wild flowers constitute one of his greatest enjoyments. At this early period he also attempted to write poetry, and produced verses on a great variety of subjects, some of which were accepted, and appeared in the newspapers of York and Leeds, but always without his name attached to them. He continued thus working, reading, rambling, and always learning, at the place of his early home, until the death of his father in 1845 A.D., when he removed to the neighbourhood of Boroughbridge, where he resided for the next fifteen years.

Many of the following facts, and dates, respecting the numerous works he has published, are also from "*The Biograph.*"

In 1853 A.D. Mr. T. S. Turner, bookseller, of Boroughbridge, published a most useful and interesting book of nearly 200 pages, entitled "The History of Aldborough and Boroughbridge,"—two of the most interesting towns, historically, in the north. No name appears as author, but the preface by the publisher, contains this passage: "In the attempt to supply the public with a complete history, within as narrow limits as possible, I have spared no labour and expense. In addition to my own attention to it, I have engaged the assistance of an individual of considerable literary merit." This has been understood to refer to Mr. William Grainge, to whose pen, therefore, the history is due, and it is the earliest of his works which has come under the writer's attention.

"The Battles and Battle Fields of Yorkshire" was published in 1854 A.D. It soon became a popular book, on a popular subject, and is now out of print. "The Castles and Abbeys of Yorkshire," a similar work, was published in 1856 A.D. Next, in 1859 A.D., appeared "The Vale of Mowbray, a Historical and Topographical account of Thirsk and the neighbourhood,"—a book of nearly 400 pages, into which is condensed a mass of information, greater than found in many books of double the size. It is admirably arranged, and pleasantly written. In 1863 A.D., published by Mr. Thorpe, of Pateley Bridge, appeared "Nidderdale," also a most valuable addition to local history and topography. "The Poets and Poetry of Yorkshire," in two volumes, was issued in 1868 A.D., published at Wakefield, and dedicated to H.R.H. the Prince of Wales. In these tasteful volumes are included biographical notices of above two hundred and forty poets of the county, from Cædmon, who died in 680 A.D., down to the present time. These are preceded by a pleasantly written preface, and well chosen introductory extracts. Each poet's works are illustrated by admirably selected specimen pieces.

At intervals between these works, Mr. Grainge sent to the press many pamphlets and tracts on kindred subjects, some of them of great interest. Such were the "Guide to Harrogate," which has gone through many editions;—"A Memoir of Sir W. Slingsby";—"A Short History of Knaresborough";—"A Tract on the Geology of Harrogate"; "An Historical and Descriptive Account of Swinsty Hall," one of the most interesting of the Old Halls of the Forest;—and, in conjunction with the late Mr. C. Forrest, "A Ramble among the antient British remains on Rombold's Moor." And also, about two years ago, appeared, published by Mr. R. Ackrill of Harrogate, "The Annals of a Yorkshire Abbey,"—a popular and most useful history of Fountains Abbey.

The work, however, which enlists a forester's attention, and which is the largest and most important that Mr. Grainge has given to the public, is the one alluded to before, viz., "*The History and Topography of Harrogate and the Forest of Knaresborough.*" It was published by Mr. T. Thorpe of Pateley Bridge, in 1871 A.D., and is a large, well got up, and well written volume of over 500 pages. Of this work and its author the following account is quoted from a discriminating reviewer, Mr. J. T. Beer, F.R.S.L.:—

"Mr. Wm. Grainge of Harrogate, the well known author of several important works, * * * * has just published a very valuable addition to his former labours, in a History and Topography of Harrogate and the Forest of Knaresborough,—a large and highly poetic district, abounding in scenes of sublimity and beauty; and dusted over, as stars upon the black dome of heaven, with a countless host of those historic associations, which bind our hearts to the scenes of their enactment long ages after the events have passed away. * * * *
Mr. Grainge had prepared himself, in a great measure by his publications, for this more complete and elaborate work, which upon every page displays evidences of erudition and laborious research, illustrating the geographical, poetical, and personal history of his chosen locality."—(*Wetherby News, March 12th,* 1872.)

No one acquainted with Mr. Grainge's writings, will be surprised to learn, that he possesses considerable poetical talent, though little of its fruits has been given to the public. The following specimen is one taken from many early productions of his pen, and has not before been published.

HAPPINESS.

What is happiness? A dream! exclaims the man
  Of high, and baffled hopes, ambition foiled,
And mighty projects blasted.—They may plan,
  Contrive, and think of happiness; 'tis spoiled
By some cross accident they cannot see;
  And when they think they grasp it, it is gone,
They know not how.—A gleam upon a sea
  Of darkness! a brain-born phantom! which none
But unlearned boys and idiots strive for!

The simple minded tell a different tale,
Of the mild power they in their hearts adore:
They say she dwells in sweet sequestered vale,
From courts and camps and cities far remote;
That virtue is her mother; labour her sire,
Temperance her sister; and her chief resort
The vales and fountains; not to aspire
Her great ambition; to bring her wishes down
Equal to her wants; in simple truth to speak
Her will,—she gains but wishes not renown,
And that she is a goddess, mild and meek.
Thus have I told what both my friends declare,
Now take thy choice and seek her *here* or *there*."

"The Widow's Lament," "The Chase of the Black Fox," and one or two other poetical pieces were contributed to Ingledew's Ballads, and Songs of Yorkshire, published in 1860 A.D. From the first mentioned the following stanzas are taken:—

"What, dost thou smile? my darling child!
Thy heavy loss thou dost not know!
Thy mother's grief is frantic, wild,
For oh, thy father moulders low!

"No more will he with kindly care,
Caress thee fondly in his arms;
His loving kiss thou canst not share,
Nor lisp to him thy vain alarms.

"Forgive me, God! I wished to die,
When thou my babe so sweetly smiled;
For thee to live in hope I'll try,
My comfort left, my darling child!"

As conscious of its parent's woe,
The artless innocent upsprung,
Its arms around her neck to throw,
While to her lips its kisses clung.

Then love dissolved the mother's grief,
What mother can desert her child?
A flood of tears now brought relief,
And hope again (though faintly) smiled.

Few, if any, living men have a more full and accurate knowledge of the biography, family history, poetry, superstitions, legends, and folk-lore of the neighbourhood, than

Mr. Grainge. Among his many manuscripts is a copy of Fairfax's Dæmonology, and of the only two now existing fo Fairfax's Eclogues. These Mr. Grainge has annotated with notes personal, topographical and literary, of the greatest value. We hope the day may come when our Northern and Forest literature will be further enriched by their publication,—and that the worthy annotater may long be spared, and encouraged, to interest and instruct his wide circle of readers, and friends, from the rich stores he has amassed, by long years of patient perseverance and research.

SONNET.

WINTER.

FROM frozen north, whence icy bleak winds blow,
Comes winter, in deathlike grasp to hold,
Alike the valley, plain, and upland wold!
Now glitt'ring in her robe of virgin snow
Earth keeps Sabbath; idle lies the plough;
The birds are mute, flocks hurtle in the fold:
Man hastens home before the biting cold,
And closer nestles to his hearth's bright glow.
O'er Nature's life hath breathed the chilling breath,
And stiff and white it rests in sleep, as death.
Yet death is but the gate of life, and sleep
The slumbers that o'er wearied nature creep.
Soon life will burst the bonds, in beauty rise,
With strength renewed, beneath Spring's genial skies.

SARAH.

"Meek souls there are who little dream
Their daily strife an Angel's theme,
Or, that the rod they take so calm
Shall prove in Heaven a martyr's palm.

And there are souls that seem to dwell
Above this earth,—so rich a spell
Floats round their steps, where'er they move,
From hopes fulfill'd, and mutual love."

—*Keble*.

SHE came upon the vision,
A school-girl bright and fair
With childhood's mirth and prattle,
And flowing flaxen hair.

With joy and laughing sunshine,
She danced along the way,
To parents and to schoolmates,
The light of brightest day.

The fairest flowers of Wharfedale,—
Where all are sweet and fair,—
Ne'er shed more joy and fragrance,
Upon the balmy air,

Than she, on all around her,
Shed, e'en in gambols wild,—
The light, and joy, and sweetness,
Of a bright and happy child.

* * * * * * * *

A maiden next we saw her,
  In all a maiden's prime;
As op'ning rose, or lily,
  In early summer time.

In form and mien, "a princess"*
  Among her youthful peers;
In thought and maiden graces,
  A girl beyond her years.

Each day revealed new beauties—
  New powers of soul and mind,—
Her presence brought the sweetness
  And balm of summer wind.

The children gathered round her,
  To win her word, or smile;
For she their tears and sorrows,
  E'en deepest, could beguile.

In school, or home, or household,
  Before her sadness fled;
Where'er she moved, the fragrance
  Of love and peace, was shed;

O'er parish, as the breezes,
  'Twas borne from door to door,
It breathed in homes of plenty,
  And cottage of the poor.

Where social duties callèd,
  And grace and wit were seen,
In gentle calm and beauty,
  She reigned, uncrowned, a queen;

And held in gentlest thraldom,
  The hearts of old and young;
While on her youthful pathway
  Were choicest off'rings flung.

* * * * * * * *

* Genesis xvii 15 (Margin).

Again the scene was changed,
Chill, adverse winds had blown ;
The flower which bloomed so sweetly,
Amid their wreck was strown.

In city's crowd and scramble,
She raised her bowèd head ;
Then forth she went, still smiling,
To win the daily bread.

For others patient toiling,
She knew no rest by day ;
E'en failing health, and weakness,
Could not her efforts stay.

Through weary nights of suff'ring,
She toss'd, in hope and fears,
Still in her step shone brightness,
And kindness through her tears.

Then on through months of labour,
Of hand, and heart, and brain,
Till not longer wearied nature
Could live, and bear the strain.

The dart of death had struck her,—
Laid prostrate ev'ry power,—
As scythe, in its summer bloom,
Strikes e'en the sweetest flower.

The form that long unquestioned,
In love its sceptre swayed,—
Now on a bed of suffering
Unconscious, helpless, laid.

The head that thought for others,
And rose at ev'ry call,—
But ceased to think of kindness,
When it ceased to think at all.

The hand that toiled for others,—
No thought of gain or pelf,—
But ceased its weary labours ;
When paralyzed itself.

The heart that beat for others,—
  Drew love with ev'ry breath,—
But ceased to shed its love-glow,
  When chill'd by cold of death.

The end! It came, and found her
  A meek and heavenly child,*
When angel-arms were closing,
  She held up hers, and smiled.

The end! No less a martyr's
  Though met in peace, at home,
Than theirs who died in tortures,
  For holy faith at Rome!

The end! No less a martyr's,
  Nor with less constance borne,
Than theirs of old, whose limbs were
  By tyrant's wild beasts torn!

While yet her day was shining,
  The sun went down in love;
But light that waned ere noon-tide,
  Must brighter shine above.

And now she rests;—the faithful,—
  Her work of love, "Well done,"
Through blood of Him who bought her,
  Her crown of life is won.

The flower, which bloomed so briefly,—
  Crushed in the Father's hand,—
Has left e'en a richer fragrance
  In this,—the mourners',—land.

* St. Matthew xviii., 3.

A POET IN THE FOREST.

THE REV. J. M. ASHLEY, B.C.L.

WHILE these Lays and Leaves have been passing under the pen of the writer, the poetic muse has again awoke in the Forest.

Transplanted, in 1873 by the present Prime Minister, the Right Honourable W. E. Gladstone, from the hot-bed of busy life,—the great metropolis,—(St. Peter's Chapel, Vere Street) to the remote but pretty Vicarage of Fewston, the Rev. John Marks Ashley B.C.L., has become one of the Forest worthies, and added no little to its fame in the field of learning and literature. His many published works had before this period stamped him, "a scholar, a ripe and good one," in fields of Mediæval Theology, and of classical and patristic lore.

The following is merely a list of such works:—"The Relations of Science," 1855; "The Victory of the Spirit," 1865; "Thirteen Sermons from the Quaresimale of Quirico Rossi," 1868; "The preparation for Death, from the Italian, 1868. A Commentary on the Epistle to the Ephesians of Thomas Aquinas"; "The spiritual exercises of St. Ignatius," 1869; "Dominical and Festival Homilies of St. Thomas Aquinas," 2 Ed. 1873; "A year with Great Preachers," 2 vols. 1872; "A Festival Year with Great Preachers," 1873; "Eucharistic Sermons by Great Preachers, 1873; "A Promptuary, for Preachers," 2 vols. 8vo., 1876; "St. Augustine, the Preacher," 1877; "Origen, the Preacher," 1878; "Studies from Dantè," now publishing in "The Churchman's Shilling Magazine," and many original essays in "The Union Review,"

"The Ecclesiastic" and other Journals. The Homilies of St. Thomas Aquinas and "The Promptuary" have had a very extensive sale.

But it is under the inspiring breezes, and beauties, of the forest valley, that the muse has awakened the sweet notes within, and stirred him to enrich the forest literature with the songs of his rural retirement.

Already he has published "Lisa," "The Burial of Polynices," both classical poems of much beauty. "The Battle of Senlac and other Poems" (in 1880), an 8vo. vol. of 175 pages; besides a large number of poetical pieces of merit, including many Hymns, in several local, and other, publications.

The following on local objects, or suggested by them, are selected as the most suitable specimens of his muse for reproduction here :—

ANNIE'S VISIT.

The churchyard lay on hilly slope,
High on the sunny side;
Below it spread the bright green fields,
And lake extending wide.

It was a summer's afternoon,
And balmy was the air;
When seated on a little grave
Was mourning maiden fair.

She sat and plucked some blades of grass,
Torn off the tiny grave;
Among her treasures sacredly
These lovingly to save.

On a like sunny afternoon,
Some months before, in spring,
Around that self-same grave she stood
In sorrow worshipping;

Which then was opened to receive
A younger sister, whom
The *Master* called,—a lovely plant,—
In paradise to bloom.

She now had come some spoil to take,
Some relic from the ground,
In which her little sister had
A place of resting found.

With brightened blush and tear-gemmed eye,
  She trembling mention made
Of one, whose little body lay
  In that small quiet grave.

Whilst health and youth and beauty graced
  The maiden who survived,
The other girl was food for worms,
  The little one who died.

Scanned by the eye of sense alone,
  Who can their lots compare?
Viewed by the eye of faith, to change
  Their portions, who would dare?

The dead child lives an angel's life,
  An angel now in light;
Removed from every earthly taint,
  With spirit ever bright.

The living child has yet to die,
  To pass through Sorrow's reign;
To learn by this world's discipline
  The sacrament of pain.

For her whom God hath taken first,
  Thanksgiving we outpour;
For her who has to follow her,
  We *pray* for evermore.

THE CRAG.

Norwood Crag, on the Farnley Estate, is situated two miles S.E. of Fewston.

On Norwood Crag I stood one winter's day;
A noble panorama round me lay;
The lovely vale of *Washburn* just below,
Flanked by the hills through which Wharfe's waters flow,
The *Calder* moors appeared beyond the rest,
With grey old *Pendle* at the further West:
Then *Simon's Seat*, the *Pock Stones* and *Greenhow*,
And the *Great Whernside* glittering with snow.
Next came the *Brimham Rocks*, whose boulders grand,
As if upheaved by some vast Titan hand;
Which blended into *Sawley's* dark firs' shade,
To which *How Hill* a pleasant contrast made.
The *Hills* of *Hambleton* across the plain,
Point to a fertile country, rich in grain:
Studded with many churches here and there,
Unlike the western view so bold and bare.

By *Harlow Hill* the eye its way can wend,
Past *Harrogate* and *Knaresborough* to spend
Its gaze upon a mass against the sky,
Which is *York's* mighty *Minster* towering high.
More toward the East, by Harewood's lordly home,
Back to the *Wharfe* and *Chevin* then we come.
The leading objects these of that fine sight,
Opening from every side on Norwood's height.
Perchance all England might be searchèd through,
For spot from which to gain like varied view.
I love full oft to climb that rocky hill,
And with its prospect sweet my soul to fill;
It ever teaches me some lesson true,
Again I come, that I may learn anew.
This winter's day, all sunshine, was so clear,
That distant hills and moors seemed very near;
From peak and mound on which the sun could play,
The pure white snow had melted quite away;
But in the small ravines and little nooks,
And in the beds of sometime running brooks
It lay; and every hollow bathed in light,
Whilst unknown dells afar came into sight;
Their purity, made lowly places plain,
They caught the eye, as white without a stain.
So holiness in thought and word and deed,
Exalts the humble when in sorest need;
They cannot murmur e'en when brought most low,
If grace their hearts has whitened like the snow.

THE CLOUD.

(The Phenomenon which suggested the following lines was seen at the Brandrith Crags on North Moor, a part of Lord Walsingham's Estate of Blubberhouses, one February morning.)

The Moor was draped with snow,
Still was the air;
The sun peeped forth at intervals,
Now here, now there.

From Brandrith's high and hoary crags,
The view stretched out,
O'er moorland hills and rocky peaks,
Dotted about.

Far southward, hidden by the hills,
Great work-towns lie;
And from their myriad shafts ascends
The smoke on high.

The smoke-cloud lighted by the sun,
Up into sight
Arose above the moorland ridge,
One mass of light:

A contrast to the sombre moor,
Silent and cold;
Region of solitude profound,
Rocky and bold.

The Spirit of the place came by,
And thus she spake;
"From yonder golden cloud do thou
Thy lesson take.

"Its birth-place tells of dirt and toil,
And of the care,
Which wears men's souls and bodies out,
As hard to bear.

"Type of the life the Spirit lives,
The whilst on earth,
It cleaveth to the lowly place,
Which gave it birth;

"And of its future glory, when
It mounts on high,
To where the Sun of Righteousness,
Is very nigh.

"From former sin and sorrow freed,
Without one stain,
To indicate the lowly place,
From whence it came;

"To shine as doth this cloud to-day,
By borrowed light;
And be, like it, to others then
A great delight."

The Spirit ceased; mist veiled the sun,
The curtain fell
On sight and sound,—yet left a thought
On which to dwell.

The reader, it is felt, will unite with the present writer in thanks to the author of these poetic thoughts and sketches, for the permission, kindly given, to enrich "Forest Lays and Leaves" by their insertion.

THE BURN IN SPRING TIME.

"Washbrook with her wealth her mistress doth supply."
—*Drayton.*

FROM its home in the heathery moorland's dark earth,
Where the curlew and moorcock alone hail its birth,
O'er pebbles and sand, bright with sparkle and mirth,
Like an infant at play,
The burn takes its way.
Where the fern is unfolding its delicate green,
'Neath the root and the rock, where the ouzel is seen,
And quick darting trout glint in silvery sheen,
It dances in May
Through the livelong day.

With the notes of the throstle, by marital bush,
Or, the lark's when uprising at morning's first blush,
Or the coo of the cushat in evening's quiet hush,
Low, dulcet, or strong,
It mingles its song.
Where the celandine gleams in its vesture of gold,
Or, the meek *marguérite*, in numbers untold,
Gems the meadows, and upland, and whin-crested wold,
Their beauties among,
It hurries along.

R

'Tween its moss-covered banks where primroses grow,
Through Bluber's dark woods where the hyacinths blow,
By hedge-rows where violets hide, meekly, and low,
O'er gravel and loams,
It ripples and foams.
Where the blossoms of spring-time yet hang on the trees,
And the air is resonant with humming of bees,
And the scent of the hawthorn still ladens the breeze,
By sweet rural homes
It wanders and roams.

Through low-lying pastures, where lambs are at play,
Through dells and green woodlands, with life on each spray,
Where maidens and youths are gathering the "May,"
In kerchief and scarf,
By coppice and barf,
By the fields where husbandmen scatter the seed,
By cottage and farm, with neither riches nor need,
It murmurs along, nought its course to impede,
Till, a wand'ring dwarf,
'Tis lost in the Wharf.

So our spring-time of life, flows on in young glee,
Now it sings with the lark, now works with the bee,
'Mid flowers it glides, ever joyous and free,
O'er rosebuds and thyme,
To manhood's short prime.
And, thus, onward it hurries, by sorrow uncrossed,
Through sunshine, unmindful of winter's dark frost,
'Till the bright days are gone, and for ever 'tis lost,
As a long ago chime,
In the ocean of time.

PART II.

THE BURN IN THE STORM.

The bleak winds of autumn sweep o'er the wild moor
'Mong the weird rocks of Brandrith they whistle and roar,
While black tempest-clouds their contents down-pour,
On heather and fern,
And home of the hern.

And black is the crown upon Lypersley Pike,
And turbid the waters in brown Greenay Sike,
As onward they foam, through brooket and dike,
An impetuous burn
Which nothing may turn.

Down rough moorland channels pour torrents, not rills
They jump from the rocks and leap from the hills,
And, foaming and fretting, they dash through the gills
Thus starts, loud and hoarse,
The burn from its source.
An imperious giant, its wrath knows no bounds,
As it sweeps o'er the hillocks, and levels the mounds
And deep scars re-echo its thunder-like sounds.
Irresistible force,
Desolation its course.

Man's puny works are swept off, as in scorn,
The monarchs of forest from firm roots are torn,
And downward, as straws on its billows, are borne.
By farmstead they flee,
O'er meadow and lea.
Onward it goes, strewing with wreckage its way,
In anger and foam, with spoil and with spray,
It bears death on its waves thro' the brief autumn day,
Till harmless they break,
Engulfed in the lake.

So dark clouds of passion, when they fall on the brow,
In torrents downpour, till irresistible they flow,
With destruction and grief their stream-bed to strow.
No appeal they vouchsafe,
But leave many a waif.
Till their powers to destroy and ravish are spent,
By Infinite Power robbed of evil intent,
And in the ocean of good effectually blent,
No longer to chafe,
The heaven-kept-safe.

A YOUNG NATURALIST.

WITH LEAVES FROM HIS DIARY AND OTHER NOTES.

"Full many a gem of purest ray serene,
The dark, unfathom'd caves of ocean bear;
Full many a flower is born to blush unseen,
And waste its sweetness on the desert air."

—*Gray.*

FROM twenty-five to thirty years ago there were few young men, in the town of Otley, better known, or more respected, than John William Brown.

He was the son of very worthy and respectable parents, though in humble circumstances of life. His health was, from his earliest years, so delicate as to preclude him from following continuously any handicraft occupation, though occasionally—whenever able—he assisted his father, in his trade of a shoemaker. He was a devoted Sunday School teacher in the Church schools, and a young man of earnest Christian life.

When the writer first knew him, about the year 1852 A.D., he was from 18 to 19 years of age, and acting as an assistant teacher at the National School at Otley, receiving, in return for his daily work in the school, tuition from the head master in Latin, and kindred subjects, after the day's duties at the school were over.

At the evening classes, held at the Mechanics' Institute, during the winter months, he was a regular attendant, especially at the Drawing and Arts Class, first as pupil and then as teacher.

With his pencil and brush he became very proficient, and several of his productions are still to be found in the neighbourhood.

His favourite pursuit, however, was *Natural History*, and particularly the branches of *Entomology* and *Botany*. To the study of these he was devoted, heart and soul. Little knowledge did he gain of them from books, for he had neither the means nor the opportunities to seek it, chiefly, there. His library was the open fields, lanes, and woods of the neighbourhood, with the blue roof of the heavens over his head, and the living objects themselves spread before him.

In the early morning, or as long as light lingered in the evening, his delicate form, somewhat stooping from physical weakness, with thin, intelligent countenance, and quick, observant eye, might almost daily have been seen searching by the woods of Farnley or Danfield, in the green lanes towards Weston or Newall, climbing the Chevin, or wandering, or sitting, among the rocks of Caley in quest of the objects of his devotion. Here he was tracking out and noting some interesting operation of nature, watching the habits or the transformations of his favourite insects, or there he was collecting some rare or new specimen of insect or plant for preservation and study at home.

His love for all the works of God was intense, and he had an eye to note them wherever he went. The writer once heard him quote with an emphasis and feeling not easily forgotten, the beautiful words of Cowper :—

> "I would not enter on my list of friends
> (Though graced with polish'd manners and fine sense,
> Yet wanting sensibility) the man
> Who needlessly sets foot upon a worm.
> An inadvertent step may crush a snail
> That crawls at evening in the public path ;
> But he that has humanity, forewarn'd,
> Will tread aside, and let the reptile live."

There was scarcely an insect, certainly no ordinary one, belonging to the district for miles around Otley, which he did not know *where* to find, and *when* to find, in its larval, or chrysalis, or perfect state. It was the same with the plants and shrubs, but more especially with the wild flowers of the neighbourhood. Each one was a friend whose nature, and habits, and habitat were well known, and whose annual return, or mutation, he would sometimes walk miles to greet and enjoy.

Having sisters married, and residing at Markington near Ripon, and Fewston in the forest of Knaresborough, he made occasional visits to these places, and greatly enjoyed the opportunities, such visits afforded him, of extending his researches and knowledge beyond the immediate vicinity of his native town.

It is to be regretted that he kept no systematic record of his observations. His diary, however (though with many gaps, and for long intervals), for the years 1852—7 A.D. inclusive, enables some idea of his researches and observations to be given, by quotations, in his own words.

First—a few general quotations are taken as showing his habits of observation, and his love for, and appreciation of, the objects and phenomena of nature around him.

"1852 A.D., Feb. 29. The Aurora Borealis has made its appearance five times this month. On Thursday night it was most splendid. It illuminated the whole heavens to a degree which has not been seen for many years. About 9 p.m. three arches appeared stretching from east to west. . . . . Streamers were sent up towards the zenith, forming and disappearing with every variety of colour mingled with flashes of red and yellow. At midnight the heavens glowed with a radiance I never saw before."

"1854 A.D., Feb. 25. While I was out rambling to-day, I gathered a few spring flowers which were peeping just above the ground, the long grass almost hiding their shining petals, but sheltering them from the chilling blasts of the wind of this season. The flowers which formed my posey were as follows:—a few field daisies, a garden daisy, a buttercup, a few primroses, and a few snowdrops. A choice collection at this early time of the year."

"Sunday, 26 (July, 1857 A.D.). At Fewston—took a stroll in the afternoon through the churchyard. There I read the following epitaphs. The first on a stone recording the deaths of three young children:—

"'I see you in your beauty;
With your waving hair at rest,
And your busy little fingers
Folded lightly on your breast;

"'But your merry dance is over,
And your little race is run,
And the mirror that reflected there
Now tells the three are gone.'

"Another one was as follows:—

'So teach us, Lord, the uncertain sum
Of our short days to mind,
That to true wisdom all our hearts
May ever be inclined.'"

"Monday, 27 (July). During my rambling this morning, I had the good fortune to find another Admiral Caterpillar (larva of the Admiral Butterfly) near Cragg Hall, Fewston. This makes up a pair. In the evening I got some caterpillars of the beautiful Vapourer Moth in Mr. Gwyther's garden."

"Wednesday, 9 (Sept. 1877 A.D.). Walked to Bolton for the purpose of sketching the abbey. Day fine but almost intolerably hot. I took a pencil sketch of the abbey, and on my way home (to his sister's, near Fewston) I took a water-colour sketch of Kexgill, a most romantic "gill" or dale, with Brandreth range of Crags above it, and a logan stone of great size, where ravens build in the cracks and holes, hence sometimes named Raven Crag. This glen is situated about half a mile west of Blubberhouses, and the Skipton road skirts the south side of it, from which a good view of the wild, romantic scenery, peculiar to this part of the country, may be obtained."

"Monday, 14 (Sept. 1877 A.D.). Visited the Holbeck Entomological Society's Exhibition, held in the National Schoolroom there. I was greatly interested with the great variety of British insects, collected and displayed in tasteful designs in large handsome cases by working men. I am glad to see that so many of our working classes are making great progress in the advancement of Natural Science and Art. What is here set forth is an example of what can be acquired by patience and industry and the cultivation of taste. There were also a beautiful collection of cured birds—British and foreign—and a good selection of paintings, both ancient and modern . . . . and also a quantity of valuable photographs."

These extracts surely show a habit, and power of observation, and a tone of thought and feeling, in a young man in J. W. Brown's position, and with his disadvantages, most admirable, and worthy to be held up as incentives and examples to all classes of readers.

One of his special pursuits was *Entomology*.

In the summer of 1855 A.D. the writer was with him on the occasion of a visit to Morecambe, then a very primitive sea-side resort, and he will never forget the delight and enthusiasm of the young entomologist at the discovery, fluttering amongst the flowers on the beach there, of a number of butterflies of a kind entirely new to him! He was not content with securing as many specimens of the insects as he required for his collection, but hour after hour, on day after day, was spent in endeavour to discover the larvæ, the plants they fed upon, specimens in the pupa state, &c. In one of his diaries there are the following remarks upon entomology generally:—

"Few persons can fail to be struck with the beauty and variety of insects, especially those of the butterfly tribe, and yet how many are ignorant of the different stages of existence they undergo, and their close analogy to the immortality of the soul. Nearly everybody regards the caterpillar as one of the greatest pests of the garden, and yet without it we should have none of those lovely butterflies which so often cross our paths in our summer walks. We first meet with a crawling caterpillar with sixteen feet, devouring everything in the shape of vegetables, until it becomes full grown. It then descends into the earth, making for itself a tomb, and there undergoes a change into the chrysalis or pupa state resembling the case of a mummy; there it remains a month or longer, and then finally bursts forth a glorious creature—perfect in all its parts, its whole time soaring aloft through the air o'er verdant meads, to sport and revel amid beautiful flowers, and extract their sweets."

In the diary, under the date "April 25, 1866 A.D.," occurs the following entry, showing his mode of observation:

"Saw a nettle tortoiseshell butterfly laying its eggs on the under side of the leaf of a nettle. Before it had finished I disturbed it and it flew away. I took the leaf with me with the eggs on it, for the purpose of watching them through all their stages."

"May 12, 1859 A.D. A warm south-east breeze and the sun shining! All nature rejoicing! The cry of cuckoo! cuckoo!

resounds from the woods on Chevin side. Hornet wasps are at work on the pales and hedges, busily collecting wood for their nests. They gnaw it with their horny mandibles, roll it up under their feet about the size and shape of a pellet, then fly off with it to their nests. They also search among the leaves of hedges and trees for caterpillars and small moths, which they roll up in the same way as they do the wood, and carry them also to their nests, for what purpose I have not yet been able to ascertain. Perhaps to feed their larvæ with. They cut off the wings of the moths and roll up only the body . . . . ."

"June 13. Whit Monday, 1859 A.D. On some hazel leaves which I got in the hedge of our garden this evening, to feed my caterpillars with, I found a very pretty larva thereon. The colour was green, with white stripes down the back and along the sides, dotted with small black spots, and covered with very short hairs; colour of the head, green."

"June 23. The caterpillar which I found in our garden feeding on the hazel, on Whit Monday, has this day spun a white silken cocoon between the hazel leaves, and is about to undergo the change into the pupa state."

"July 21st. A moth, which is a fresh kind to me, has come out of the pupa this morning, produced from the caterpillar which I found on the hazel in our garden on Whit Monday evening. Colour of the moth: upper wings, greenish grey, marked faintly, almost like the Angle shade-moth; under wings, golden ochreous yellow. The pupa was of a purple colour, enclosed in a white silken cocoon between two hazel leaves, on which the caterpillar fed."

Such entries as these, showing minute and painstaking observations, might be multiplied to almost any number. The extent to which these observations were pursued may be gathered, in some measure, from the following inventory of the specimens, all reared or caught with his own hand, which were in J. W. Brown's possession in March, 1856 A.D.:—

Seven Years' Collection of Insects.

Case	No. I.	contains	71	Moths and Butterflies.
,,	No. II.	,,	51	,, ,, ,,
,,	No. III.	,,	54	,, ,, ,,
,,	No. IV.	,,	266	,, ,, ,,
,,	No. V.	,,	122	,, ,, ,,
,,	No. VI.	,,	46	,, ,, ,,
,,	No. VII.	,,	149	Beetles, Flies, &c.

Total 761 specimens.

These include 61 varieties of moths, 53 of which are nocturnal and 8 diurnal.

Three varieties of sphinxes—all nocturnal: and 15 varieties of butterflies.

Case No. VII. contains 7 insects of the class *Neuroptera;* 17 of the class *Diptera;* 19 of the class *Hymenoptera;* 20 of the class *Coleoptera;* 87 of the class *Orthoptera.*

"These have all been collected by myself in the neighbourhoods of Otley and Fewston, in Yorkshire, and Morecambe Bay, in Lancashire. "J. W. BROWN."

Probably the most valuable, because the most systematic, notes penned by J. W. Brown, relate to the *Botany* of that portion of Wharfedale in which Otley is situated. The small MS. book containing them bears the title, "Natural History of Otley," and is in the possession of its author's brother, still residing there, and himself no tyro in entomology. The author no doubt intended, had life and health been spared him, to include in the notes a full account of the natural history of the neighbourhood; but as it is, it is a mere fragment of that extensive subject, and embraces only a portion of the botany, viz., the wild flowers, mosses and lichens.

In some preliminary remarks, the field of his researches in this subject is thus described:—

"At no great depth from the surface of the soil on Chevin, lies a series of rocks of millstone grit formation, which in many places appear above the surface in the form of huge crags. One of these, which bears the name of Pelstone Crag, is celebrated as affording one of the finest panoramic views of the valley—with its numerous mansions, its shady woods, and its beautiful clear river gracefully wending its course through the verdant fields. . . . There is another large crag in the deer park (Caley), named Middle Crag, &c. . . . There are also many other interesting rocks on the Chevin, most of which are in the woods on the sides of the steep declivities; many are overgrown with beautiful varieties of mosses and lichen worthy of the botanist's notice."

And again, upon the subject on which he writes, he says:—

"Our valley is rich in the treasures of flora. On woodland and moor, in fields, by the river's bank and beneath the hedgerow's shade, are scattered in rich and varied profusion those lovely flowers indigenous to our soil, and which are such a source of admiration and pleasure in our country rambles. In all the above situations, at the different seasons of the year, the botanist may always find abundance of wild flowers from which to select suitable and beautiful specimens for his herbarium. Botany is ever an interesting branch of natural history, and the collecting of plants for study forms a very pleasing and entertaining amusement during the hours of leisure and recreation. If we examine the structure of flowers, and consider the uses to which many of them are applied, we are at once led to admire and adore the wisdom and goodness of Him who had created them and all things, for our enjoyment and use. The beauty of form and colour with which many flowers are arrayed, delights the eye and calls to mind the beautiful words of our Saviour, 'Consider the lilies of the field, how they grow; they toil not, neither do they spin: and yet, I say unto you, that even Solomon in all his glory was not arrayed like one of these.''

As to the *form* into which his wide general and local knowledge has been thrown in these notes, the following extracts will serve as examples.

"THE VIOLET. *(Viola Odorata.)*

"This lovely flower may be found on hedge-banks, partly hidden among the herbage, where its small blue flowers scent the air around. White violets also grow in the same situations. Both kinds flower in March and are plentiful in the fields and lanes of our neighbourhood. Those persons who are unacquainted with the localities, will be able to find them on the southern banks of Weston Lane, Farnley Lane, and in the fields on both sides of these lanes, also in Pool Road and in Caley Fields."

"The violet belongs to the class *Pentandria*; order *Nonogynia*.

'The violet in the greenwood bower,
Where birchen boughs with hazel mingle,
May boast herself the fairest flower,
In glen, or copse, or forest dingle.' "

"CROSS-WORT. *(Galium Cruciatum.)*

"Class *Tetrandria*; Order *Monogynia*. This is a little plant with small yellow flowers, and leaves disposed round the stem in the form of a cross, hence its name. It appears in flower in May, on hedge-banks, in Curtis's gardens, Caley Fields, Farnley Lane, and near the mill-dam stones."

"ST. JOHN'S WORT. *(Hypericum Perforatum.)*

"Class *Polyadelphia*; Order *Polyandria*. This plant may be found in tolerable abundance on the river's bank, by the sides of ditches, in Caley Fields, and Bush Lane, in August. Its leaves are full of little holes, which are only seen when held up to the light, hence its name 'Perforated St. John's Wort.' The flowers are yellow, and in clusters on the stem."

After this manner the manuscript contains descriptions of the plant, the flower, the time of flowering, the place in which it is to be found, with, here and there, interesting associations or remarks on about eighty species of wild flowers. Also similar accounts of six species of ferns, six of mosses, and ten of lichen, are given, all of which are to be found around Otley. Several of these are illustrated by extremely accurate and tasteful water-colour drawings.

"The plants thus described," again writes the author, "form but a very small portion of the numerous species which flourish in, and deck with their varied beauties, every open field and wood, and heath and hedge of one of the most lovely and fertile valleys of Great Britain. In the study of a little of its botany the writer has spent very many pleasant hours, and in rambles, with companions interested in the same pursuits, and often alone, to the objects of search. Some of the results are here noted, and, though only small, will, it is hoped, lead others into the path of this most interesting branch of natural history, from which they will derive no small amount of pleasure and instruction. The book of nature is ever open to all; and let those who desire to peruse its countless pages, go forth into the fields, and there, with the blue canopy of heaven above them, and the green sod, smiling with flowers of every hue, beneath their feet, and surrounded by all that is lovely and grand in nature, let them study and admire the glorious works of the all-wise Creator; and let them exclaim with the inspired psalmist, 'O Lord, how manifold are Thy works! In wisdom hast Thou made them all! The earth is full of Thy riches!'"

In studies and recreations, such as these, did the youth of precarious health, and strength, spend the hours and days in which he was precluded from the labour by which the family bread was won. The date, at which the manuscript on botany was compiled, does not appear upon the face of the book itself, but, from certain indications, it was probably written about the year 1853 A.D. or 1854 A.D., when its writer would be from 20 to 21 years of age.

During the last few years of his life, J. W. Brown was, in a great measure, denied even his favourite studies. The gradual failure of already delicate health, with corresponding decrease of bodily strength, interfered with the active pursuit of them, and precluded him from the long walks and rambles of former years. Numerous friends, however, and sympathizers, to whom his tastes were known, continued to bring to him whatever objects or curiosities in nature they found, that were likely to be new to him, or worthy of his interest. Among other things thus conveyed to him, I find mention in his diary of the larva of a rare sphinx moth sent to him, in August, 1856 A.D., by the late Henry Brown, Esq., then Mayor of Bradford—a relative.

In William Duckworth, M.D., a near neighbour, he ever found a kind, liberal, and judicious friend, in whose possession are some of his best sketches and paintings.

In the summer of 1859 A.D. the end was clearly drawing on. His passion, however, was strong even to the last. On the 15th of July, in that year, when it had become no longer desirable that he should go out alone, there is the following suggestive entry in the diary :—

"Mother, myself, and William B. took a walk as far as Hell-hole Gill, for the purpose of getting some six spotted Burnet moths in a dry hilly pasture there, on the right-hand side of the road going towards Shipley. Being afflicted with an affection of the heart and lungs, I was not able to pursue the moths, and only caught a pair which flew close to me. B. kindly gave me some good specimens out of the number which he caught. They looked exceedingly pretty as they ever and anon darted through the air, or alighted on the pink flowers of the betony, displaying their bright scarlet wings; and were very numerous. . . . . We returned home both pleased and refreshed with our out, the day being a fine one, with a mild western breeze."

By a remarkable coincidence the two last entries, made by the poor young enthusiast in his diary, seem as if entirely prophetic of his own approaching end.

"August 4 (1859 A.D.).—This morning the last of my Poplar caterpillars, reared from the egg, has *gone into the earth to undergo the change into the chrysalis state.*"

"August 5.—My brother's Eyed Hawk caterpillar has *descended into the earth to undergo the change into the pupa state.*"

On the 19th of the same month (August, 1859 A.D.) he entered into rest, at the age of twenty-five years. Three days afterwards the mortal remains were laid in the earth in the full hope of a bright and glorious resurrection.

Had life been spared to him, and health given him, in all probability his name would have found a place in the proud list of "the worthies" of his native county. Ought it not to find a place in that honourable list as it is? He certainly gathered more knowledge of his native vale than men usually acquire in a lifetime; and, at least, he demonstrated what might be done in a short life, and under the most adverse circumstances, by industry and perseverance. Making allowance for the difference in age, in education, in general circumstances and advantages, the extracts which have been given can scarcely fail to call to mind the popular naturalist of the South—the gentle, devout Gilbert White. And, even under all disadvantages, had not the hand of death intervened, one is inclined to ask — 'Might not Otley, in the beautiful valley of the Wharf, have become a Selborne of the North?

THE TRYST; A FOREST IDYL.

PART I.

"A simple child,
That lightly draws its breath,
That feels its life in every limb,
What should it know of death?"
—*Wordsworth.*

THE sun was quickly hast'ning down,
O'er Roggan's heath-clad brow,
The western sky was blushing deep,
In his departing glow;
The cooling breeze that fans the cheek,
With freshness from the lake,
Just breathed enough, among the trees,
To make the aspen shake.

The Washburn slowly murmured on,
'Mong rocks in leafy dell,
Then o'er the bye-wash, 'neath the trees,
In silvery splashes fell;
No sound but these disturbed the hush
Of evening's gentle sough,
Save from the Gill, or Lane Ends Wood,
Came cushat's softest coo.

Three youthful sisters, happy, fair,
  Blithe as the birds of May,
In blush of waking girlhood's life,
  Through forest groves did stray.
A youth their sole companion was,
  A neighbour's son was he,
Their childhood's friend and playmate oft,
  The sharer in their glee.

With careless steps they sauntered on,
  Where grow the tow'ring pine,
Or, ling'ring, stood where roses sweet,
  Their arches wildly twine.
And flowers, that meek in pathway bloom,
  Bedeck'd the velvet sod,
While foxglove tall, and waving fern,
  O'erhung the path they trod.

The dancing wavelets on the lake,
  In sunset's golden ray,
Now soft in shade, now bright in gleam,
  Were not more bright than they,
As through the glades their ringing laugh,
  The breeze *now* bore along;
Then, soft and sweet, as distant lute,
  Their notes of evening song.

A rustic seat, but newly made,
  Stood 'neath a spreading lime,
And there they paused to rest awhile,
  At the hour of curfew's chime.
The soothing calm, which breathed around,
  O'er buoyant spirits fell;
Some time in silent thought they sat,
  None cared to break the spell.

At length the youth address'd the one,
  More pensive than the rest,
" Dear Coz, your thought pray tell us,
  We know it is the best?"—

She slowly raised the drooping fringe,
  Of a dark and thoughtful eye,
Her look! it stopp'd the rising smile,
  Though scarcely knew they why.

" The thought you ask to know," she said,
  " But ill befits your glee,
O, why, upon this evening sweet,
  Should it have come to me?
Is it some angel's voice that speaks
  In this still, tranquil, hour?
Or, is't some evil portent's hand
  That casts its shade before?

" Ten years have passed while children here,
  In wood, and field, we've played,
Ten summers, morn, and noon, and night,
  By stream and lake we've strayed,
The tale of happy hours is told
  By every path and glen,
When thrice ten years have come and gone,
  Oh, where shall we be then?"

The words so guileless and so frank,
  Scarce on her lips had died,
When one, the youngest,—yet a child—
  With childlike haste replied;
" Where shall we be? at home, of course,
  Or, (this with mirthful eye),
Perhaps Anna at yon old grey house,
  And *you*,—O very nigh!"

" Ho, Ho, you forward sister mine!
  Who taught you that to say?
Retract! retract! Away! away!
  Or you a forfeit pay!"
Then 'mong the dewy grass and flowers,
  Began a merry chase,
But e'en their youthful, flying, steps,
  Soon flaggèd in that race.

As from a bow at venture drawn,
  Its goal to archer dark,
The arrow, quiv'ring through the air,
  Unerring strikes its mark ;
So then a chord, at random struck,
  Vibrated in each breast,
The words in each an echo found,
  That marr'd the girlish jest.

Yet part in jest, in earnest part,
  The youth thus made reply,—
" Oh, we can set the doubt at rest,
  When th' years are passèd by,
Beneath this tree we then will meet,
  Where'er we scattered be."
They part in jest, in earnest part,
  To the fair tryst agree.

'Mid sobered thought, and kindly words,
  They whil'd the hours away,
And spake of schemes, and hopes, and joys,
  For many a coming day.
Thus long, till waning light was gone,
  They sat in converse sweet,
And stars were sparkling clear on high,
  While dew-drops kissed their feet.

A stalwart yeoman and his sons,
  Detained in hay-field late,
With cheerful greeting hurried by,
  And through his homestead gate.
They rose and took their homeward path,
  Unmindful of the past,
Nor feared the dark of sorrow's night,
  Nor felt yet life's chill blast.

Yet heaven in pity seemed to yearn,
  And earth to breathe a sigh,
As hand in hand, that night they stood,
  At last to say "Good-bye."

The youth, unwilling, slowly turned,
  And at the closing door,
With lingring looks, *he went,—they went,*—
  To meet on earth no more.

PART II.

"I have had playmates, I have had companions,
In my days of childhood, in my joyous school-days;
All, all are gone, the old familiar faces,
Gone before
To that unknown and silent shore."
—*Charles Lamb.*

"The aged farmer tott'ring o'er the green
Leans on his staff, recounts the days he's seen."
—*Anonymous.*

'Twas on another summer's eve,
  Long years had come and gone,
Again the heath was tinged with gold,
  The west in glory shone.
The linden tree in vigour stood,—
  Its branches wider threw,
The eglantine still spann'd the path,—
  Its tendrils wilder grew.

The breath of even rose and fell,
  As heave of maiden's breast,
The river chaunted in its bed
  The song of nature's rest.
While calm, as wrapped in childhood's sleep,
  Lay lake, and wood, and moor,
Above, below, around, was peace,
  As thirty years before.

With rev'rent step and thoughtful brow,
  A stranger trod the way,
He bore the marks of manhood's prime,
  Tho' slightly streaked with grey.

Three boys, his sons, in youthful glee,
  Were by their father's side,—
To them, 'twas joy 'mong trees to wind,
  And through the green shaws glide.

He led them on, nor question asked,
  By paths no stranger knew;
'Till soon by glades and ferny banks,
  To boyish sports they flew.
A broken seat in linden shade,
  With moss and lichen grown,
He found, and rais'd with rev'rent care,
  And, lonely, sat him down.

An agèd man there slowly came,—
  His form was bent and low,
His hair was white, his cheeks were shrunk,
  Time's furrows mark'd his brow.
"Mine agèd friend," the stranger said,
  "By years and toil oppressed,
Your tott'ring staff pray lay aside,
  And sit by me and rest."

"Ah, Sir," he said, "the thanks I give
  Of one whose work is done;
Full fifty years this path I've trod,
  But now my course is run."
He came, and by the stranger sat,
  And watched the boys at play,
But mem'ries seemed within him stirred,
  Of some far distant day.

"Methinks," ere long the old man said,
  "You are no stranger here,
Yet 'tis a dream,—my senses fail,—
  And memory is not clear,
But in its page of later days,
  Shall I the record seek,
Or, in the far off years of youth,
  Ere manhood clothed your cheek?"

"It may be true," he quick replied,
"That we before have met,
Though 'tis a mirage oft that's seen
Of things we don't forget.
If fifty years you here have dwelt,
Remote from busy town,
Then every neighbour you'll have seen,
And many changes known?"

"Aye, Sir, I have, and I can say,
Though, Sir, it be with woe,
Not many's left of those I knew,
E'en thirty years ago."
"Then worthy friend, no doubt you knew,
There dwelt in yonder hall,
Three sisters once,—some years ago,—
Can you their fate recal?"

He gave a dubious glance, then said,
"Alas, I knew them well,
Though now 'tis many, many years,
Since there they ceased to dwell.
Aye, oft, as home from work we came,
(I'd wife and children then)
With cheery words they hailed us here,
Or in yon forest glen.

"One night, Oh, I remember 't well,—
(My wife was then at home,
And, Sir, nigh thirty years ago,
We laid her in the tomb,
My children since have gone afar,
Of all I am bereft,—
Of all, who gathered round our hearth,
But I, alone, am left).

"We passed along this well-known path,
(My steps were not then slow),
An eve like this,—'twas calm and still,—
They sat where we do now.

I thought how happy was their lot,
  They seemed to know no care,
But pure and free, in thought and word,
  As moorland's morning air.

"But sir, as summers passed away,
  (And Oh, how quickly flown),
First one was called, from hence away,
  To yon great smoky town;
A few years passed; a message came,
  That ill did her betide,
Her strength was gone, her bloom was fled
  Though almost still a bride.

"She slowly drooped, and meekly bowed
  Beneath the hand of God;
They brought her home, and soon she lay
  Beneath our churchyard sod.
The youngest next, in wedlock's bond,
  To distant city went;
But in its hurry, strife, and noise,
  Her lamp soon, too, was spent.

"Upon a bleak cold winter's day,—
  All things around seemed dead,—
They brought her, too, and laid her down
  By her dead sister's bed.
In church-yard yonder on the hill,
  On stones 'neath drooping tree,
You'll find the dates, and names, and age,
  If them you wish to see.

"The other, do you ask of, Sir?
  Her I remember well,
Her kindly words, and kinder deeds,
  Could all the neighbours tell.
She stayed with us much longer, Sir,
  And wept her sisters' loss,
And like our Heavenly Master, Sir,
  She had to bear 'the cross.'

" She went at last to city crowds,
  Where vice and sorrow blend,
To nurse the sick, and tend the poor,
  Thus life for Christ to spend;
And there she laboured long, they said,
  The friend of young and old;
And blessings bore to squalid homes,
  More rich than finest gold.

" Yet, Sir, in time there came a change,
  They hardly noticed how,
And she who long had nursed the weak,
  Herself grew weak and low;
Then home she fled to rest, and breathe
  Our forest air so clear,
As to its native covert flies
  The arrow-stricken deer.

" Still oft she came to read to me,
  And spake of days gone by,
And told of Him who died for us,
  And of the Home on High.
Then, Sir, she went away again,
  To try new scenes and air,
But, Sir, she only went to die,
  And strangers laid her *there*.

" Now, Sir, I've told you what I know,
  I'll try to toddle home,
But home is not what once it was,
  It's drear and very lone.
The dark'ning hours around me close,
  I'm looking for the morn,
To bring its light, and new-born strength,
  To the weary and the worn.

" I then shall meet them all again,
  My wife that's gone before,
My sons, who're now beyond the seas,
  Meet them to part no more.

Good night, dear Sir, good night again,"
With faltering voice he spake,
"Methinks e'en now o'er Almas Cliff
The light begins to break."

He rose, and moved with tott'ring step,
Toward his lone house door,
Not as, with sons in strength, he went,
Those thirty years before,
When with life's gifts around him shed,
In pride he raised his brow,
No thought, no hope, of home beyond,
That home so precious now.

PART III.

"Oft in the stilly night
Ere slumber's chain has bound me,
Fond memory brings the light
Of other days around me;
The smiles, the tears,
Of boyhood's years,
The words of love then spoken;
The eyes that shone
Now dimm'd and gone,
The cheerful hearts now broken!"

—*Moore.*

Adieu, my friend of old, adieu;
Thy tale of bygone years,
Might well arrest a wand'rer's step,
Or move a stranger's tears;
To me it speaks with deeper voice,
To pierce the inmost breast;
It thoughts awakes, and strikes a chord,
Where sacred memories rest.

Eyes dark with their excessive bright
  I see, dark eyes of truth,
And forms, lithe, moldèd, moved,
  With fire of early youth;
And happy smiles, and merry glance,
  Yet live in memory clear,
And ringing laugh, and joyous song,
  Still linger on my ear.

And are they gone! How once we played,
  As only children play;
And, wand'ring through these meads and paths,
  Spent many a holiday!
How oft o'er hill and moor we strayed,
  With hand in hand together,
Among the yellow gorse-bush bloom,
  Or 'cross the purple heather!

We plucked in Spring the primrose pale,
  In alders' grateful shade,
By Washburn's heath-dyed waters' side,
  Or Green Beck's leafy glade;
We gathered many a bluebell fair,
  Along the steep Side-Bank,
And many a meek forget-me-not,
  In Delf-Close bottoms dank!

And by the pleasant summer-seat,
  On hill above the "Cut,"
We loved to see the shadows flit,
  Cross Bluber Hall, or hut;
Or sat, or played, beside the gate,
  On Autumn's evening's wane,
While homeward toiled the harvest-men
  By kindly Hopper Lane;

And often by the crag we watched,
  The river wind along,
Where Fairfax tuned his British lyre
  To Tasso's sacred song.

Or, by the old Church-porch we met,
  With lengthening shadow falling,
As Sabbath bells to Evensong *
  The foresters were calling.

And oft we sought the ferns and flowers,
  Where Kexgill's echoes wake,
Or list to love's first murm'ring notes,
  By Bluber's sylvan lake.
How quickly thus, though childhood's days,
  As days of childhood flew,
We into youth and maidenhood,
  Together unconscious grew!

Since then, what changes time hath wrought!
  What hopes have passed away!
How oft the dark of sorrow's night
  Hath come o'er youth's bright day!
How young-life's dreams, which seemed so real,
  And here were felt and told,
Are now "forgotten as a dream,"
  When the dreamer's heart lies cold!

Oft summer flowers have faded,—died,—
  Along the Well Close side,
And autumn leaves been scattered, sere,
  O'er Clifton's meadow wide;
Oft ferns have drooped their golden fronds,
  In Kexgill's rocky dell,
And 'neath the alder bushes bare,
  Run Washburn's angry swell.

And oft the hay's been gathered in,
  And reaped the golden grain,
And weary reapers wended home,
  By the Inn at Hopper Lane;

---

* "Those evening bells! Those evening bells!
How many a tale their music tells!
Of youth, and home, and that sweet time
When last I heard their soothing chime."—*Moore.*

And oft another reaper's come,
  With fabled scythe in hand,
And reaped a precious harvest here,
  For the holy, better, land!

Here hectic blush hath burnt on cheeks,
  As glow of closing day,
Lithe forms have faded, drooped, and sunk
  In slow unfelt decay;
And life, that throbbed in every vein,
  Hath waned with every breath,
Till eyes, whence flashed once souls so deep,
  Have brighter flashed for death.

As winter storms have fallen, bleak,
  Have gentle spirits fled,
And sisters, one by one, been laid
  In their cold churchyard bed.
With pure white snow for winding sheets,
  More soft than eider down,
They rest in Him "Who giveth rest,"
  And wait the golden crown.

* * * * * * *

I stand,—by memory's power, the gulf
  Of years behind is past!—
I go,—by faith the stream before
  Is bridgèd o'er at last!
Life's duties call: "A little while,"
  And then the lost are found,
And every holy hope is grasped,
  And broken tie re-bound.

* * * * * * *

Long musing thus the stranger sat,
  Till stars shone bright on high;
A hand, laid gently on his arm,
  Told that his sons stood by.
"Papa," said they, "Oh, why so sad,—
  A tear is in your eye,—
Three times we spoken now to you,—
  You've made us no reply?"

"Yes, boys, I thoughtful was, and sad,
And you may wonder why;
To me there speaks a voice of days
Far off, yet very nigh.
But come now, let us haste away,
What know you of the past;
The future's yours; till time has fled,
You do not feel its blast.

"To you all speaks of joy and life;
With me it is not so;—
The forms I see, the sounds I hear,
Are those of long ago:
And still so clear, so near, so real,
Now hov'ring round they seem,
That I, to them, might, in the morn,
Awake as from a dream."

* * * * * * *

Yes, eve of life, as eve of day,
Is pledge of coming light,
And that we lose in ev'ning's gloom,
We find in morning's bright;
And mem'ries dear whose roots lie deep,
In days and years of yore,
The brighter burn, as nearer comes
The morn, which lies before.

And friends, and ties, asunder far,
By death or distance riven,
Though ne'er on earth they meet again,
A trysting have in Heaven,
Where gathered all, in that pure home,
Afar from sin and strife,
No change they'll know,—no death is there,—
But rest, and endless life.

BOLTON PRIORY: ITS LEGENDS AND ASSOCIATIONS.

> "All lovely Bolton! though no incense roll,
> O'er cloistered courts by holy footsteps trod,
> Where from earth's thousand altars could the soul
> Hold a more rapt communion with its God?"
>
> —*Earl of Carlisle.*

THE mouldering walls of "Bolton's ruined priory" stand about two miles from the western boundary of the forest—and its owners, in the olden times, possessed rights of pasture for their flocks on the forest's moors and hills. The ruins have, in the opinion of Dr. Whitaker, the historian of Craven, "for every purpose of picturesque effect no equal among the northern houses—perhaps not in the kingdom." Most men who have visited them would probably endorse his words.

They are, as yet, away from the pollutions of modern manufacture, on the banks of the crystal Wharf, amid rich meadows, with background of dark woods and heather-capped hills, in the rich pastoral district of Craven, of which, one, well acquainted with it, and who loved it, the late Earl of Carlisle, sang,—

> "Vaunt not Helvetian hills, Ausonian vales,
> Vaunt not each painted, each poetic scene,
> Still, still I cling to Craven's past'ral dales,
> Their purple heather and their emerald green."

Turner loved to paint Bolton. Landseer has depicted it in its prosperity, and in a manner suggestive of the fruitfulness of its forests, its granges, and its waters. Wordsworth and Rogers, and a host of minor poets, have immortalized its legends and its beauties.

The history of the origin of the priory, and the tradition as to the selection of its charming site, are alike characteristic of the monastic foundations.

William the Conqueror granted large possessions in Craven to William de Romille. His daughter and heiress, Cicely, and her husband, William de Meschines, founded, about 1120 A.D., a house for Augustinian canons at Embsay, a remote spot in the hills between the valleys of the Aire and the Wharf. The churches of Skipton and Carleton, and afterwards of Kildwick in Airedale, and Harewood, were bestowed, along with other possessions, as an endowment.

The two daughters of the founders of this house, Adeliza and Avicia, retained their mother's name of De Romille—an indication of the importance of her family. The possessions in Craven descended to Adeliza or Alice, the elder, who married William Fitz Duncan, nephew of David, King of Scotland. One son alone survived of this marriage—the last hope of the De Romilles. From the place of his birth—one of his parents' manors in Cumberland—he was known as the "boy of Egremond."

A little over a mile from the ruins of the priory, in the deep solitude of the woods, is the well-known "Strid." Here the valley is suddenly closed in by immense rocks of millstone grit. Through a channel worn, or rent, in these, and not more in some places than four or five feet in width, the whole of the waters of the Wharf are poured with terrific force.

While on a hunting expedition in the year 1251 A.D., the boy of Egremond, accompanied by huntsmen and with hound in leash, came to this romantic spot. Fearlessly he attempted to step across the seething channel of the Strid. Like several persons who have attempted the same feat in modern times, he paid the penalty of foolhardiness. The hound in leash suddenly held back and checked its master's step, and he fell into the abyss and perished. The affrighted forester, who had accompanied his master, hurried to the Lady Adeliza. Probably the dismay on his countenance told the sad story, to an anxious mother, more plainly than his significant inquiry, "What is good for a bootless bene?" which Wordsworth interprets,—

"Whence can comfort spring
When prayer is of no avail?"

Her despairing response was "Endless sorrow."

When she realised that she was indeed childless, she vowed "that many a poor man's child should be her heir."

To accomplish this object she removed the religious house, founded by her parents at Embsay, to the nearest available spot to that at which the young Romille was lost, namely, the present site of the ruins at Bolton. She also increased the endowments of the brotherhood, giving to them "the whole of the vill at Bolton, and the place called Stede, and the land between Poseford and Spectbek, and the rivers Wharf and Washburn." To these, other possessions at Harewood, Keighley, and elsewhere, were liberally added afterwards by other donors.

This legend of the foundation, or rather re-foundation of the priory, has stirred the poetic genius of two of our sweetest poets, Wordsworth and Rogers, each of whom, in his own inimitable way, has given it a prominent place in English literature. The latter thus sings:—

"'Say, what remains when hope is fled?'
She answered, 'Endless weeping!'
For in the herdsman's eye she saw
Who in his shroud was sleeping.
At Embsay rung the matin bell,
The stag was roused on Barden fell;
The mingled sounds were swelling, dying,
And down the Wharf a hern was flying;
When near the cabin in the wood,
In tartan clad and forest green,
With hound in leash and hawk in hood,
The boy of Egremond was seen.

Blithe was his song, a song of yore,
But where the rock is rent in two,
And the river rushes through,
His voice was heard no more.
'Twas but a step, the gulf he passed;
But that step—it was his last!
As through the mist he winged his way
(A cloud that hovers night and day),
The hound hung back, and back he drew
The master and his merlin too;
That narrow place of noise and strife
Received their little all of life.
And now the matin bell is rung,
The "miserere" duly sung;
And holy men in cowl and hood
Are wand'ring up and down the wood.
But what avail they?"

Wordsworth, under the title, "The Force of Prayer," treats the tradition more fully, and at greater length:—

"'What is good for a bootless bene?'
With these dark words begins my tale;
And their meaning is, whence can comfort spring
When prayer is of no avail?

"'What is good for a bootless bene?'
The falconer to the lady said;
And she made answer, 'Endless sorrow!'
For she knew that her son was dead.

"She knew it by the falconer's words,
And from the look of the falconer's eye;
And from the love which was in her soul
For her youthful Romilly.

"Young Romilly through Barden Woods
Is ranging high and low;
And holds a greyhound in a leash,
To let slip upon buck or doe.

"The pair have reached that fearful chasm;—
How tempting to bestride!
For lordly Wharf is there pent in
With rocks on either side.

"This striding-place is called 'the Strid,'
A name which it took of yore;
A thousand years hath it borne that name,
And shall a thousand more.

"And hither is young Romilly come,
And what may now forbid
That he perhaps for the hundredth time
Shall bound across the Strid?

"He sprang in glee—for what cared he
That the river was strong, and the rocks were steep?
But the greyhound in the leash hung back
And checked him in his leap.

"The boy is in the arms of Wharf,
And strangled by a merciless force,
And never more was young Romilly seen
Till he rose a lifeless corse.

"Now there is stillness in the vale,
And long unspeaking sorrow;
Wharf shall be to pitying hearts
A name more sad than Yarrow.

"If for a lover the lady wept,
A solace she might borrow
From death, and from the passion of death;—
Old Wharf might heal her sorrow.

"She weeps not for the wedding day
Which was to be to-morrow;
Her hope was a farther-looking hope,
And her's is a mother's sorrow.

"He was a tree that stood alone,
And proudly did its branches wave;
And the root of this delightful tree
Was in her husband's grave.

"Long, long in darkness did she sit,
And her first words were, 'Let there be
In Bolton, on the field of Wharf,
A stately priory!'

"The stately priory was reared,
And Wharf, as he moved along,
To matins joined a mournful voice,
Nor failed at evensong.

"And the lady prayed in heaviness,
That looked not for relief;
But slowly did her succour come,
And a patience to her grief.

"Oh! there is never sorrow of heart
That shall lack a timely end,
If but to God we turn, and ask
Of Him to be our friend!"

The priory appears to have been at the height of its prosperity about the beginning of the fourteenth century. In 1299 A.D. the annual value was £865 17s. 6d., which, at the dissolution in 1540 A.D., had diminished, probably through the ravages of the Scots after the battle of Bannockburn, to £298 15s. 11d.

We learn, from the various books and accounts yet extant, that the establishment usually consisted of the prior, eighteen monks or canons, and two or three conversi; the Armigeri, or gentlemen dependent on the house; the Liberi Servientes, or free servants, "inter curiam" and "extra curiam." There were about thirty of the former, amongst whom were the master carpenter, master and under cook, brewer, baker, smith, Hokarius Fagotarius, and the Ductor Succorum. These received wages of from three to ten shillings per annum. The Liberi Servientes "extra curiam," numbered from seventy to one hundred, and were employed in husbandry on the farms and granges. Besides these, there appears to have been also a considerable number of "garciones," or household slaves.

At the dissolution in 1540 A.D., when the priory was surrendered to the king's commissioners by Richard Moon, the last prior, there were but thirteen brethren or canons.

The following list of "the stock" of the priory in 1301 A.D. is very suggestive of the prosperity depicted in Landseer's "Bolton Abbey in the Olden Time."

In that year, at Bolton and the Granges, which were the outlying farms of the house, "there were 713 horned cattle, of which 252 were oxen; 2,193 sheep, 95 pigs, and 91 goats." And there were slaughtered in one year for consumption, "besides *venison*, *fish*, and *poultry*, 64 oxen, 35 cows, 1 steer, 140 sheep, and 69 pigs." The quantity of wheat flour used in the same period was 319 quarters; of barley and oatmeal for household purposes, 192 quarters,

There was made into malt (oats or barley), for ale, 636 quarters. The quantity of wine purchased was seven *dolia.* A dolium was 2 pipes. Taking a pipe at 126 gallons, we have a total of nearly 1800 gallons for the year. No doubt one great virtue of the brotherhood was generous hospitality.

It must not be thought, however, that all these "good things of the earth" necessarily secured peace and good-will among their possessors. Glimpses of a very different state of feeling are occasionally to be caught.

The learned author of "Fasti Eboracensis" (Canon Raine), from the register of Archbishop Giffard, gives a report of certain investigations made, by that archbishop's authority, into the condition of some of the northern monasteries in the years A.D. 1274—1276. The entry in this report respecting Bolton may be taken as a specimen.

"Bolton - in - Craven. The whole convent conspired against the predecessor of William de Danfield, the present prior. Nicholas de Broc, the sub-prior, is old and useless. Silence is not observed, and there is much chattering and noise. John de Pontefract, the present cellarer, is incompetent. The cellarer and sub-cellarer are often absent from service and refections, and have their meals by themselves when the canons have left the refectory. The house is in debt to the amount of £324 5s. 7d."

Much of the leisure time of at least some of the monks was devoted to the study of astrology and alchemy, and they embodied their knowledge of these mystical sciences in long metrical narratives still extant, but perfectly, or nearly so, unintelligible to the common sense of modern readers.

One of their nearest neighbours, in the latter part of the fifteenth and the beginning of the sixteenth century, was Lord Clifford of Barden Tower, known as "the shepherd lord," who, after a life of study and rural retirement, was called to a chief command at the battle of Flodden in 1513 A.D. To the days of his retirement near the priory Wordsworth thus alludes :—

"And choice of studious friends had he
Of Bolton's dear fraternity,
Who, standing on the old church tower,
In many a calm propitious hour,
Perused with him the starry sky;
Or in their cells with him did pry
For other lore, through strong desire,
Searching the earth with chemic fire."

There was one circumstance which interrupted, sadly, the happiness of the nobleman's retirement, and probably, also the peace of his monastic neighbours, and that was the conduct of his scape-grace son, who equally with his father, has shared the tradition of being the hero of the old ballad of "Ye nutte browne maide." A letter from the Shepherd Lord to one at the Court of the king—Henry VIII.—is preserved by Whitaker, in the which, Lord Clifford bitterly complains of "the ungodly and ungudely conduct of his son, Henrie Cliffordе." He states that this mad-cap son sets at nought his commands, threatens his servants, and with his own hand, had struck his "poore servaunt Henrie Popeley in peryl of dethe, w'ch so lyeth, and is lyke to dye"; besides this the father complains of his son's thefts committed to support his inordinate pride and riot; and that notwithstanding he had given him £15, "and over that his blessyng upon his gude and lawful demeanour," desiring him to forsake the evil company of certain evil companions, "as well yonge gents as oth's," lest, "he sholde bee utterlie undone for ev'r, as well bodilie as ghostlie," yet that he continueth his course of disobedience, "and troblith divers housys of religioun, to bring from them their tythes, shamefully betyng ther tenaunts and s'vants, in such wyse as some whol townes are fayne to keype the churches both nighte and daye, and dare not come att ther own housys."

On such an expedition, W. H. Leatham, Esq., in a pretty ballad entitled "Henrie Cliffordе and Margaret Percy," makes Henrie present himself at midnight, as a wayworn and pilgrim, at the gates of the Priory, and ask a lodging from the prior. The prior (Moon)

"Spake, and straightway entrance gave;
The pilgrim held his sturdy stave
Within the opening door,
Then turning, whistled loud and shrill,
Till answering from the woodland hill,
Rose laughter's frantic roar;
And troop on troop, came hurrying down,
But ill concealed in palmer's gown,
With staff, and scallop shell.
The wilder still the chiding broke,
Till ilk' affrighted Friar woke,
Within the peaceful dell.
"How, now? good Father Moyne!" quoth they,
"One hundred marks of thee,
"Or thou shall wend with us away,
"Under the green-wood tree!"
Then one by one, with haggard mien,
Each sleep-awakened monk was seen,
With ghost-astounded air;
For when he viewed the burly knaves,
Bearded and bronzed, with secret glaives,
Stand with uplifted, oaken staves,
He mote, in sooth, despair!
* * * * * * * * *
"Now, Prior Moyne! we must away,
To the green-wood, ere break of day,
And thou with us shalt go!"
The priest is loth, but yield he must,
Or, pay one hundred marks on trust,
With mickle wrath, and woe.
The bag is brought—the coin is told,
And doubly curst the sinners bold,
Who, robb'd the church, and filch'd her gold."

While quoting this ballad by Mr. Leatham, the following description of Barden in the early morning from it can scarcely be withheld:

"Now, round about old Barden's towers,
Round ivied wall, and leafy bowers,
Light mists are hovering thin,
Or falling soft, in silver showers,
The Wharfe's deep vale within;
Now walks abroad the glorious sun,
Scattering away the dawn-clouds dun;
And with the birth of day is heard,
The piping of each minstrel bird.

Where stately oaks, in forest pride,
  Rise from yon river's bed,
Mantling the hills on either side,
  In one broad covert spread,
Old Clifforde's Hall, and chantry's aisle,
  Lattice, and solemn tracery,
Basking like youth in love's first smile,
  Glow beneath the golden sky."

After these glimpses of monastic life within, and at the priory, and its surroundings, a passing look may now, in conclusion, be taken at the ruins:

"O Bolton, what a change! but still thou art
Noble in ruins, great in every part!
When we behold thee, signs of grandeur gone,
Live on thy walls and shine in every stone."

Only sufficient fragments of the domestic buildings remain, in foundations and scattered buttresses, to show how extensive they must have been.

The principal parts of the *church*, however, are yet standing. The *nave* is appropriately fitted up and used as the parish church. And, only two or three years ago, a beautiful screen and reredos, shutting off the nave from the ruined central tower, have been erected by the liberality of the noble owner of Bolton,—the owner, also, of princely Chatsworth.

The *central tower* appears, for some reason, never to have been carried much above the roof of the nave, nor completed. In 1521 A.D., Richard Moon, the last prior, commenced to build a tower at the west end of the nave. This, too, was unfinished when he and the brethren were dispersed at the dissolution. It bears the inscription in Old English letters, "In the yer of our Lord MDCXX, R‿. begann thes fondachon, on qwho soul God haue marce. Amen." While forming now the west entrance to the church, this tower entirely hides the original west front.

The *nave* contains specimens of every style of architecture, from that of transitional to that immediately preceding the Reformation.

The walls of the *north transept* remain tolerably perfect; those of the *south* one are completely gone.

The *chancel* walls also remain. It has been of the Decorated period, but little, unfortunately, of its once beautiful tracery is now to be seen. The magnificent east window contains the only fragments left, and those only sufficient to show how exquisitely beautiful it must have been when perfect. The peep of scenery—mountain, wood and water—which is obtained through the archway of the window—one of nature's most pleasing pictures in one of art's most graceful frames—is alone worth a visit to Bolton.

In both the nave and chancel were *chantry chapels*. One, at the east end of the aisle of the nave, was founded by an early benefactor of the monastery,—a Mauleverer of Beamsley. The Mauleverers were succeeded by the Claphams of Beamsley. Beneath this chantry chapel is the family vault, in which, according to tradition, those who were interred were always placed in an upright position. It is said that modern examinations have confirmed the truth of the tradition. However, the poet has utilized it:—

"Pass, pass who will, yon chantry door,
And through the chink in the fractured floor
Look down, and see a grisly sight—
A vault, where the bodies are buried upright!
There, face by face, and hand by hand,
The Claphams and Mauleverers stand;
And in his place among son and sire,
Is John de Clapham, that fierce esquire,
A valiant man, and a man of dread
In the ruthless wars of the White and Red;
Who dragged Earl Pembroke from Banbury Church,
And smote off his head on the stones of the porch."

Within a few years of the dissolution the site of the deserted priory, with the chief part of its late possessions, was granted for a nominal sum of money to Henry Clifford, Earl of Cumberland, who already had possessions in the vicinity, and from whom it has descended, in the female line, to the present noble owner.

In the middle of the seventeenth century the heiress of the family was the Lady Anne Clifford, upon whom, by marriage or otherwise, had accumulated the titles of Countess of Pembroke, Dorset and Montgomery, Baroness Clifford, Westmoreland, and Vescie. This lady was evidently a strong upholder of women's rights in her own days. "She had been an independent courtier in the court of the haughty Elizabeth; she personally resisted an award of her family property by King James; she re-fortified her castles in defiance of Cromwell; and when the *secretary* of Charles II. wrote to her, naming a suitable candidate for one of her parliamentary boroughs," she replied,

"Sire, I have been bullied by a usurper, I have been neglected by a court, but will not be dictated to by a subject. Your man shan't stand.—Anne, Dorset, Pembroke, and Montgomery."

It is impossible to turn away from this place without recalling the tradition of the "White Doe of Rylstone," and the world-wide poem which Wordsworth founded upon it.

Rylstone—the home of the Nortons—is upon the fells some five or six miles above the priory.

Standing among the ruins, by the priory church, it is not difficult to realize the scene, on the Sabbath morn, so sweetly pictured by the poet:—

"From Bolton's old monastic tower
The bells ring out with gladsome power;
The sun is bright; the fields are gay
With people in their best array
Of stole and doublet, hood and scarf,
Along the banks of the crystal Wharfe,
Through the vale, retired and lowly,
Trooping to that summons holy.
And up among the woodlands see
What sprinklings of blithe company!
Of lasses, and of shepherd grooms,
  That down the steep hills force their way,
Like cattle through the budded brooms;
  Path or no path, what care they?
And thus in joyous mood they hie,
To Bolton's mouldering priory."

There are still the tangled paths through the moorlands, —the fells,—the woods,—and the meadows,—all before the eye. Along them, or across them, members of the congregation are still to be seen wending their way to the House of God. The white doe, which after the death of its gentle mistress, Emily Norton,

"Maid of that blasted family,"

sought, every Sabbath day, a place by her grave in the shadow of the church, may, without any great stretch of the imagination, be pictured there also,

"Right across the verdant sod,
Toward the very house of God,
Comes gliding in with silvery gleam,
Comes gliding in serene and slow,
Soft and silent as a dream,
A solitary doe;
White she is as lily of June,
Beauteous as the silver moon
When out of sight the clouds are driven,
And she is left alone in heaven."

Then—

"When from the temple forth they throng,
* * * * *
Her work, whate'er it be, is done,
And she'll depart when they are gone."

Well! gone is the Bolton of monastic times; gone those days of the grim Claphams and the dark Cliffords; gone the white doe and its gentle mistress; gone, as some may perhaps yet think it, that "sunrise time of zeal,"—

"When faith and hope were in their prime,
In great Eliza's golden time."

And yet, of Bolton, in the words of another true poet of the north, (the late Canon Parkinson), it may be said,—

"Here nature smiles as bright as when
Thy towers first rose amid the glen;
Sweetly still the stream rolls on,
Though many an imaged arch is gone.
The sheep still graze this velvet ground,
The oak and ash still flourish round;
And still the bridled current roars,

And through the pass as wildly pours
As when, check'd by his timid hound,
The boy of Egremont was drown'd.
Unchang'd in voice, young Echo still
Is heard to shout round Barden hill.
And daily from yon scar's proud crown,
The untarned cataract pours down.
The sunshine casts as sweet a smile,
On ruined walls and moss-grown aisle,
As when its rays more proudly shone
On glittering vane and sculptured stone.
And wandering eyes still love to gaze
On thee, thou child of other days,
And treasure up, for years to be,
A kindly memory of thee!"

THE SNOWDROP.

WE hail thee, pearly snowdrop dear,
  In dress of virgin white;
Herald amid the winter's gloom
Of spring's returning light!

In sheltered dell by Green Beck side,
  Thou lift'st thy humble head,
And gently spring'st in new-born life,
  From dust of last year's dead.

Like tear of faith in sorrow's eye,
  Like hope on mourner's brow,
Thou spak'st of life and summer bloom
  Where yet lies winter's snow.

Then hail thee, pearly snowdrop dear,
  The first of Flora's train,
In forest dell and woodland nook,
  Or on the open plain!

Yes, hail thee, meek and lowly flower,
  In dress of virgin white,
Herald amid the winter's gloom,
  Of spring's returning light!

THE HAREBELL BY THE SPRING WELL.

HAREBELL! thou meek blue harebell!
With infant hand I pluck'd thee,
Then growing here by the spring well,
Under the green forest tree.

When on me youth had cast its spell,
With loved ones then I found thee,
Then growing here by the spring well,
Under green forest tree.

Thirty years! and, in this dell,
With tear-dimmed eye I hail thee,
Growing here by the spring well,
Under the brown forest tree.

Dead mem'ries rise perforce and tell,
Of those who ne'er may hail thee,
Here growing still by the spring well,
Under the brown forest tree.

Emotions deep my bosom swell,
As now my children pluck thee,
Still growing here by the spring well,
Under the old forest tree.

When in a higher world I dwell,
Their children too may find thee,
Then growing here by the spring well,
Under the dead forest tree.

Harebell! meek and fragile harebell!
Fair emblem of *death* to see,
As *plucked* to-day by the spring well,
Under the old forest tree.

Harebell! perennial harebell!
Thou speak'st of *life* to me;
Ever growing by the spring well
Under the green forest tree.

A DIRGE FOR THE VALLEY; OR A FORESTER'S LAMENT.

"And thus with gentle voice he spoke,—
'Come lead me, lassie, to the shade,
Where willows grow beside the brook;
For well I know the sound it made,
When dashing o'er the stony rill,
It murmured to St. Osyth's mill.'

"The lass replied,—'The trees are fled,
They've cut the brook a straighter bed;
No shades the present lords allow,
The miller only murmurs now;
The waters now his mill forsake,
And form a pond they call a lake.'"—*Crabbe.*

BROTHER, dost thou remember
The valley bright and fair,
Where ran the sparkling river,
And breath of peace was there?

The pastures rich where browsed,
In the sweet summer time,
Fair herds, at noon and evening,
And in the morning's prime;

The meadows, where in hay-time,
We tossed the new-mown grass,
And whence, with shouts, we homeward
Then bore the fragrant mass?

Brother, dost thou remember,
  The dark, thick Lane Ends Wood, *
Where, by the slippery pathways,
  Our fav'rite nut-trees stood;

The hollies and the brambles,
  Where built the birds in spring;—
The green "shaw" at the bottom,
  With mystic "fairy ring;"

That pine where built the magpie
  Her nest thick year by year;
That hawthorn-shaded hollow,
  Where the Green-Well bubbled clear?

Brother, dost thou remember
  "The Busks" and "Coppice" glade,—
Where hyacinth and primrose
  Bedecked the hazel shade;

The pool in winding river,
  So clear, and cool, and deep,
Where in the hot June weather,
  Were washed the bleating sheep:

The long "reach" in "the alders,"
  And birch of silvery grey,
Where sat the proud kingfisher,
  To watch his finny prey?

Brother, dost thou remember
  The "Green Beck" and "the Gill;"
The dear old homestead, nestling,
  Beneath the sandstone hill?

---

* All the words written as proper names are the names of fields and places which have been engulfed by, or their appearance materially altered by, the new reservoirs constructed by the Leeds Corporation in the valley of the Washburn, and which now occupy a very considerable portion of that valley.

Ah, dost thou not remember
  The "Delph," "the Holm," "the Garth;"
The "Side-Bank" and "the Bottoms,"
  Their flowers and velvet swarth;

The hedge-rows, where the rabbits,
  On summer ev'ning played,—
The tree, in which the "owlets"
  Their wintry lodgings made?

Brother, dost thou remember
  The "Thackray" homestead, well;
Where, near its wood, the brooklet
  Into the Washburn fell?

And further down the river,—
  By the brown moorland side,—
The "New Hall" famed in story,
  For deeds that darkness hide;

Where dwelt immortal Fairfax,
  And tuned his British lyre,—
Our chill cold north'rn song to warm,
  With Tasso's southern fire?

And yet a little further,—
  So dark and thick, and tall,—
The woods of grand old Swinsty,
  Descending from the Hall,

To where the river gurgled,
  Along its stony path,
From the dark and slipp'ry "hippins,"
  By side of Rowton Wath?

The dear old church, too, brother,
  Where long our fathers prayed,
And round whose sacred walls now
  Their mould'ring dust is laid;

Ah, dost thou not remember,
  How, throned upon the hill,
It looked o'er meads and cornfields,
  O'er wood, and hall, and mill?

And then the quaint bright village,
  On terraced hill-side won,—
With gardens trim and sloping
  To meet the mid-day sun :

High up, the thatchèd schoolhouse,
  The "Green," where oft we played,
The "Shop" where Robin Hardisty,
  His feathery "tackle" made ;

The path near which the "webster,"
  His noisy shuttle plied,—
The house upon whose chimney
  The "signal broom" was tied ?

Brother, dost thou remember
  These landmarks in the vale,—
These haunts of early childhood,
  In sunny Washburn dale ?

Does not the mere recital
  Of things familiar then,
Awake a loving memory,
  E'en now, when we are men ?

Our fathers, long before us,
  Much loved these rural shades,
And in *their* youth and manhood
  Oft paced the well-known glades ;

In them, when youth smiled brightly,
  They told their tales of love ;
Of them, in old age prattled
  Ere called to homes above.

No spot to us familiar,
  But known to them before ;
And brook and field and pathway
  Were loved by them of yore.

All are gone or going, brother !
  And most are swept away !
And o'er the vale and homesteads,
  The waters roll to-day.

Our children ne'er may know them,
  Nor see as we have seen;
Except from love's reporting,
  Ne'er know that they have been!

The "holms" and dark green pastures,
  Where sheep and cattle fed;
The "busks" and sloping meadows,
  With many a thymy bed;

The clear pools in the river,
  The banks aud braes so steep,
Are buried 'neath the waters,
  Full fifty fathoms deep!

The hollies and the hazels
  Are stript from Lane Ends Wood,
"The coppice" and its flowers
  Are far beneath the flood.

The "shaw," where danced the fairies,
  The "gap," where rabbits played,
The hedge, and dark green alders,
  In watery depths are laid.

"The gill" is filled with waters,
  Where but the Green Beck ran;
And from Low Cragg to Ridsdale
  Waters the valley span.

Cragg Hall, now lone and dreary,
  Which from Eliza's day
Hath looked o'er vale and woodland,
  Sees but the waters' play.

And quiet "Thackray" homestead,
  Whence sprang a race of fame,
Its wood, and holm, and brooklet
  Have perished but in name.

And o'er the spot where Fairfax
  First taught his nephew brave,
And lived, and sung, and died,
  There beats the rip'ling wave.

And where, hard by, the mill race,
  The mill and bridge were known,
There now are raised great earth-works,
  Or lake rests, deep and brown.

And now the woods of Swinsty,
  Are swept away, and gone;
The Hall but stands to mourn them,
  Majestic still, but lone.

And up the deep Gill Bottoms,
  And o'er the Wath and stones,
The water, calm, is resting,
  Or in the tempest moans.

The dear old church yet reigneth
  Upon its hill-side throne,
And o'er the waters smileth
  As once o'er fields, its own.

But, ah, the village changeth,
  Its rural life hath fled;
The villagers are moving,
  And some, alas, are dead.

Its fields and paths are heaving,
  By unseen power toss'd,
Its homes and cots are ruins,—
  Another Auburn lost!

The lake of deep brown waters,—
  Expanding far and wide,—
Now holds the forest valley
  In all-engulphing tide.

These scenes of rural beauty,
  Which once we thought our own,
Are swept off quick and ruthless,
  For needs of distant town!

No doubt, a sense of grandeur
  The wide-extending lake—
Its wood-clad banks and islets,—
  In strangers will awake.

Though by this innovation,
  Fair scenes have here arisen,
Yet old associations,
  Before them out are driven.

"No man who'th drunk the old wine,
  Straightway desireth new,
He saith 'the old is better,'"—
  So 'tis with I and you.

To us who knew the "older,"
  This new thing ne'er can be
The sweet pastoral valley,
  Now sleeping 'neath *this sea!*

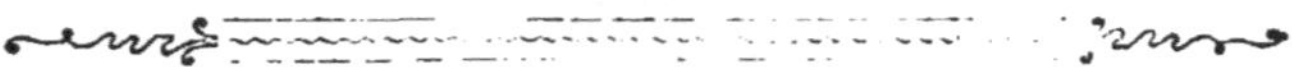

A SONNET.

CRAGG HALL.

CRAGG Hall! To memory sacred and affection dear,
  I leave thee. My dead fathers loved thee well,
  And thou their joys, and sorrows too, could'st tell!
They loved thee through Spring, and Summer, Autumn sere,
And Winter's death, of many a circling year.
  Their birth thou hailed; then list' their marriage bell;
  Young voices again thou heard:—then hark! the knell
Thy lord was fatherless; there fell the widow's tear;
  I leave thee; home where all their joys and fears
  And footfalls fell for twice a hundred years.
I leave thee; for another owns thee now,—
For him, and his, thy hearths with welcome glow,
  For them thy roofs resound, and shelter spread;
  I leave thee,—but, *as the widow leaves her dead.*

CHILDREN.

I.

Like plants are little children who,
  In this world's garden grow ;
For good or evil on them, we
  Our care and pains bestow.

II.

Fresh showers of love alone can keep
  Them happy, pure and bright ;
By these they grow in gentleness,
  God's children of the light.

III.

Weak in themselves, they seek the help,
  Which a strong arm can give ;
On us, their elders, it depends,
  How well or ill they live.

IV.

The food of knowledge they demand,
  Their little minds to fill ;
To make them clever, good and wise,
  To discipline the will.

V.

Oh ! blessed ministry is it,
  Christ's lambs to fondly tend ;
That as they grow in moral health
  They may fulfil the end

VI.

Their heavenly Father had in view,
  When He unto our care,
A precious trust committed them,
  That they one day may share

VII.

In all our joys and sorrows, whilst
  We here with them may stay ;
And afterward together dwell,
  In God's home far away.

VIII.

Lord, give us grace at home, at school,
  To train them so, in love,
That present blossom may bear fruit,
  Which shall be reaped above.

Fewston. J. M. A.

LAYS AND LEAVES.

HARROGATE:
R. ACKRILL, PRINTER AND LITHOGRAPHER
"HERALD" OFFICE.

LIFE'S DAY.

"Can there be anything great in a little time? for This whole time between childhood and old age, in relation to eternity would be something very small."
PLATO. Republic, 608. c.

How small the interval that lies between,
The blushing dawn of childhood and old age!
Contrasted with Eternity's vast range
It is a nothing—a mere vapour seen
To vanish in a breath: now less, now more:
Gone, ere our vision can its form define!
Man's life, indeed, when measured e'en by time
Is lost amidst the "after" and "before."
Is then this "little while" of no concern,
Unworthy of a struggle or a thought,
The same, with noble, or base deeds inwrought?
Ah! no, it is a time in which to earn
The wages that Eternity will pay
So lasting are the issues of Life's day.

Fewston.

J. M. A.

S. Matt.,

I.

And "from afar" Thy blessed steps shall I,
Follow with tardy feet,
And not at Thy dear side be ever found
Danger to share and meet?

II.

I would be with Thee, but my nature fears,
Where death and sorrow are;
Grace hath not wrought its perfect work, and so
I follow "from afar."

III.

Moment of action—with no time for thought,
Strong impulse holds her sway;
Her will is law—she bids me let Thee go,
Alone on Thy sad way.

IV.

I love Thee Lord! Alas! my love is cold,
And faith is weak in me;
Whilst selfishness absorbs my better self,
I am "far off" from Thee.

V.

Grant me to follow Thee not "afar off,"
But step by step behind;
To place my feet in every print of Thine,
That I by love can find.

VI.

Thus may my earthly life a copy be,
By grace dear Lord of Thine;
So that when called, by Thee, unto Thy home,
Thou wilt be ever mine.

Fewston.

J. M. A.

ORIGINAL POETRY.

THE PASSAGE TO PARADISE.

"May enter in through the gates into the city."

I.

Afar the golden city shines,
All glorious within;
Its pearly gates wide open stand,
O may I enter in.

II.

Onwards, and upwards, have I fought,
Through sorrow, fear, and sin;
Through darkness into light at last,
O may I enter in.

III.

In silence with submission deep,
Unto Thy Cross I cling;
With head bowed down and broken heart,
O may I enter in.

IV.

Over temptations sore and strong,
The victory to win;
Became my portion through Thy grace,
O may I enter in.

V.

Others into the "narrow way"
Of life, I sought to bring;
I helped them in their weakness, Lord!
O may I enter in.

VI.

To gaze upon the gates without,
Guarded by Cherubin;
Were loss eternal with despair,
Lord! let me enter in.

Fewston. J.M.A.